Balthasar at the End of Modernity

D. M. M.
1913–1994

Balthasar at the End of Modernity

Lucy Gardner
David Moss
Ben Quash
Graham Ward

T&T CLARK
EDINBURGH

T&T CLARK LTD
59 GEORGE STREET
EDINBURGH EH2 2LQ
SCOTLAND

First published 1999

ISBN 0 567 08671 2 (HB)
ISBN 0 567 08704 2 (PB)

British Library Cataloguing-in-Publication Data
A catalogue record for this book is available from the British Library

Typeset by Waverley Typesetters, Galashiels
Printed and bound in Great Britain by Bookcraft, Avon

✤

Contents

Preface and Acknowledgements

Hans Urs von Balthasar is a theologian whose time appears to have come. Across a broad theological spectrum there is a growing interest in his thought, an interest which crosses older conservative/liberal, ecclesio-political boundaries in a surprising manner. In the English-speaking world this fascination has grown markedly in the past decade. In response to this phenomenon we have come to ask, 'Why here, why now?'

In particular, the reception of Balthasar's work has been coupled with varied attempts to explore how theology is to be conducted responsibly by those who understand themselves to be 'at the end of modernity'. New philosophical attitudes and themes, many openly critical of various versions of 'modernity', seem to find a ready partner in Balthasar's theology. The authors here have found themselves drawn into a similar engagement, and yet recognize that these questions will yield to no hasty answers. Of particular importance in these essays is the strong belief that to criticize modernity and its philosophies cannot involve any unproblematic return to the pre-modern; our task is rather to find appropriate ways of receiving the theological tradition in this situation and at this time. Post-modern philosophical resources thus provide a background to, and dialogue partners for, our work, and the various authors have indicated the particular ways in which they undertake this possibility and task.

While a growing number of volumes are being published on Balthasar's work, many of these are primarily expository and exegetical. The summaries of Balthasar's theology and explorations of his sources are indeed good, but we do not aim here to add to them. Rather than attempting to comment on Balthasar's work from the outside, the authors of this volume have attempted to write as it were from within his thought, both to discover its fundamental dynamics and to see how it may be pushed and tested. In some ways this book represents four different theologians attempting to develop their own theological voices and themes in critical engagement with Balthasar's thought. Accordingly, although we are all fascinated by this man's achievement, it would be a mistake to see these chapters as attempting either to sanctify or to bury Balthasar; we wish rather to encourage rigorous theological engagement with his work.

We are especially grateful to Rowan Williams, who supported the project from the first and has provided an interpretative Afterword to the essays; and also to Fergus Kerr, whose considerable familiarity with the development of Roman Catholic theology in the 1960s is brought to bear in an introductory essay which situates Balthasar's historical achievement.

We should like to thank T&T Clark, especially Stratford Caldecott, for their support and encouragement. Early discussions of these papers took place at a special seminar at the 1996 Society for the Study of Theology conference in Cambridge, and were developed, through the generous help of Stratford and T&T Clark, over three days at St Stephen's House, Oxford.

From amongst those who have brought Balthasar to the attention of the English-speaking world, our second word of thanks goes to the late Donald MacKinnon. With the breadth, vision and incisiveness which were always a feature of his own work, MacKinnon grasped several decades ago the importance of Balthasar's work for the unfolding of theology. We dedicate this work to his memory.

Abbreviations

References to works by Balthasar are given, where possible, in parentheses in the text of the book. The authors have used both German originals and English translations and, where appropriate, references to both German and English editions are provided.

In the following list the German original and abbreviation is followed immediately underneath by its English equivalent (where possible).

BN   *Bernanos: An Ecclesial Existence*, tr. Erasmo Leiva-Merikakis (San Francisco: Ignatius Press, 1996)

CL   *Cordula oder der Ernstfall* (Einsiedeln: Johannes Verlag, 1966)
CW   *The Moment of Christian Witness*, tr. R. Beckley (San Francisco: Ignatius Press, 1994)

ED   Elisabeth of Dijon, tr. A. V. Littledale (London: Harvill Press, 1956)

GOW   *The Grain of Wheat: Aphorisms*, tr. Erasmo Leiva-Merikakis (San Francisco: Ignatius Press, 1995)

H I   *Herrlichkeit* Bd I (Einsiedeln: Johannes Verlag, 1969)
GL 1   *The Glory of the Lord. A Theological Aesthetics. I: Seeing the Form*, tr. Erasmo Leiva-Merikakis (Edinburgh: T. & T. Clark, 1982)

H II.1   *Herrlichkeit* Bd II.I (Einsiedeln: Johannes Verlag, 1969)
GL 2   *The Glory of the Lord. A Theological Aesthetics. II: Studies in Theological Style: Clerical Styles*, tr. A. Louth *et al.* (Edinburgh: T. & T. Clark, 1984)

H II.2   *Herrlichkeit* Bd II.2 (Einsiedeln: Johannes Verlag, 1969)
GL 3   *The Glory of the Lord. A Theological Aesthetics. III: Studies in Theological Style: Lay Styles*, tr. A. Louth *et al.* (Edinburgh: T. & T. Clark, 1986)

H III.1/1 *Herrlichkeit* Bd III.1/1 Teil (Einsiedeln: Johannes Verlag, 1965)
GL 4   *The Glory of the Lord. A Theological Aesthetics. IV: The Realm of Metaphysics in Antiquity*, tr. B. McNeil *et al.* (Edinburgh: T. & T. Clark, 1989)

H III.1/2   *Herrlichkeit* Bd III.1/2 Teil (Einsiedeln: Johannes Verlag, 1967)
GL 5   *The Glory of the Lord. A Theological Aesthetics. V: The Realm of Metaphysics in the Modern Age*, tr. O. Davies *et al.* (Edinburgh: T. & T. Clark, 1991)

H III.2/1   *Herrlichkeit* Bd III.2/1 Teil (Einsiedeln: Johannes Verlag, 1969)
GL 6   *The Glory of the Lord. A Theological Aesthetics. VI: Theology: The Old Covenant* (Edinburgh: T. & T. Clark, 1991)

H III.2/2   *Herrlichkeit* Bd III.2/2 Teil (Einsiedeln: Johannes Verlag, 1969)
GL 7   *The Glory of the Lord. A Theological Aesthetics. VII: Theology: The New Covenant*, tr. B. McNeil (Edinburgh: T. & T. Clark, 1989)

HW   *Herz der Welt* (Schwabenverlag: Stuttgart, 1988)

KB   *Karl Barth: Darstellung und Deutung Seiner Theologie* (Einsiedeln: Johannes Verlag, 1951)

B   *Karl Barth: Exposition and Interpretation*, tr. E. Oakes (San Francisco: Ignatius Press, 1992)

MH   *Man in History* (London/Sydney: Sheed & Ward Ltd., 1968)

MP   *Mysterium Paschale*, tr. A. Nichols (Edinburgh: T. & T. Clark, 1990)

P   *Prayer*, tr. G. Harrison (San Francisco: Ignatius Press, 1986) [tr. of *Das Betrachtende Gebet* (1955)]

PT   *Presence and Thought: An essay on the Religious Philosophy of Gregory of Nyssa*, tr. M. Sebanc (San Francisco: Ignatius Press, 1988)

ST I   *Verbum Caro, Skizzen zur Theologie I* (Einsiedeln: Johannes Verlag, 1960)
ExT 1   *Explorations in Theology I: Verbum Caro*, tr. B. McNeil (San Francisco: Ignatius Press, 1993)

ST II   *Sponsa Verbi, Skizzen zur Theologie II* (Einsiedeln: Johannes Verlag, 1960)
ExT 2   *Explorations in Theology II: Spouse of the Word*, tr. B. McNeil (San Francisco: Ignatius Press, 1991)

ST III   *Spiritus Creator, Skizzen zur Theologie III* (Einsiedeln: Johannes Verlag, 1967)
ExT 3   *Explorations in Theology III: Creator Spirit*, tr. B. McNeil (San Francisco: Ignatius Press, 1993)

ST IV   *Pneuma und Institution, Skizzen zur Theologie IV* (Einsiedeln: Johannes Verlag, 1974)
ExT 4   *Explorations in Theology IV: Spirit and Institution*, tr. B. McNeil (San Francisco: Ignatius Press, 1993)

TD I   *Theodramatik* Bd I (Einsiedeln: Johannes Verlag, 1973)
ThD 1   *Theo-Drama: Theological Dramatic Theory: I. Prolegomena*, tr. G. Harrison (San Francisco: Ignatius Press, 1988)

TD II.1   *Theodramatik* Bd II.1 (Einsiedeln: Johannes Verlag, 1976)
ThD 2   *Theo-Drama: Theological Dramatic Theory: II. Dramatis Personae: Man in God*, tr. G. Harrison (San Francisco: Ignatius Press, 1990)

TD II.2   *Theodramatik* Bd II.2 (Einsiedeln: Johannes Verlag, 1978)
ThD 3   *Theo-Drama: Theological Dramatic Theory: III: Dramatis Personae: Persons in Christ*, tr. G. Harrison (San Francisco: Ignatius Press, 1992)

TD III   *Theodramatik* Bd III (Einsiedeln: Johannes Verlag, 1980)
ThD 4   *Theo-Drama: Theological Dramatic Theory: IV: The Action*, tr. G. Harrison (San Francisco: Ignatius Press, 1994)

TD IV   *Theodramatik* Bd IV (Einsiedeln: Johannes Verlag, 1983)

TL 1   *Theologik* Bd I (Einsiedeln: Johannes Verlag, 1985)

TL 2   *Theologik* Bd II (Einsiedeln: Johannes Verlag, 1985)

TL 3   *Theologik* Bd III (Einsiedeln: Johannes Verlag, 1987)

Th   *Thérèse von Lisieux* (Köln: Jakob Hegner Verlag, 1950)
             Thérèse von Lisieux, tr. Donald Nicholl (London: Sheed & Ward, 1953)

Contributors

LUCY GARDNER is Tutor in Christian Doctrine at St Stephen's House, Oxford.

FERGUS KERR OP is Regent of Blackfriars, Oxford.

DAVID MOSS is Director of Studies at St Stephen's House, Oxford.

BEN QUASH is Dean of Peterhouse, Cambridge.

GRAHAM WARD is Professor of Contextual Theology and Ethics at the University of Manchester.

ROWAN WILLIAMS is Bishop of Monmouth in the Church in Wales.

1

❧

Foreword:
Assessing this 'Giddy Synthesis'

FERGUS KERR

'We here attempt to develop a Christian theology in the light of the third transcendental', Hans Urs von Balthasar declares at the beginning of *Herrlichkeit*; 'that is to say: to complement the vision of the true and the good with that of the beautiful *(pulchrum)*'.[1] The logical and ethical perspectives in which theology was practised needed to be supplemented by the aesthetic: a supplementation which would be corrective, even therapeutic, since 'neglecting one can only have a devastating effect on the others'. In 1961, this was a provocative challenge to the ruling neo-scholasticism in Roman Catholic theological institutions, which it is difficult to reconstruct now. While the essays in this book build on Balthasar's immense theological legacy in order to take some of his themes further, it seems appropriate to begin by recalling the originality of his first major intervention on the theological scene. Identified now, even by sympathetic readers, as a conservative, even reactionary and sectarian figure, in the supposedly liberal and ecumenical environment of post-Vatican II academic theology, it is important to recall the radically adversarial dimension of his theology and its indebtedness to his friendship with his Calvinist contemporary Karl Barth.

Balthasar insists, as he opens his great work, on how 'impoverished Christian theology has been by the growing loss of this perspective'. As regards Protestant theology, the absence of the aesthetic perspective begins with the Reformation itself: 'It appeared to Luther that the Death-and-Resurrection dialectic of the Christ-event had been replaced by the non-dialectical schemata of Neoplatonic aesthetic metaphysics.'[2] In the end, the elimination of the aesthetic from Protestant theology and Christian life as a whole means that Protestants have lost the contemplative dimension of the act of faith.[3] It takes twenty-five pages to survey the devastation of Protestantism, less than ten to discuss the absence of

---

1 *The Glory of the Lord: A Theological Aesthetics. I: Seeing the Form*, tr. Erasmo Leiva-Merikakis (Edinburgh: T. & T. Clark, 1982), p. 9.
2 Ibid., p. 45.
3 Ibid., p. 70.

1

the aesthetic in post-Reformation Catholicism. That does not mean, however, that it is not a waste land. As late as the fifteenth century, in Nicholas of Cusa, 'the normative tradition of thought remains the integrated philosophical and theological method common to both the Platonic–Aristotelian and the Augustinian–Dionysian streams'.[4] In the seventeenth century, however, after Descartes, philosophy yields to the charms of the natural–scientific ideal of knowledge, and philosophers, evidently including Catholic apologists, 'become eager to experiment with the question of what reason can accomplish without the aid of revelation and what the possibilities are for a pure nature without grace'.[5]

With that last phrase, in particular, Balthasar must have known that he would be perceived as taking sides in the acrimonious debate that had raged within Roman Catholic theology for the previous twenty years, over the proper understanding of the relationship between nature and grace.[6] Without naming names, and allowing that Catholic theology 'still today produces great achievements', Balthasar goes on to say that modern Catholic theology 'accepts the dire consequences of the fact that ever since Luther and Jansen, on the one hand, and Descartes, on the other, theology has defined itself in contrast with philosophy'.[7] This means, for example, that dogmatic theology is practised merely as history of doctrine; theological ethics, 'losing its all too philosophical character', is becoming situation ethics; Catholic biblical scholars, who adopt 'with relish' the categories of Protestant biblical criticism, are now captivated by the alleged distinction between Hellenistic and Hebrew thought; and so on.[8] Balthasar inveighs at length against trends in Catholic biblical scholarship – with a certain prescience, since he must have had little enough evidence in 1961 for the suspicions that would become a clamour fifteen or twenty years later. Professors of systematic theology in the neo-scholastic tradition would no doubt have endorsed his hostility to their colleagues in biblical studies; but they would hardly have welcomed his implication that the practice of critical–historical exegesis illustrated the post-Cartesian rift between theology and 'what the possibilities are for a pure nature without grace'. The very idea of 'a pure nature without grace' could only have been calculated defiance of the then vociferous and well-placed adversaries of *la nouvelle théologie*, who sought to hold on to the possibility, and indeed the indispensability, of philosophy as the preparation for, and in a real sense the foundation of, systematic theology.

As it happened, however, Balthasar's challenge to the theological establishment went almost unnoticed. Preparations for the Vatican Council were already attracting the attention of most theologians, and it

4 Ibid., p. 72.
5 Ibid., p. 72.
6 See Fergus Kerr, 'French Theology: Yves Congar and Henri de Lubac', in *The Modern Theologians: An introduction to Christian theology in the twentieth century*, ed. David F. Ford (second edition, Oxford: Blackwell, 1997); Joseph A. Komonchak, 'Theology and culture at mid-century: the example of Henri de Lubac', *Theological Studies* 51 579–602; Etienne Fouilloux, 'Dialogue théologique? (1946–1948)', in *Saint Thomas au XXe siècle* (Paris: Saint-Paul, 1995), pp. 153–95.
7 GL 1, p. 74.
8 Ibid., p. 75.

soon became clear, in any case, that neo-scholasticism had many other enemies, above all among the bishops. Ironically, by the time that Roman Catholic theologians became aware of the importance of *Herrlichkeit*, Balthasar was perceived on all sides, somewhat to his embarrassment, as the leading adversary of trends in post-conciliar Catholicism.[9] The shock waves that *Herrlichkeit* should have had in Roman Catholic theology were overtaken by unanticipatable events. It is hard, now, to understand how significant Balthasar's work is, negatively in its rejection of neo-scholasticism, positively in its opening towards the theology of Karl Barth.

One of the implications of Balthasar's project was that 'so-called "fundamental theology"' would not be distinct from dogmatic theology[10] – a cryptic aside, it may seem, but heavily charged with meaning for neo-scholastic theologians, on the one hand, for whom natural theology was conceived, not as the Pelagian project so vehemently denounced by Karl Barth, but certainly as a separate study of the *praeambula fidei*; as well as for Barthians, on the other hand, who regarded the *analogia entis* as 'the invention of the antiChrist'.[11]

Balthasar's alternative to neo-scholastic theology emerges much more confrontationally in his series of monographs on figures who have shaped (Western) theology – Irenaeus, Augustine, Denys, Anselm, Bonaventure, Dante, John of the Cross, Pascal, Hamann, Soloviev, Hopkins and Péguy. Denys, whose radically aesthetic worldview 'becomes after that of Augustine', Balthasar says, 'the second pillar of Western theology',[12] would not have been so welcome to exponents of Aristotelian–Thomistic theology.[13] In the reference to the 'giddy syntheses' of Bonaventure's 'cathedral-like theology' Balthasar must have known that he was teasing all sides in the neo-scholastic citadel.[14] More inflammatorily, Thomas Aquinas is omitted for the same reason as Origen, Gregory of Nyssa, the Florentines (Petrarch and Marsilio Ficino) and the Cambridge Platonists: 'It may be that a deep and lucid philosophical aesthetics has been developed, but that it has failed to achieve a theological translation, that is, to be seen as the unfolding of a theology based on the biblical revelation.'[15]

---

9 With *Cordula oder der Ernstfall*, published in 1966, a ferocious attack on Karl Rahner's theology, Balthasar established himself as the first major theologian to come out against what seemed a betrayal of traditional Catholicism in the aftermath of Vatican II; tr. Richard Beckley as *The Moment of Christian Witness* (New York: Paulist Press, 1969).

10 GL 1, p. 9.

11 Karl Barth: 'I regard the *analogia entis* as the invention of Antichrist, and I believe that because of it it is impossible ever to become a Roman Catholic, all other reasons for not doing so being to my mind short-sighted and trivial', originally in 1932, *Church Dogmatics* I/1 (Edinburgh: T. & T. Clark, 1975), p. xiii.

12 GL 2 (1984), pp. 17–18.

13 See Wayne Hankey, 'Denys and Aquinas: antimodern cold and postmodern hot', in *Christian Origins: Theology, Rhetoric and Community*, ed. Lewis Ayres and Gareth Jones (London and New York: Routledge, 1998).

14 GL 2, p. 18.

15 Ibid., p. 21; Aquinas is, of course, studied at length in GL 4: *The Realm of Metaphysics in Antiquity*, under the rubric of 'The theological a priori of the philosophy of beauty'. See James J. Buckley, 'Balthasar's Use of the Theology of Aquinas', *The Thomist* 59 (1995), pp. 517–45, for a judicious discussion.

Balthasar invokes what could only have seemed a very eccentric list of modern shapers of Catholic theology. J. G. Hamann, 'the Magus of the North', one of the progenitors of the *Sturm und Drang* movement and a great adversary of the Enlightenment, was, of course, a Lutheran. Vladimir Soloviev, whatever his personal relationship to the Roman Catholic Church, would not have struck many neo-scholastic theologians as 'a thinker of universal genius', and it would not have been much comfort to learn that he 'anticipates the vision of Teilhard de Chardin'.[16] Whether Gerard Manley Hopkins, a poet no doubt 'of the highest calibre', may intelligibly be said to represent 'the English theological tradition' is another matter; its difference from Continental thought is allegedly that 'there has never been any opposition between image and concept, myth and revelation, the apprehension of God in nature and in the history of salvation', thus he is able to 'build a bridge between poetic aesthetics and the Ignatian exercises'.[17] English theology, 'reared in an hereditary empiricism', alive in such works as Austin Farrer's *The Glass of Vision* and Eric Mascall's *Words and Images*, involves mistrust of the value of universal concepts, sensitivity to the uniqueness of the individual, and is traceable back to Milton, Purcell, Shakespeare and, behind them, to Duns Scotus.[18] Interesting as Balthasar's reading of Hopkins is, of course, the assumptions about Englishness would need a good deal of discriminating attention. No Continental neo-scholastic theologian would have regarded British empiricism as a receptive environment for Catholicism.[19] Duns Scotus, it was generally thought then, rightly or wrongly, created the metaphysical conditions for the work of William of Ockham, acknowledged as a mentor by Luther and, equally unwelcome to neo-scholastics, widely credited with the triumph of nominalism, supposedly the arch-error. In so far as Catholic theologians paid any attention at all to what went on in English philosophy in 1961, they regarded 'linguistic analysis' as a continuation of nominalism. Here again, Balthasar was teasingly flying a kite that could not but irritate the neo-scholastic fraternity.

What was happening in England, in philosophy, theology, or anything else, was of little interest to Catholic theologians on the Continent.[20] French theology, from the 1890s until the eve of Vatican II, was the centre of attraction, no doubt because the controversies were conducted with such passion. Charles Péguy, an ardent socialist and Dreyfusard, much influenced by the philosophy of Bergson, and an anticlerical who remained unreconciled to the Church for domestic reasons (he was killed on the Marne in 1914, aged forty), had been far too controversial a figure for decades in French Catholic circles for his inclusion in Balthasar's list to be anything but extremely provocative. Above all, the inclusion of studies

---

16 GL 2, p. 19.
17 Ibid., p. 19.
18 GL 3, p. 355.
19 It may be that such English neo-scholastics as Martin D'Arcy SJ and those described by Aidan Nichols, *Dominican Gallery: Portrait of a Culture* (Leominster: Gracewing, 1997), show more sympathy.
20 Or in North America, where neo-scholasticism was perhaps even more entrenched than in France, Germany, Italy, Spain, Poland, etc.

of 'lay styles' – the very idea of *lay* theological styles – could have been perceived as little more than a calculated insult in the entirely clerical neo-scholastic establishment of the time.

Karl Rahner's *Schriften zur Theologie*, of which the first volume appeared as early as 1954, seemed to informed readers an audacious subversion of many neo-scholastic positions; but he was almost obsessively careful to open his essays with respectful allusions to current neo-scholastic literature and to remain within the conventional bounds of the prevailing theology. Balthasar, by comparison, was reckless in his disregard for the theological establishment. True enough, *la nouvelle théologie*, with its patristic *ressourcement* appeal to philosophical pluralism and opening towards Orthodox and Protestant theologies, was to triumph over neo-scholasticism. No doubt, most of the desiderata of *la nouvelle théologie* were acknowledged at Vatican II. But that could not have been predicted in 1961. After all, there had been a decade of neo-scholastic triumphalism, and intimidation and repression of exponents, however tentative, of alternative theological projects. In 1950, in his encyclical *Humani generis*, Pope Pius XII had warned against excessive emphasis on divine revelation to the detraction of human reason; distrust of systematic theology as inadequate to the language of Scripture and the Fathers; and, in particular, indifference to philosophy, by which he meant Thomist realism. In 1961, when *Herrlichkeit* began to appear, few expected much of the Council, and many influential theologians hoped for reiterated anathematizations of the errors of modern – in effect Modernist – theologies.

That Balthasar was not reluctant to shock neo-scholastic and ultramontane sensibilities at the time might be illustrated by his substantial essays on ecclesiology, such as 'Casta Meretrix', first published in 1961.[21] But the most flagrant challenge to neo-Thomist theology was his essay 'Fides Christi', in the same volume, in which, directly contradicting Thomas Aquinas (and invoking Buber and others including Lacan's Cistercian brother Marc-François), Balthasar argues that Christ had faith, a harmless thesis some might think today, but that would only show how deaf they are to the resonances of Balthasar's interventions in the great intra-Catholic theological controversies of those days.[22]

At the time, of course, Balthasar was a lonely figure, theologically, supported principally by his friend Adrienne von Speyr, to whom he said later that he owed his most distinctive theological insights; without her, he claimed, though she had no part in the writing, 'the basic perspective of *Herrlichkeit* would never have existed'.[23] He also noted, however, perhaps somewhat ingenuously, that 'it is almost unnecessary to set out how much I owe to Karl Barth: the vision of a comprehensive biblical

---

21 In *Sponsa Verbi, Skizzen zur Theologie II*, 1961, tr. as *Explorations in Theology II: Spouse of the Word* (San Francisco: Ignatius Press, 1991), pp. 193–288; the Catholic Church as 'holy whore' was not a familiar notion among Roman Catholics in 1961.

22 Ibid., pp. 43–79; the counter-attack has been a long time coming but see Henry Donneaud, 'Hans Urs von Balthasar contre saint Thomas d'Aquin sur la foi du Christ', *Revue Thomiste* 97 (1997), pp. 335–54.

23 *First Glance at Adrienne von Speyr* (San Francisco: Ignatius Press, 1981), p. 13.

theology, combined with the urgent invitation to engage in a dogmatically serious ecumenical dialogue'.[24] Barth

> joyfully greeted and endorsed my book about him, followed my subsequent works with some suspicion, but perhaps never noticed how much a little book like *Love Alone* sought to be fair to him and represents perhaps the closest approach to his position from the Catholic side.[25]

Moreover, in the preface, Balthasar says that *Love Alone*, this 100-page 'sketch', follows the pattern of *Herrlichkeit* – as if we might be allowed to regard it, if not as a substitute, at least as an introduction to the great work itself. Finally, in *Love Alone*, Balthasar insists that his 'theological aesthetics' has 'a purely theological sense'; it centres on 'the perception in faith of the self-authenticating glory of God's utterly free gift of love'[26] – which sounds a fairly characteristic Barthian note.

The basic perspective of *Herrlichkeit* surely owes far more to Barth than to Adrienne von Speyr. In 1941 Balthasar was invited to take part in Barth's seminar on the Council of Trent – 'The enemy is listening in', Barth said, welcoming him. In return, Barth attended the lectures in 1948–9 which Balthasar gave on 'Karl Barth and Catholicism', finding in Balthasar a theologian who 'envisaged a kind of reformation of the Catholic Church and of Catholic theology from within'. To bring about this 'reformation', Barth adds that he himself 'was to be introduced like a new Trojan horse ... (against Thomas and against Augustine)' – joking, no doubt, in a letter to his son Christoph, yet presciently anticipating Balthasar's later assault on the citadel of neo-scholasticism.[27] By this time, the two theologians had become close friends (Barth's famous love of Mozart owed much to Balthasar, an accomplished musician).[28] More to the present point, however, though Balthasar offered criticisms of Barth's interpretations of Catholic doctrine in the seminar in 1941, 'there was no really impressive counter-attack', Barth notes: 'Perhaps he had been reading my *Dogmatics* too much (he dragged around II/1 especially, in his briefcase, like a cat carrying a kitten).'[29]

Whatever the dependence of the two theologians on one another, Balthasar comes close, in the introduction to the first volume of *Herrlichkeit*,[30] to saying that the very idea of contemplating the divine glory, and thus of reconceiving Christian theology in the light of the

---

24 'Rechenschaft 1965', tr. Kenneth Batinovich, in *The Analogy of Beauty*, p. 220.

25 Ibid., p. 220; *Love Alone: the Way of Revelation* (London and Dublin: Sheed & Ward and Veritas Publications, 1968), tr. anonymously with a few minor additions to the original *Glaubhaft ist nur Liebe* (Einsiedeln: Johannes Verlag, 1963).

26 Page 9: 'der nur im Glauben wahrnehmende Empfang der sich selbst auslegenden Herrlichkeit der allerfreiesten Liebe Gottes'; more literally: the perceptive reception – in faith alone – of the self-interpreting majesty of God's utterly free love.

27 Eberhard Busch, *Karl Barth: His Life from Letters and Autobiographical Texts* (London: SCM Press, 1975), p. 362, letter dated 30 December 1948.

28 Ibid., p. 362.

29 Ibid., p. 302.

30 GL 1, pp. 52–6.

transcendental of beauty, comes precisely from Barth's *Church Dogmatics* II/1. In that volume, Barth deals with the perfections of the divine freedom – God as 'One, constant and eternal, and therewith also omnipresent, omnipotent and glorious'. The treatise culminates in the claim that the biblical concept of God's glory, if it is to mean 'something other and more than the assertion of a brute fact', requires the complement of the concept of *beauty*: to say that God is beautiful is to say 'how He enlightens and convinces and persuades us'.[31] What the thesis means is as follows:

> It is to say that God has this superior force, this power of attraction, which speaks for itself, which wins and conquers, in the fact that He is beautiful, divinely beautiful, beautiful in His own way, in a way that is His alone, beautiful as the unattainable primal beauty, yet really beautiful.[32]

Barth continues, for fifteen or sixteen pages, often in this same lyrical vein, about the beauty of God as the radiance of his glory.

Of course Barth cautions us against bringing contemplation of God 'into suspicious proximity to that contemplation of the world which in the last resort is the self-contemplation of an urge for life which does not recognize its own limits'.[33] This would be to bring God 'in a sinister because in a sense intimate way into the sphere of man's oversight and control'.[34] Nevertheless, however carefully, we have to say that God is beautiful and in saying this, Barth goes on to note, 'we reach back to the pre-Reformation tradition of the Church'.[35] Here, then, at the conclusion of his treatment of the doctrine of the divine perfections, in Balthasar's cherished volume of the *Dogmatics*, Barth refers back to Augustine and Pseudo-Dionysius, insisting on great caution in taking on board this 'hardly veiled Platonism', but finally deciding that 'biblical truth itself' does not 'permit us to stop at this point because of the danger' – we have to say that 'God is beautiful'. The motif is rare in the ancient Church, Barth says, and 'completely ignored' in Protestant theology. 'Even Schleiermacher, in whom we might have expected something of this kind', he says, perhaps a little slyly, 'did not achieve anything very striking in this direction.'[36] Indeed, post-Reformation Catholic theology did not feature this notion either, Barth says, until Scheeben (in 1874). But, for all 'the danger that threatens from the side of aesthetics', there is no reason, despite the history of Protestantism, 'to shrink back at this point with particular uneasiness or prudery, suppressing or dismissing out of sheer terror a problem that is set us by the subject itself and its biblical attestation'.[37]

31 *Church Dogmatics* II/1 (Edinburgh: T. & T. Clark, 1957), p. 650 (published in German 1940).
32 Ibid., p. 650.
33 Ibid., p. 651.
34 Ibid.
35 Ibid.
36 Ibid.
37 Ibid., p. 652.

Here, Balthasar thinks, Barth achieves a 'decisive breakthrough'.[38] The terror of corrupting evangelical theology by Platonizing philosophy is understandable but needs to be resisted. Barth recognized that his appeal to 'an authentic theological aesthetics' had 'no roots within the realm of Protestant theology' but required him to retrieve 'those elements of Patristic and Scholastic thought which can be justified from revelation itself and which, accordingly, are not suspect of any undue Platoniz- ing'. Balthasar rejoices in Barth's return to a pre-Reformation theology of the divine beauty; but one wonders how far Balthasar's project of writing a theological aesthetics was shaped, and even perhaps prompted, by his delight in Barth's treatise on the divine perfections. Since it came out in 1940, the year that Balthasar arrived in Basle, he could not have had any influence on *Dogmatics* II/1. It seems likely, on the other hand, that Balthasar found in Barth's theology of the glory and beauty of God the strategy to dethrone the neo-scholasticism – 'sawdust Thomism' – which he hated so deeply.[39] The Reformed theologian's reopening of a patristic/scholastic theologoumenon enabled the Catholic theologian to drive coach and horses through the neo- scholastic establishment.

In addition, Balthasar claims to find a movement within Barth's theology from the 'first stage', 'a phase whose inner form lay in the over- powering and uncompromising rhetoric of Luther and the Reformation', with an emphasis on the scandal of the Gospel and plenty of anti-Catholic rant, to a 'second stage' laying claim to 'pre-Reformation theology' in a 'tranquil, attentive contemplation *(theoria)* of revelation'. He even sees this movement from polemics to contemplation 'from volume to volume of the *Dogmatics* ' (by 1961 Barth had published IV/3, the last volume, as it turned out, except the 'fragment' on baptism which appeared in 1967, a year before his death). Luther's theology, though rooted in Scripture, was 'basically anti-contemplative'.[40] Modern Protestant theology, remaining subservient to Bultmann's dualism of biblical criticism and *sola fide* existentialism, is immune to this 'contemplative' (quasi-Catholic!) Barth.[41] So Balthasar concludes.

Barth did a good deal to establish Balthasar's reputation as an unconventional theologian. He first mentions him in *Dogmatics* IV/1 (1953). Lamenting the papal encyclical *Mystici Corporis* (1943), Barth concludes that 'for the moment it is hard to see how there can be any further discussion with the official Roman Catholic doctrine of the Church when it so obviously continues to harden in this way'.[42] On the other hand, there are hopeful signs:

38 GL 1, p. 56.
39 'I could have lashed out with the fury of Samson. I felt like tearing down, with Samson's own strength, the whole temple and burying myself beneath the rubble. But it was like this because, despite my sense of vocation, I wanted to carry out my own plans, and was living in a state of unbounded indignation'; recalling in 1975 his years of study as a Jesuit in the 1930s, cited by Edward T. Oakes, *Pattern of Redemption: The Theology of Hans Urs von Balthasar* (New York: Continuum, 1994), p. 2.
40 GL 1, p. 57.
41 Ibid., p. 56.
42 *Church Dogmatics* IV/1, p. 659.

We must not overlook the fact that within modern Roman
Catholicism there are those who think and speak of the Church in
a way which is very different and which seems to give fresh life
to the *fide solum intelligimus*, cf. the stimulating writings of H. U. v.
Balthasar (*Geschleifte Bastionen*) and F. Heer (*Das Experiment
Europa*).[43]

Later in the same volume, in the course of attacking (a little bizarrely)
Bultmann's 'existentialist translation of the sacramentalist teaching of the
Roman Church', Barth refers again to Balthasar: 'In modern Roman
Catholic theology there is a promising but, of course, unofficial movement
which is apparently aiming in the direction of what we might call a
christological renaissance.'[44] He mentions Balthasar's book on his own
work – 'an understanding ... incomparably more powerful than that of
most of the books which have clustered around me'. Mainly, however, he
is out to demolish Balthasar, who has 'with him and under him quite a
chorus of German and especially French friends' (alluding, teasingly, to
the generation of *la nouvelle théologie*, of whom, as he must have known,
most were under a cloud):

> this promising new beginning in Roman Catholic theology is in
> danger of returning to, or it may be has never left, the well-worn
> track on which the doctrine of justification is absorbed into that of
> sanctification – understood as the pious work of self-sanctification
> which man can undertake and accomplish in his own strength.[45]

Barth cites Balthasar's studies of the Carmelite nuns Thérèse of Lisieux
(1950), and Elisabeth of Dijon (1952) and the layman Reinhold Schneider
(1953), alleging that their stories are told with 'such positive and stimulating force' that the Holy One 'fades into the background as compared
with His saints'. Barth, here, is countering Balthasar's famous remark
about the 'christological constriction' of the *Dogmatics*; but it is surely
outrageous to claim that the figure of Christ is occluded in Balthasar's
biographical studies of some saints.

However all that may be, it is not absurd to see Balthasar's magnificent
attempt, in *Herrlichkeit*, to expound a theology centred on the glory of
God, as an extension of Barth's reflections on the beauty of God in *Church
Dogmatics* II/1. In fact, Balthasar himself confirms this. In the introduction
to the final volume of *Herrlichkeit*, which deals with the motif of glory/
beauty in the New Testament, Balthasar reverts to *Dogmatics* II/1 at some
length, saying that Barth's theology of glory 'agrees with our own overall
plan' and that outlining it, as Barth does, offers 'an overview that we

43 Balthasar's book, actually entitled *Schleifung der Bastionen* (1952), was the
'programmatic piece ... which blew the last, impatient trumpet blast calling for a
Church no longer barricaded against the world, a trumpet blast that did not die
away unheard, but which has subsequently forced the trumpeter himself to pause
and reflect'; see *The Analogy of Beauty*, p. 196.
44 *Church Dogmatics* IV/1, p. 767.
45 Ibid., p. 768.

ourselves can approach only slowly'.[46] Thus, in effect, *Herrlichkeit* is a slow, patient and much more elaborate working out of Barth's conception of the divine beauty.

Balthasar's dependence on Barth for inspiration has been noted by Noel Dermot O'Donoghue: '*Herrlichkeit* is in some ways a rewriting of Barth's *Church Dogmatics*', he says, without specifying further, but adding that

> a lot of the excitement of the book comes from the tension between the Barthian theology of discontinuity (and the total Otherness of God in Christ) and that Platonic and Aristotelian strand in Catholic theology which sees nature and grace as somehow continuous, and so defends the basic goodness and beauty of human life.

Furthermore, 'part of the background (or horizon?)' of Balthasar's work is 'the Luther–Kierkegaard–Barth theology of discontinuity'.[47]

It sounds as if O'Donoghue finds, in Balthasar's *Herrlichkeit*, a strenuous attempt to integrate with traditional patristic/medieval theology the occasionalism, the monism of the Word of God invading a hostile world, the actualistic theopanism, etc. of which Catholic theologians have frequently complained, perhaps with some justification as regards Barth's *Epistle to the Romans* and even the first volume of *Church Dogmatics*. O'Donoghue accuses Balthasar of being so captivated by Barth's 'theology from above' that, for all his being 'deeply imbued with traditional Marian piety', his treatment of Mary's *fiat*, while seeming to insist on human initiative, 'shows on closer reading an undertow of the kind of theology in which man is passively receptive and does not in any real sense work out his own salvation'.[48] O'Donoghue wants to 'push Balthasar back to some of his acknowledged sources', who turn out to be all modern Catholic (Scheeben, Karl Adam, Romano Guardini, Erich Przywara), in order to secure 'the place of the human in the divine–human encounter', and to bring forward the synergic theology which is in the background of Balthasar's work but clearly, O'Donoghue thinks, somewhat threatened by 'the Barthian "monergic" strand'.[49]

Perhaps. But if *Herrlichkeit* is inspired by Barth's appeal to a pre-Reformation theology of glory/beauty, it is, on the contrary, a 'contemplative' and quasi-'patristic' Barth on whose insights Balthasar is drawing. Of course, in the divine economy of salvation, Plato's *imago* metaphysics and Aristotle's *causa-et-finis* metaphysical realism come together on a higher level, as Balthasar says, which means that we cannot approach Christian love and beauty in merely Platonic terms.[50] We are not succumbing to 'the false kind of enthusiasm which hovers about suspended on aestheticist and idealistic proleptical illusions' (!). Rather, 'as Karl Barth has rightly seen', we must never speak of God's beauty

---

46 GL 7, p. 23.
47 In *The Analogy of Beauty*, p. 3.
48 Ibid., referring to GL 1, p. 485.
49 Ibid., p. 4.
50 GL 1, p. 123.

'without reference to the form and manner of appearing which he exhibits in salvation-history' – including the Cross and everything else which 'a worldly aesthetics ... discards as no longer bearable'.[51] God's attribute of beauty can certainly be treated in the context of a doctrine of the divine perfections, Balthasar says (where else did he find it in Barth?); it could be examined as manifested in creation, it might be 'deduced' from the doctrine of the Trinity; but none of these considerations would speak to us, Balthasar insists, unless at every stage of reflection the *theologia* is never detached from the *oikonomia* but is, on the contrary, 'accompanied and supported by the latter's vivid discernibility'.[52] Balthasar, there, could hardly be more 'Barthian'.

There are many other references to Barth's *Dogmatics* in *Herrlichkeit*. Three are particularly relevant here. In connection with 'the dynamic interrelationship of classical theo-philosophy and the Christian theology of revelation', illustrated by the 'bold paradox' in which Thomas Aquinas declared that 'it belongs to the nobility of human nature that we can attain perfection in our *desiderium naturale* for the very Highest only through a free self-disclosure of God' (another glance at the controversy over Henri de Lubac's attacks on the Thomist commentators), Barth reappears as 'significantly and prophetically' transcending the dogma-free Christianity of the Enlightenment and German idealism by permitting 'a feeling for "glory"' to emerge 'in a new and elemental way'.[53] Secondly, insisting on the 'Catholic' claim that 'if God speaks his word to created men and women, surely it is because he has given them an understanding which, with God's grace, can achieve the act of hearing and comprehending', but insisting equally on the 'Barthian' point that this cannot occur on the basis of a neutral foreknowledge of what 'truth' is, Balthasar writes as follows:

> Such encounter with God cannot take place on a dialogical plane which has been opened in advance; it can occur only by virtue of a primary sense of being overawed by the undialogical presupposition of the dialogue that has started, namely, the divinity or glory of God.[54]

Finally, discussing the 'allocation of the love of God in Christ, which however contains within the gift the requirement which corresponds to it' – 'the decisively Christian element in a theological aesthetics' – 'because its essential basis is the inner Trinity of God and the coming-forth of this Trinity in the Incarnation', Balthasar refers us once again to the remarks, 'quoted at the beginning', about the beauty of God in his Trinity and his incarnation, in *Dogmatics* II/1.[55]

Suppose, then, that Barth's doctrine of the divine perfections played a decisive part in shaping Balthasar's alternative to neo-scholastic theology,

51 Ibid., p. 124.
52 Ibid., p. 125.
53 GL 5, pp. 14–15.
54 GL 6, p. 11.
55 GL 7, p. 314.

does it follow that, if the impact of *Herrlichkeit* had not been forestalled by the Council, neo-scholasticism would have collapsed? Were the adversaries of *la nouvelle théologie* entirely misguided in their fears that the attack on the neo-scholastic dichotomy between the orders of grace and of nature would lead, not to an equilibrium which would balance the natural and the supernatural in a living unity, but rather, as O'Donoghue contends,[56] to a thoroughgoing supernaturalism? No doubt the apologetics, metaphysics and non-biblical ethics practised with such gusto in the pre-Vatican II era often left the specifically Christian doctrines in the shadows. No doubt, also, in the continuing anti-Modernist mode in mainstream theology, with its fears of 'experience', 'tradition', 'life' and so on (subjectivism, historicism, vitalism, pragmatism, etc.), neo-scholasticism often tended towards a certain rationalism. But the deepest problem in Roman Catholic theology, since Vatican II, has been the disappearance of serious engagement with *philosophy*.

Given the lengthy examination of the history of the contemplation of beauty in the central volumes of *Herrlichkeit*, from Homer and the Greek tragedians through Plato and Plotinus to Heidegger, it may seem inappropriate, in connection with Balthasar, to raise questions about the absence of philosophy in theology today. But that is the problem. Balthasar's history of the metaphysical tradition comes to a head in his claim that it is now the Christian who 'remains the guardian of that metaphysical wonderment which is the point of origin for philosophy and the continuation of which is the basis for its further existence'.[57] A little further on he says: 'the responsibility for developing a comprehensive and contemporary metaphysics falls to the Christian'.[58] Behind this claim that, as it seems, philosophy must now be conducted within the context of faith, there lies Balthasar's assumption that the Western metaphysical tradition centres on 'the authentic metaphysical question': 'Why is there anything at all and not simply nothing?'.[59]

Balthasar's history of metaphysics is thoroughly imbued with Heideggerian language and insights. Here, of course, he is denying Heidegger's thesis that Christians cannot take the question why there is anything rather than nothing seriously since (as Heidegger thinks) they already have the answer. On the contrary, Balthasar contends, Christians are the only ones who are capable of the 'wonder at Being' which is fundamental to metaphysics. Moreover, it is not, as Heidegger thinks, that authentic philosophy is rooted simply in wonder at beings in their difference from being. Rather, it is that 'Being as such by itself to the very end "causes wonder", behaving as something to be wondered at, something striking and worthy of wonder'. But this 'primal wonder' which is 'the fundamental aim of metaphysics' turns out, Balthasar contends, to be 'that which in the realm of metaphysics deserves the authentic name "Glory"'.[60] In other words, philosophy is always already theology –

56　*The Analogy of Beauty*, p. 5.
57　GL 5, p. 646.
58　Ibid., p. 652.
59　Ibid., p. 613.
60　Ibid., pp. 614–15.

nature, so to speak, is always already grace. The 'miracle of Being', Balthasar says, is 'the site of glory in metaphysics'.[61]

For Balthasar, metaphysics seems to be absorbed into theology, in just the way that an opponent of *la nouvelle théologie* would anticipate. No doubt neo-Thomists were mistaken to speak of 'a pure nature without grace', but it is equally mistaken to allow the discourse of the economy of grace to dictate and even replace the open-ended investigations of philosophy. It is not only survivors from the neo-scholastic era who would regard this as short-circuiting matters of importance – of importance also for *theology*. These days, in the 'Continental' tradition as well as in the 'analytical' tradition, metaphysics is a flourishing discipline. All the main traditional topics are under discussion: the problem of universals, the nature of abstract entities, the problem of individuation, the nature of modality, identity through time, the nature of time, of meaning and of truth, etc. and especially (in this context) the realism/ antirealism debate in English-speaking philosophy, logocentrism and deconstruction in Continental terms.

It is hard to see much development of Catholic Christian theology, or of Balthasar's theology in particular, taking root in the English-speaking world without serious re-engagement with metaphysics.[62] It is not that the work of contemporary philosophers should be confronted for apologetic purposes. Rather, as Donald MacKinnon (one of the first to introduce Balthasar's work to English-speaking students) tactfully pointed out, in connection with Balthasar's Christology, 'it is arguable that a greater philosophical expertise would have helped his exposition'.[63]

Similarly, as the essays in this book show, Balthasar's work can be continued in new directions only by engaging with current projects in philosophy which, while no doubt rightly described as poststructuralist and postmodernist, take us back, in the wake of Nietzsche and Heidegger, to German idealism, the movement with which, in different ways, Barth and Balthasar both strove to come to terms, and the impact of which in Catholic theology neo-scholasticism was invented to avoid.[64]

---

61 Ibid., p. 613.
62 One place to start would perhaps be Hilary Putnam's 1989–90 Gifford Lectures at St Andrew's, *Renewing Philosophy* (Cambridge, MA, and London: Harvard University Press, 1992).
63 *The Analogy of Beauty*, p. 172.
64 The place to start here would be *Post-Secular Philosophy: Between philosophy and theology*, edited by Phillip Blond (London: Routledge, 1997).

2

꙳

Kenosis:
Death, Discourse and Resurrection

GRAHAM WARD

There is a museum in Florence, situated on the Via Romana, beyond the Ponte Vecchio and just past the Palazzo Pitti. The Palazzo Torrigiani is a natural history museum built in the closing years of the eighteenth century, like so many other museums in European cities. And in the Museo Zoologico there is a prize exhibit – a rather grey-looking rhinoceros. It is the oldest extant stuffed animal, one of the first in what was to become a new art form: taxidermy.

W. Swainson, who wrote a definitive account of the art, *A Treatise on Taxidermy*, published in Glasgow in 1840, lists at the back of his volume two famous collectors of the sixteenth century, one Ulysses Aldrovandi, an Italian, the other Pierre Belon, a Frenchman. He does not record the story a French taxidermist in 1687 relates about the first collection of natural exhibits. According to this story, which ties in well with the growth of trade in the sixteenth century, a Dutch nobleman in 1518 brought back from India many beautiful tropical birds. He built a heated aviary for them and put them on public display. But one evening a servant left open the door of the furnace which was used to keep the room warm. In the morning the birds were all found dead from suffocation. Distraught, the nobleman combed the city of Amsterdam for chemists who could restore his birds to the resemblance of life. A crew of such chemists was assembled. They skinned and wired and stuffed the bodies with Indian spices, mounting them in such a way that the aviary, though now silent, was once again full of their colourful presences.

Throughout the seventeenth century, the number of collectors listed grows considerably. By the late seventeenth century England has its own taxidermists. In the eighteenth century learned treatises, particularly in France, were published by Ferchault de Reaumur (in 1748), M. B. Stollas (in 1752), by E. F. Turgot (in 1758), by the Abbé Manesse (in 1786). The first English treatise appears in 1794, written by one E. Donovan, 'Instructions for collecting and preserving various subjects of natural history'. The account of the operation is graphic and tactile:

[F]irst open the skin with a pair of sharp-pointed scissars [*sic*], in a straight direction from the vent to the throat, and take away all the inside, scoop out the brains, take away the eyes, and with the scissars cut off whatever flesh you can from within the head, as the tongue, &c., but leave the skull; during this operation be careful to preserve the mouth, snout, feet, and claws perfect, and if any blood, or slimy matter adheres to the hair, wash it off with a sponge and warm water: the skin must then be laid on a flat board, or table, and rubbed on the inside with some composition liquor, or powder, until it feels perfectly dry to the hand.

The emphasis is upon control. The presupposition is a realm of natural, self-defining entities upon which operations can commence. The tone of the instructions is almost objective, the operation almost mechanical, but not quite. Certain shivers of sensation emerge with contact: those scissors have edge, the brains are scooped, certain slimy matter adheres. It is as if science's newly emerging discrete and inert objects, based upon atomistic conceptions of matter,[1] are not quite dry – a certain stickiness pertains and the subject cannot quite absolve himself from it to enable the illusion of objectivity. Nevertheless, the aim of the technology is perfect replication, identical repetition – for preservation, for acquisition. But for what reason and for whom? These were the years that saw the rise of 'Cabinets of Curiosity' owned by the wealthy, later to become, or be bequeathed to, museums. The treatment – its method, its tone – manufactures objects frozen in time, objects to be acquired, possessed, exchanged, 'articles of commercial speculation', Swainson notes,[2] articles to be tabled, labelled and arranged (with wires and staves) in 'natural positions'.

Swainson sums up this developing 'art', the aestheticization of the natural: taxidermy 'teaches the various processes by which the form and substance of animal bodies may be preserved from decay, and rendered subservient to the studies of the naturalist in his closet'.[3] The art is an exercise in power and governance. Knowledge is mastery and reasoning is instrumental in obtaining that mastery. Swainson's account includes tips on hunting the animals, explains the difficulties to be encountered and overcome in India, Africa and South America, and describes the best means of shipping and importing bodies. What is being offered is a manual on trading in death. It is a death glorified, heightened and yet curiously concealed. The taxidermist produces forms akin to those great obelisks and mausoleums in cemeteries of the same period. William Hornaday, in a treatise published in 1891 entitled 'Taxidermy and Zoological Collecting', writes against those who 'collect' indiscriminately.

---

1 In her *New Maladies of the Soul*, tr. Ross Guberman (New York: Columbia University Press, 1995), Julia Kristeva writes: 'Galileo's Copernican heliocentrism, which was eventually accepted by the Church, does not seem to have been the primary focus of the accusations brought against him, which were provoked rather by his conception of matter' (p. 180). Science could not proceed until matter was viewed atomistically, rather than capable of transubstantiation and an allegorical reading. At the heart of this essay is a rereading of 'matter'.
2 W. Swainson, *A Treatise on Taxidermy* (Glasgow, 1840), p. 3.
3 Ibid., p. 1.

The collector should first know how to collect, for 'to collect' has become a cognate of 'to quarry'. The observance of this principle would have saved the useless slaughter of tens of thousands of animals. What is voiced in the taxidermist's employment of words like 'preservation' and 'perfection' is a secularized form of eternal life, a technology of resurrection devised in the all too evident climate of death. But the bodies produced are silent and lifeless, universal specimens not particular and contingent.

I employ taxidermy – its development, its practices, its desires – as a cultural metaphor for modernity. By cultural metaphor I mean a cultural event or activity which stands for some symptomatic value in any particular *Zeitgeist*. If, following Clifford Geertz, we can understand different cultures in terms of different languages, then in this way we can draw an analogy between the way powerful, expressive and condensed figures of speech act as focuses for significance and the way specific cultural phenomena relate to the general cultural climate. By modernity I mean the modern age as Balthasar characterizes it in volume 5 of *The Glory of the Lord* (H III.1/2). It is the age when man becomes the measure of all things:

> Around the centre of this man, Pico gathers together all arts and sciences, philosophy, mysticism and magic, and finally also Christian theology. The ideal of the *uomo universale* seeks for a time to realise in life this great man who will be equal to every intellectual [*geistigen*] exercise, like Leonardo da Vinci or even Erasmus, Paracelsus, Milton, Goethe. In order to probe [*ergrunden*] his metaphysical being and at the same time his fitness for achievement, he is – like a chemical – isolated in strange retorts; on the island Utopia (Thomas More), in the kingdom of the Sun (Campanella), in New Atlantis (Francis Bacon), he is to prove how far he can create a society out of his own powers. (H III.1/2, 632; GL 5, 286)

This is the age of metaphysical speculation, of self-regulating 'nature, of scientific positivism, of social contracts, of liberal humanism, of aesthetics divorced from the transcendentals of truth and goodness'. It is also, to return to my cultural metaphor, the age of death.

At a time when infinity (and its implications) was being discovered and, concomitantly, appalling fears of finitude, humanity dreamed of boundless freedom, limitless development, evolving perfection, secular eternities (Spinoza), secular kingdoms of God (Kant), secular self-transcendence (Heidegger). The denied, repressed and therefore obsessive scene – as historians such as Philippe Ariès, Michel Vovelle and social theorists like Jean Baudrillard have shown[4] – was death. The psychologies of death (Freud), philosophies of death (Heidegger) and theologies of death (Hamilton, Altizer) are only three of the

---

4 See Philippe Ariès, *The Hour of Our Death*, tr. Helen Weaver (London: Penguin, 1983); Michel Vovelle, *La Mort et L'Occident de 1300 à nos jours* (Paris: Gallimard, 1983); and Jean Baudrillard, *Symbolic Exchange and Death*, tr. Iain Hamilton (London: Sage Publications, 1993).

twentieth-century trajectories of this repressed scene. They each, like the art of taxidermy, announce a paradox of modernity – a certain necrophilia issuing from a profound necrophobia. We can locate the art of taxidermy within one recent scholar's account of the movement.

> [F]rom the funeral excesses of the baroque, the perfected technique of embalming, to the ghastly tableau of a corpse preserved in his favourite armchair reading the newspaper, practices which on the surface appear as fetishizations of death act as consolations which parade personal extinction as an illusion of art.[5]

Consciously, the death-bound subjectivities of modernity[6] imagined forms of absolute power, total control. They conceived the cult of the inert object, science's inert object extolled and validated as Nature. In the wake and pull of the infinite, the recognized vulnerability and the awesome alienation led to a new concern with desire – desire as lack, as yearning for the moon (see Blake's cartoon of the ladder set up upon the earth). The subject's life in the *Bildungsroman* stretched out in one long aching for the never-to-be-achieved consummation.[7] Balthasar will draw attention to metaphors of modernity's heroic *eros* – Racine's Phèdre, Kleist's Penthesilea, Byron's Cain, Wagner's Tristan. He will point out how the presentation of *eros* here 'in its self-glory and autonomy' (H III.1/2, 624; GL 5, 279) is linked both to post-Christian notions of integration and apotheosis and also to madness, Dionysian power, passion and death. Modernity's Prometheus unbound is an apocalyptic figure modelling himself on a Titan and, like the Titan Cronus, consuming all his children.[8] Here Balthasar's work began with an examination of the Prometheus principle in Western European literature from the sixteenth century, in the first volume of his dissertation *Apokalypse der deutschen Seele* (Salzburg: A. Pustet, 1937). Here, forty years later, in a chapter entitled 'Titanisms' in his *Theodrama* his examination remains central (TD II.1, 385–91; ThD, 2 420–6).

Prometheus' tool is mimesis – for he himself was modelled and expresses modelling. The 'art' of taxidermy replaces the ergon of a living entity with an aesthetics of the object, with a soulless materialism. The technologies of production and reproduction dominate a culture of

---

5 Catherine Pickstock, *After Writing: Language, Death and Liturgy* (Oxford: Blackwell, 1997), p. 102.
6 See A. Lingis' book, *Deathbound Subjectivities* (Bloomington: Indiana University Press, 1992) for an account of the *eros–thanatos* preoccupation of philosophy from Descartes to Derrida.
7 Ben Quash's treatment of Balthasar's ecclesiology and doctrine of the eucharist (Chapter 4, below) demonstrates that the thought of consummation and the question of its place and nature in Christian thought remains an important motif in his work.
8 See Edith Wyschogrod's book, *Spirit in Ashes: Hegel, Heidegger and Man-made Mass Death* (New Haven: Yale University Press, 1985). She traces the reification of the objects and persons, the spiritual and material sources which brought about modernity's death-world, and provides a genealogy for the 'Present-day myths which organise existence in terms of annihilation' (p. 29). These myths are apocalyptic and reflect 'a wholly new immanent totality'.

representation in which the subject is sharply divided and placed in authority over the object. It is a culture in which endless reproduction of the same gives the illusion of time passing, of life.

It is within the logic and economies (monetary, metaphysical and libidinal) of such a culture that the doctrine of kenosis – the self-emptying of God in Christ – becomes the focus for philosophical, ethical and theological attention. This essay is concerned with the nature and implications of that doctrine and its refigurations in modernity. It will argue for the importance of Balthasar's re-examination of that ancient teaching, at the end of modernity's imaginings, as a way beyond the impasse of the 'death-world' (Edith Wyschogrod's term).[9] It will argue for a theological account of resurrection which pushes beyond Balthasar, after him; an account which takes up and refigures the preoccupations of modernity – with representation and the natural order, with the passing of illusion, with the logic of production, alienation and synthesis, with desire, death and subjectivity – within a Christian, eschatological horizon. It will argue for a resurrection of the body on the far side of modernity's culture of necropolis. This body, contingent, particular and yet in its contingency and particularity elected to the supernatural, issues from a reconception of materiality. This body is permeable, frangible and distributed across other bodies – spiritual bodies, physical bodies, ecclesial bodies, political bodies, the eucharistic body of Christ, the bodies of specific discourses which articulate any one body's constantly shifting identity. This body is *corpus*, and I will argue for a cultural movement towards 'transcorporality'[10] within which Balthasar's theological corpus can be relevantly situated, though I leave to Ben Quash's essay any elucidation of Balthasar's theology of the eucharist.

Kenosis: Philippians 2.5–11

Much of what follows rests upon an interpretation of seven verses in this Pauline epistle (in the Jewish context of Isaiah's Suffering Servant). Therefore we begin our exploration of the configurations of the doctrine of kenosis with exegesis. This is not because my exegesis can avoid being any less impartial than anyone else's, but because we need at the outset a detailed map of the kenotic trajectory. In this way we can locate particular emphases placed by theologians on one part of the trajectory and, consequently, critique their blindness to other parts. More importantly, this is not simply an essay in the history of a doctrine from the beginning to the end of modernity. This essay is also an attempt, following Balthasar

---

9 The 'death-world' (modelled on the world and values of the extermination camp) and the 'death-event' (the staging and imagining of mass death in manifold forms – man-made starvation, nuclear war), Wyschogrod believes, constitute a new grid through which all experiencing now takes place. They are historical a priori which lie behind our culture of necropolis.

10 The word was coined by Kristeva (who may be quoting James Joyce), *New Maladies of the Soul*, p. 188. I employ it to suggest a permeable, frangible set of overlapping bodies and the movement of relations – biological, erotic, agapiac, epistemic, political – between and within them. See my essay 'Transcorporeality: The ontological scandal' in Grace Jantzen (ed.), special issue of *John Rylands Bulletin on Representation, Gender and Experience* (Manchester University Press, 1999).

and developing his insights, to configure a postmodern doctrine of kenosis which takes biblical exegesis as its starting-point.

According to the *carmen Christi* of Philippians 2.5–11, the *locus classicus* for Christian teaching on kenosis, it is the incarnation, the Word becoming flesh, which allows us to trace the association between kenosis and naming, the event of God's love and the taking of form:

> Have this mind among yourselves, which is yours in Christ Jesus, who, though he was in the form of God, did not count equality with God a thing to be grasped, but emptied himself, taking the form of a servant, being born like other human beings. And being recognised as a man, he humbled himself and became obedient to the point of death, even death on a cross. Therefore God has highly exalted him and graciously bestowed on him the name which is above every name, that at the name of Jesus every knee should bow, in heaven and on earth and under the earth, and every tongue confess that Jesus Christ is Lord, to the glory of God the Father.

In the descent Christ empties himself, makes himself void. The verb *kenoō* is related to the noun *kenos*, meaning 'vain', 'devoid of truth' or 'without a gift'. With the doctrine of kenosis, then, we investigate exactly what it is to be incarnate. Put systematically, Christology grounds a theological anthropology, and a theological account of what we know of God and how we know it. The kenotic myth concerns the nature of theological naming or discourse and the nature of nature itself. As John Macquarrie has recently observed, the importance of the teaching lies in its insistence upon the importance of the material, the historical and the embodied. It offers a 'safeguard against those docetic tendencies which seem to have dogged the classical christology through the centuries'.[11] With this teaching we are concerned with the relationship between the Logos and mediation.

Kenosis is a doctrine of divine representation. But as the account of the act of divine representation it calls into question the nature and status (ontological and epistemological) of human representations before and following the incarnation. Furthermore, if Christology grounds a theo-logical anthropology, the God who becomes form grounds the human capacity to make forms. Being *homo symbolicus* is integral to being made 'in the image of God'. It is therefore significant that the *carmen Christi* of Paul's letter reveals a concern with representations and consciousness, human and divine. 'Be mindful', verse 5 exhorts, and *phroneo* is both intellectual understanding and the ability to think. The verse enjoins that we have the same consciousness as Christ. Verses 6 and 7 delineate that consciousness in terms of a certain morphology and a certain action. He

---

11 John Macquarrie, *Jesus Christ in Modern Thought* (London: SCM Press, 1990), p. 245. For a contemporary and feminist approach to the doctrine of kenosis see Sarah Coakley's penetrating essay '*Kenosis* and Subversion: On the Repression of "Vulnerability" in Christian Feminist Writing', in Daphne Hampson (ed.), *Swallowing the Fishbone: Feminist Theologians Debate Christianity* (London: SPCK, 1996), pp. 82–111.

existed in the form of God (*en morphē theou*) but in the emptying he became the form of a slave (*morphēn doulou*). We will return to these phrases. In this morphology, though he was equal to God he did not reckon (*hegesato*), think or consider that as something to be used for his advantage.[12] In this morphology he took on the likeness (*homoiomati*) of human beings and was found in human form (*schēmati*). In verse 7, the 'taking form' and the 'becoming like' are both modalities of the main verb *kenoō*. Christ's kenosis is his incarnation (death and resurrection)[13] – that is the point. Christ's kenosis is not concerned with the abandonment of divine properties. It actually reveals something about God that would otherwise be concealed – his powerlessness in his giving of himself as servant. The effect of kenosis is a renaming of the world, a world embraced by the Word, again. God gives Christ 'the name above all names' (*to onoma to uper pan onoma*); a name before which all others will bow and each tongue confess (*exomologēsetai* – speak out publicly) the Lordship of Christ. Again, humiliation or submission (not Christ's this time, but ours) leads directly to acts of representation, to speaking out publicly. The site for the continuation of the renaming of the world in terms of the Word is the Church – its liturgies, its sacraments, its office. Quash will say more about this public and liturgical speaking in Chapter 4.

One of the main shifts within the hymn is from the language of form (*morphē* and *schēma*) to the act of naming. The act of naming is made to participate in the form of revelation – for the name revealed, and then confessed, is God's own name, Lord. Furthermore, its concern with representation and human consciousness is worked out in terms of a poetic performance. The Christian reader learns by reading. The reading is part of the theological practice. Since Ernst Lohmeyer's study of the hymn in the 1920s, these lines have been understood to constitute a poetic unit composed with ellipsis, 'rhythm, parallelism, and strophic arrangement'.[14] In other words, the hymn re-presents. It is not separated as an act from the action it tells. It is a poetic enactment reflecting upon three enfolded forms of representation – the divine representation of God in Christ, the exemplary nature and vicarious representation of Christ's self-giving for the Philippians (see 2.1–4) and the act of naming and speaking as a response to the reception of what is given. Gardner and Moss' essay develops this notion of reception with respect to Balthasar's theology and demonstrates the connection between reception, participation and analogy. For this essay it is sufficient to show how the kenotic hymn is characterized by a self-reflexive meditation upon theological, ethical and

---

12 See P. T. O'Brien, *The Epistle to the Philippians* (Grand Rapids: Eerdmans, 1991), pp. 211–16, on interpretations of this phrase '*ouk harpagmon hegesato*'.

13 J. Jeremias, on the basis of a comparison between this action and the pouring out of the Suffering Servant's soul in Isaiah 53, argues that the kenosis is not the incarnation, but only the death. See 'Zu Phil 2,7 ... EAUTON EKENOSEN' in *Novum Testamentum* 6 (1963), pp. 182–8. This would associate him with the culture of necropolis, modernity. Central to my thesis is that an act of incarnation is also an entry into death, but the two moments of this economy are summed up in the third, resurrection, which is an eternal living beyond oneself.

14 O'Brien, *Philippians*, p. 198. Although it still remains contentious how many strophes there are – two (Martin) or three (Dibelius).

linguistic imitation: salvation, the appropriate behaviour of those being saved, and language.

The kenotic economy turns, then, upon four key words associated with representation: *morphē, homoiōma, schēma* and *onoma. Morphe* is an unusual word in the New Testament – it appears only once more in the longer ending of Mark's Gospel (16.12). According to Lightfoot it 'implies not the external accidents but the essential attributes'.[15] Much has been written concerning the dative *en* and several commentators have stressed its importance for the interpretation of the whole passage.[16] *En morphē theou* – the Godhead as a sphere within which Christ dwells – would then be the equivalent of the Johannine 'that glory I had with you before the world began' (17.5). The *en* as such would then suggest trinitarian participation by the Son in the Father. Following Lightfoot, a host of more recent scholars have confirmed this reading by pointing out the affinity between *morphē* and *eikōn*, where *eikōn* suggests not a distinction between form and substance, but a participation of one in the other. Furthermore, *eikōn* is associated in both the LXX and elsewhere in the New Testament with the glory of God, his *doxa*.[17] In the kenosis this participation is poured out and Christ clothes himself (*lambano*) in the essential attributes, *morphē*, of slavery. Note the connection here between slavery and glory in the Godhead – both are icons of trinitarian procession. As F. F. Bruce put it, challenging nineteenth-century kenotic Christologies which saw in Christ as servant the abandonment of his divine properties in the form of God: 'The implication is not that Christ, by becoming incarnate, exchanged the form of God for the form of a slave, but that he manifested the form of God in the form of a slave.'[18] Bruce pinpoints a certain concealment and therefore agnosticism pertaining to this form which Balthasar's doctrine of analogy develops: 'Christ's *morphē* exists within a tension unique to it which is intelligible only in a Christological sense: it … presents itself primarily as its opposite and as the uttermost concealment of this divine form' (H I, 645; GL 1, 670). The Pauline language suggests an antithesis of 'God' and 'slave', but the repetition of *morphē* identifies the two in the way that John in his gospel identifies crucifixion with exaltation.

As this icon of slavery Christ was born in the likeness (*homoiomati*) of humankind. *Homoiomati* is an ambivalent word in the New Testament (and the history of Christology). Battles have been fought over how to translate it. Lightfoot again points the way: 'Thus *homoiōma* stands midway between *morphē* and *schēma*.'[19] *Schēma* denotes the outward appearance, the accidents, in the Aristotelian sense, of human nature. But these appearances are not manifestations of the substance, they are rather

15 J. B. Lightfoot, *St. Paul's Epistle to the Philippians* (London: Macmillan, 1894), p. 108.
16 R. P. Martin, *Carmen Christi: Philippians 2. 5-11 in Recent Interpretation and in the Setting of Early Christian Worship* (Cambridge University Press, 1967), p. 99; O'Brien, *Philippians*, p. 206.
17 See Martin, *Carmen Christi*, pp. 99–119 for a detailed discussion of the association. See also 2 Cor. 4.4 and Col. 1.15 for Christ as *eikōn tou theou*, developing a Second Adam Christology. The association is important for Balthasar's own concept of Christ as the revelation of God's glory.
18 'St. Paul in Macedonia. 3. The Philippian Correspondence', in *Bulletin of the John Rylands Library* 63 (1980–1), p. 270.
19 Lightfoot, *Philippians*, p. 110.

signifiers distinct from but detailing the signified substance. Human forms, natural forms are appearances not self-defining matter. *Homoiōma* operates at the threshold between the essential manifestation of the form, the icon, and the external appearances. The first, *morphē*, is identical with the original, its ontological extension. The second, *schēma*, is an image or resemblance, which is emphasized by the comparative *hos* – he was found *hos anthropos*, bearing all the hallmarks of a human being. A note of separation from the essence, the original, is evident. But *homoiomata* can suggest both full identity with and difference from. R. P. Martin, in his extended analysis of the *carmen Christi* in Paul's letter concludes: 'The sharp alternatives are: its meaning as "identity" or "equivalence" and its meaning as "similarity" or "resemblance".'[20] The dative here, *en homoiō-mati*, is both a dative of respect ('with respect to being human') and participation ('entering into the condition of being human'). 'By *homoioma*, however, Paul doubtless wishes to say more than this, namely, the process whereby the thing itself impresses its form on us on its own initiative [*ein sich-Ausprägen der Sache selbst und von ihr selbst her*]', Balthasar remarks, emphasizing both similarity and identification (H I, 556; GL 1, 578).

The move from *morphē*, through *homoiōma* to *schēmati* expresses a deepening progression towards externality, secondariness and appearance – towards a human externality which manifests the essential nature of being a slave, towards a world in which what appears is not what is. There is a descent from a logic of identity into a world of shifting appearances and, with verse 9, there is a return to the logic of identity when the Father crowns the Son with his name; a name they share, Lord, Yahweh. In this presentation of kenosis, then, an economy of representation is outlined – form, analogy and figuration give way to the stability of denomination and identity, the names above all names. The return to the Father is a return to the 'form of God' from which he descended – the glory of self-identification within trinitarian difference. This economy of representation is framed within a rhythm of exchange, acts of the giving and receiving by both God and Christ. We will return to this later.

There remain, though, two important aporia in this mimetic economy. The first, we have drawn attention to – the ambivalent and yet pivotal word *homoiōma*, where presence becomes representation for what is absent. For at what point in the word 'likeness' does identity shift towards resemblance? The second aporia also involves an absenting, a cancelling of presence. For the doctrine of kenosis makes the descent into death inseparable from the incarnation. The ultimate descent into non-being and non-identity is part of, though not the end of, the kenotic trajectory. Dispossession lies at the centre of incarnation. This is important for understanding the nature of *homo symbolicus*, the one 'made in the image of' who subsequently makes images of or resemblances. It is important because in so far as Christ's humanity is true humanity and true image of God, the kenosis of incarnation defines the human condition – its physical appearance, its representations of those appearances – as crucified, as constantly abiding in a state of dispossession and resemblances. We

---

20 Martin, *Carmen Christi*, p. 200.

descend, in the hymn, from true presence in God into the symbolics of being human, into textuality. From textuality we move out again into the silent margin of death which erases both our humanity and our representations. Crucifixion presents a moment when the sacramental is eclipsed.

Not that crucifixion, absence and autism is the end of the kenotic story. There is resurrection, a renaming and a re-empowerment to speak. We pass, with Christ, through the textuality of the cosmos from one margin of transcendence to another; we move towards and then beyond death. In the middle, in the textuality of the cosmos, is the incarnation–crucifixion–resurrection of the form. Of course, the other way of seeing this would be to say that the textuality of the cosmos is the single aporia transgressed by the Trinity which frames it. We exist, then, in the aporia created by God, in the initial *diastasis* that opens with creation itself: we exist only to the extent we receive.[21] Only *post mortem* are we re-empowered to speak in the name of Christ. Only *post mortem* is identification possible: 'this inexact [*ungefahre*] word is replaced by the exact Word [*durch das exakt Wort ersetzt wird*], which is uttered precisely where the word passes over into silence [*in Todesschweigen*]' (H III.2/2, 76; GL 7, 84–5). We find the same sentiment expressed in the Book of Revelation, in the letter to the angel of the church at Pergamum: 'To him who conquers ... I will give a white stone, with a new name written on the stone which no one knows except him who receives it' (Rev. 2.17). *Post mortem* one is given the personhood one always knows is possible; *ante mortem* it is a process of becoming through obedience, humility and descent. *Ante mortem* is the time for realizing our dispossession, our secondariness; realizing, what Emmanuel Levinas describes as our position as accusative in a transcendental grammar. The dispossession is integral to the fact we are 'in the image of' and image makers. It is an expression of that initial *diastasis* separating the uncreated creator from the created creation. The *ante-mortem* realization of our dependence, though, and the secondariness of our representations, is lived within the horizon of *post-mortem* hopes. The economy of our representations and self-representation is, theologically, inseparable from our eschatological participation in the Godhead. In the words of Balthasar: 'Only in death, through divine judgement, does a man receive his definitive orientation' (MP 13).

The final moment of the kenotic economy is, then, the resurrected body of Christ, his Church, those whose knees shall bow and whose tongues confess that Jesus Christ is Lord. A continuum is established between the named Christ, the true image of God, and those who worship that name through their own acts of naming; being incorporated into that name through their verbalized response to and reception of it. The textuality of the cosmos is woven into the discourse of heaven, the wording of the world is enfolded within the Word of God through this resurrected body

---

21 This concept of *diastasis* will become important for our understanding of Balthasar's work. For Balthasar it goes back to exploration into the work of Gregory of Nyssa, published as PT. Lucy Gardner and David Moss continue treatment of this theme of *diastasis* as the creation's relationship to God, its reception of the divine gift of its being, in Chapter 3.

of Christ and the Church. The Church's confession and worship of Christ centres on its own act of representation, the eucharist which enacts Christ's kenosis and our kenosis in Christ through the Spirit. Through this representative act the body of Christ is distributed through the body of the Church which is made up of individual bodies located in social and political bodies. The resurrected *corpus Christi* enfolds all other bodies within it, like the Word enfolding all our words. All other bodies become sites of mystery.[22] The Church, in its response of serving the one who became a servant, receives its identity as the community of the resurrection, a body located within resurrection life which is its truth, its beauty, its goodness. Bodies as such are always transcorporal, existing simultaneously as physical, spiritual, ecclesial, sacramental and verbal bodies. This transcorporality is the enfleshment of Christ's givenness to the Father. Creation is Christ's eucharistic confession to the Father. It has no independent meaning; there is no *natura pura*. The world is an allegory of love to be interpreted by love.

Kenosis and modernity

The doctrine of kenosis was not a point of intense theological debate until the seventeenth century. Significantly, the debate raged among Lutheran theologians and its roots lay in the christological differences between Lutheran and Calvinist theology. It is, then, a particularly Protestant debate and its history and developments are important in revealing not only the associations between kenosis and modernity but the refiguration of the doctrine at the end of modernity. Calvin's own thinking is firmly in line with patristic accounts of the incarnation. Both in his *Institutes* (Book II, 13, 2–4) and in his *Commentary on Philippians* Calvin argues against the docetists that Christ was fully human and, furthermore, that this full humanity was not constraining or limiting for the Godhead. The Word is not subordinate to the flesh. The full glory of God was incarnated in the form of a man.

> For even if the Word in His immeasurable essence united with the nature of man into one person, we do not imagine that He was confined therein. Here is something marvellous: the Son of God descended from heaven in such a way that, without leaving heaven, He willed to be borne in the virgin's womb, to go about the earth, and to hang upon the cross; yet He continuously filled the world even as He had done from the beginning.[23]

This is possible because the generation of man is not unclean and vicious of itself. Athanasius would have concurred with this. Whether the logic of this teaching is coherent without a doctrine of the immaculate conception and what Balthasar terms 'marian faith' is another question, one which

---

22 See my essay 'Bodies' in Graham Ward, John Milbank and Catherine Pickstock (eds.), *Radical Orthodoxy* (London: Routledge, 1998).
23 *Institutes of the Christian Religion*, vol. 1, ed. John T. McNeill, tr. Ford Lewis Battles (London: SCM Press, 1961), p. 481.

returns in the inquiries of Gardner and Moss in this volume (Chapter 3). Calvin's emphasis is upon a trinitarian kenosis, with the sanctification of creation through the Spirit. There is no room for Mary as co-redemptrix because there is no room for a positive account of post-lapsarian creation. In fact, the fallenness of creation seals Calvin's man in an autonomous world of immanent and deluded (because godless) values. Modernity's atheistic concern with the immanent powers and secularity of the state is, theologically, all in place.

Nevertheless, it is Luther who radically reconceives the doctrine of kenosis and it is Luther's line of thinking which will trigger the 'kenosis controversy' between the Lutheran theologians of Giessen (especially Balthasar Menzer and J. Feuerborn) and the Lutheran theologians of Tübingen (especially Theodor Thummius and Melchior Nicolai) in the early seventeenth century. This, in turn, will govern the nature and development of the doctrine throughout the nineteenth century when the controversy will flare once more. It will also govern the kenotic economy as it has been reconceived most recently by a number of late twentieth-century, so-called postmodern, theologians – Thomas J. J. Altizer and Mark C. Taylor most prominent among them.

What marks distinctively Luther's understanding of kenosis is a preoccupation with finitude and death. Kenosis takes on its meaning with reference to Luther's wider *theologia crucis*. Luther is concerned with the kind of union or communication between the two natures, the divine and human. If the attributes of divine identity are eternal – absolute goodness, omnipotence, omniscience and omnipresence – in what way are these attributes related to the man Jesus? Luther, developing a nominalist position, distinguished between divine nature (*göttliche Wesen*) and divine form (*göttliche Gestalt*). The form is visible, but not the nature. Christ, Luther writes, '[t]ook the form of a servant and yet remained God and in the form of God'.[24] What this involves is that

> he has not so laid aside the divine form to the point that he can no longer feel it, or see it. If that were so no divine form would remain. But he does not take it up nor use it to lord himself over us, rather he serves us with it.[25]

What Luther emphasizes, then, is the paradox of the hidden, omnipotent, omniscient, majestic God and the revealed servant. The emphasis threatens the coherence of his two-nature Christology – for in what sense is Christ fully human if, in taking the form of a servant, he remains nevertheless always in contact (feeling and seeing) with his form as God? The question need not be tackled, only raised, here.

Significant for this essay is that the hidden God is incomprehensible and withdrawn from us because of our sin. The point at which revelation is possible, then, is the point of redemption, the crucifixion of Christ. The christological paradox is the grammar of salvation, but as a theology of

24 *D. Martin Luthers Werke: Kritische Gesamtausgabe, Abteilung Werke*, vols 1– (Weimar, 1883–), 17. 2. 243, 4.
25 Ibid., 17. 2. 243, 19.

the cross it is the annihilation of that which is human. The focus for the experience of this salvation through the cross, this dying, is the subject who believes and, in believing, is justified. As such, the human being imitates the man Jesus who is also, as understood by faith, Christ the Son of God. In his important 1520 tract 'Christian Liberty', where he quotes and employs the argument from the kenotic hymn of Philippians, Luther's emphases are upon servitude, suffering and subjection – Christ's first and then ours through faith in Christ.[26] The same note is struck in his theses 94 and 95, calling Christians to follow Christ through 'penalties, deaths and hells', entering heaven through many tribulations. The contradiction of Jesus as the Christ, the *Deus humanus*, and almighty God, *Deus absconditus*, the impotent man as the revelation of the omnipotent God, is resolved through the act of believing, which is an imitation of his dying to self.

Kenosis as self-emptying is here a putting to death of the self. Kenosis is servitude and bondage (in Luther's theological understanding of bondage as freedom). Several shifts have occurred here. First, Luther's doctrine is established within a framework of hierarchical polarities: death/life, man/God, time/eternity, slavery/freedom, grace/nature. Secondly (and consequentially), there has been a shift of emphasis in the doctrine of kenosis away from incarnation towards sacrifice. The question then becomes, what is sacrificed? As Barth records it, the question which arose between the divines of Giessen and Tübingen, 'which arose only on the specific Lutheran presupposition', was:

> Whether the man Jesus exalted to unity with the Son of God and therefore divinised – according to the logic of the Lutherans – was even in the state of His humiliation secretly present to all His creatures and ruled the world?[27]

Thirdly (and consequentially), there has been a move made towards the isolating of events in time, a movement towards theology grounded in revelation as a distinct, punctiliar event. Patristic doctrines of incarnation related the coming of the Christ and his crucifixion to the economy of salvation as an act of the triune God through time and creation. It was not an event to be isolated for forensic theological analysis, ripped atomistically from the fabric of history. Now the crucifixion becomes *the* defining theological moment, separated from time and creation, fixed eternally.

Luther's teaching on kenosis is therefore concomitant with a culture obsessed with, and fearing, death. It is a culture which develops out of the melancholy *eros* which Balthasar traces throughout the late medieval and Renaissance periods (H III.1, 498–503, 616–30; GL 5, 147–52, 264–84). The glorification of death, that paradox of necrophilia/necrophobia, is played out in Luther's *theologia crucis*. The cross is clung to as the only possibility,

---

26 See Marc Lienhard, *Luther, Witness to Jesus Christ: Stages and Themes in the Reformer's Christology*, tr. Edwin H. Robertson (Minneapolis: Augsburg Publishing House, 1982), p. 173. For a specific discussion of Luther on *kenosis* see pp. 172–6, 390–1.

27 *Church Dogmatics* IV/1, tr. G. W. Bromiley (Edinburgh: T. & T. Clark, 1985), p. 181.

through the sacrifice of what is seen and what is reasonable, of certainty. And such certainty is the only means of escaping fears, errors, death and the overwhelming darkness of this world. The finitude of the human is opposed by the eternity of God. The preoccupation with our fallenness, sinfulness and godlessness is a preoccupation with the existential structure of the human condition as, to put it in later Heideggerian and Freudian terms, being-towards-death. This is not to say that there is no hope, no resurrection, no heaven or eternal rest in Luther's theology, only that the emphasis does not lie here. The emphasis is quite plainly upon *deus crucifixus et absconditus* – an emphasis that we shall see again with the doctrine of kenosis as it is understood by the death-of-God theologians.

At the origins of modernity Luther's theology announces both important supports for the new orientation towards the autonomous self and an important critique of metaphysics. His God is beyond metaphysics and is the antithesis of the philosophically conceived God of the Enlightenment. Theology begins in divine revelation, not human speculation. Nevertheless, as B. A. Gerrish has recently pointed out, the new emphases upon the existential, the experiential, the excessive examination of the human condition, the reflectiveness upon what it is to believe, are all indices on the route towards Protestant liberalism and the metaphysical concern with consciousness. '[F]aith itself is less an act than an orientation of self';[28] Luther and Melanchthon are skilled physicians of the soul; 'the content of doctrine is precisely religious subjectivity'.[29]

It is exactly the new lines of thought on sacrifice and subjectivity, death and consciousness that later discussions of kenosis take up. By the nineteenth century this will lead to a concentration upon the religious self-consciousness of Jesus, but the intermediate stage was the 'kenotic controversy' of the seventeenth century. The Giessen school propounded the view that, in what was termed the *exinanitio*, Jesus partially refrained from employing his omniscience, omnipotence and omnipresence. Thus they drew a distinction between the potential possession of majesty and conscious restraint in exercising it. The Tübingen school, drawing upon Luther's repudiation of visibility as a criterion for theological truth, countered with the view that Jesus did in fact exercise his majesty as Son of God but it was concealed from those who did not first believe. The Lutheran *Decisio saxonica* in 1624, made by the Lutheran theologians of Saxony, endorsed the Giessen view. As Gottfried Thomasius understood, this was a decisive turning point in Lutheran Christology.[30] Karl Barth notes that the development of liberal Protestantism hangs upon this decision.[31] There is in the Giessen view a consideration now of the historical consciousness of Jesus, the religious subjectivity of Jesus. Furthermore, and again concomitant with the developing mind-set of modernity, the identity of this subject rests upon the possession and use

28 *Continuing the Reformation: Essays on Modern Religious Thought* (University of Chicago Press, 1993), p. 29.
29 Ibid., p. 52.
30 *Christi Person und Werk* (Erlangen, 1853). For a translated selection from *Christ's Person and Work*, see C. Welch, ed. and tr., *God and Incarnation: In Mid-Century German Theology* (New York: Oxford University Press, 1965), pp. 23–101.
31 *Church Dogmatics* IV/1, p. 182.

of certain properties. Theologians are concerned with the identification and definition of this distinct object, the man–God.[32]

It is the content of Jesus the Christ's consciousness as the focus for understanding the man–God paradox which dominates the next wave of debate on the doctrine of kenosis, which ranges from E. Sartorius' book *Lehre von der heiligen Liebe*, published in 1844, through to W. F. Gess' work, *Das Dogma von Christi Person und Werk*, of 1887. The most significant development in this treatment of the doctrine comes from the contemporary concerns with historicism, biography and *Bildung*. The treatment of kenosis is a theological aspect of the search for the historical Jesus and discussions concerning the evolution of Jesus' messianic consciousness.

The most systematic and theologically rigorous of these accounts came from the pen of Gottfried Thomasius. For Thomasius, what Christ 'poured out' was certain properties of his divine nature, two in particular: omnipotence and omniscience. God is treated as absolute subject and the subject is a self with certain dispositions and attributes that are essential to its nature and the way that self will develop. Thomasius does relate kenosis to a trinitarian operation, for 'being man becomes a moment of the inner–divine relationship'.[33] But his concept of the Trinity focuses upon two subjects (Father and Son) and a relationship (Spirit). He distinguishes between what is an essential attribute and what is a relative attribute in God. The essential attributes are freedom, holiness, absolute truth and absolute love. The relative attributes are omniscience, omnipotence and omnipresence. These God possesses only in relation to the world and it is these that Christ relinquishes.[34] There are obvious theological difficulties with this account, not the least of which is the division in God himself caused by the existence of a world he brought into being. Alois Emmanuel Biedermann's observation is accurate: 'the relative attributes . . . [God] can surrender, because the world and thus the relation to it is not necessary to Him'.[35] Biedermann views this as a step on the road to gnosticism.

As far as this project is concerned, all that needs to be noted is Thomasius's inadequate trinitarian reading of kenosis, his attention to subjects with essential and relative attributes and the absence of any necessary connection now between the incarnation and the passion. Kenosis begins to label a certain diminishment of faculties. Time and creation prevent God from being God. Charles Gore draws this out in that *locus classicus* of British kenoticism, 'The Holy Spirit and inspiration', published in the *Lux Mundi* volume. There, in the context of developing the thesis that no 'spiritual illumination, even in the highest degree, has any tendency to lift men out of the natural conditions of knowledge that belong to their time',[36] he explains that even Christ experienced historical contingency and possessed a historically governed consciousness.

32 See my 'Divinity and Sexuality: Luce Irigaray and Christology', in *Modern Theology* 12 (1996), pp. 221–38, for a discussion of the way modern theologians deal with Christology in terms of a divided subject.

33 Welch, *God and Incarnation*, p. 83.

34 Ibid., pp. 67–72.

35 Ibid., p. 303.

36 *Lux Mundi*, 8th edition (London: John Murray, 1890), p. 354.

When he speaks of the 'sun rising' He is using ordinary human knowledge. He willed so to restrain the beams of Deity as to observe the limits of the science of His age, and He puts Himself in the same relation to its historical knowledge.[37]

Where Thomasius' teaching on kenosis failed to give an adequate account of the Trinity, Gore's emphasis on the person of Christ fails to give an adequate Christology. Human nature is simply a vessel God uses (Gore makes much of God using the trappings of history and nature). A certain Nestorianism haunts his pages. For both of them it is human finitude that is uppermost, a human finitude to which their models of Christ draw attention. Death is the release from such finitude. Hence, because of their attention to attributes of Christ's person, the crucifixion is not a further moment in the outworking of the incarnation, a movement in God himself; it is merely the cancellation of the human consciousness and its limitations. With this attention to the attributes of Christ's person and the emphasis on historical contingency in the developing liberal humanist Christologies, the *Myth of God Incarnate* simply awaits its writing. Developments in the doctrine of kenosis will lead to the death of God and atheology.

It was Hegel who first announced this possibility. The tragic fate of the Unhappy Consciousness, in which the self aims to be absolute, in which the human absorbs the divine, announces 'the hard saying that "God is dead"'.[38] Hegel prophesies here the atheistic apotheosis of liberal humanism. Prior to Thomasius or even Sartorius, Hegel propounded a view of kenosis in one of the closing sections of *The Phenomenology of Spirit*, 'The revealed religion', which was to be highly influential in the development of twentieth-century Christologies. Prior to the nineteenth-century kenoticists, he was nevertheless more radical in suggesting the complete surrender by Christ of all divinity or the complete identification of Christ with all things human.[39] The closing sections of *The Phenomenology of Spirit* are vague, elliptical and suggestive. They are notoriously difficult texts to elucidate. But it is important to understand Hegel's recapitulation of kenosis, not only in order to see how modernity's preoccupation with death culminates in the semi-readings of Hegel by death-of-God theologians, but also in order to recognize the parallels between Hegel's thinking and Balthasar's teaching on kenosis.

In *The Phenomenology of Spirit* Hegel employs the word twice in his highly abstract account of Christ's birth, death and resurrection. The abstract nature of the account, while difficult, is methodological – the concern of the dialectical movement of spirit is always to move beyond its representations of itself. Hegel wishes, then, to concentrate upon what he calls the 'Notion of Spirit' rather than 'picture thinking' – a move similar

---

37 *Lux Mundi*, p. 360.
38 *The Phenomenology of Spirit*, tr. A. V. Miller (Oxford University Press, 1977), p. 455. See Quash's essay (Chapter 4) for an analysis of Hegel and Balthasar in terms of the aesthetics (and theology) of drama.
39 'Hegel ... must be regarded as the primogenitor in modernity of the espousal of a thoroughly radical interpretation of kenosis', Cyril O'Regan, *The Heterodox Hegel* (State University of New York Press, 1994), p. 219.

to Bultmann's project of demythologization, a move in which (or so it seems) speculative philosophy becomes the hermeneutical key for understanding the revelation of God in the narrative accounts of Jesus Christ. I write 'so it seems' because following the considerable reappraisal of Hegel as a theologian,[40] it appears that the judgement of Jean Hyppolite that religion is 'prefigurative representation of philosophical thought'[41] cannot go unchallenged. The revealed status of the Christian religion for Hegel privileges and universalizes its claims to truth. The narrative of Christ can be seen as offering a hermeneutical key for the condition of being human. That is, the trinitarian account of Christ's kenotic descent and return to the Father presents us with an account of selfhood. Rather like Augustine's *De Trinitate*, therefore, it is not the structure of being human which offers us a revelation of the Trinity, but the Trinity offers us the revelation of the structure of being human. Theology precedes, in this model, and provides the possibility for understanding, and the condition for the existence of, the philosophical and anthropological.

In developing the Notion of Spirit Hegel draws upon metaphors culled from a biblical soteriology – Adam's fall, Christ's coming, Christ's return to the Father – and understands the structure of what was later termed *Heilsgeschichte* as the structure of mind itself, our mind and the mind of God. Unlike the Greek religious Spirit which gave rise to an aesthetic representation (in works of art), the Christian man–God was actualized in history. Hegel does not doubt this. In the former religion the absolute self-consciousness of the Spirit is figured forth by the finite Spirits of artists. In the latter the absolute self-consciousness of the Spirit manifests itself. The former represents human knowledge of the divine. The latter is God's presentation of his own self-knowledge. Hence Christianity is a revealed religion and the *'content* of this picture-thinking is absolute thinking'.[42] We can observe here the radical difference between the Lutheran Hegel and Luther's own emphasis upon divine concealment. For Hegel, '[t]his concealment ceases when the absolute Being *qua* Spirit is the object of consciousness'.[43] There are theological, though not philosophical, difficulties here. If all is revealed then there is no transcendence. If there is no transcendence, if all is immanent, then all is indifferent. We shall return to this. Are we moving towards a form of total integration where difference collapses and absolute knowledge is oblivion – a form of death *à la* Spinoza's third degree of knowledge? Is the resurrection, then, the ultimate death, for Hegel?

---

40 See O'Regan and also the detailed analysis of the religious context of *The Phenomenology of Spirit* in Laurence Dickey, *Hegel: Religion, Economics, and the Politics of Spirit 1770–1807* (Cambridge University Press, 1988). For theological accounts of Hegel see Albert Chapelle, *Hegel et la religion, t. 1: La problematique; t. 2: La dialectique; Dieu et la Creation, t. 3: La dialectique; La Théologie et l'Église; Annexes* (Paris: Editions Universitaires, 1963–71); Emilio Brito, *Hegel et la tache actuelle de la christologie*, tr. Th. Dejond SJ (Paris: Editions Lethielleux, 1979).

41 Jean Hyppolite, *Structure and Genesis of Hegel's* Phenomenology of Spirit, tr. S. Cherwiak and J. Heckman (Evanston: Northwestern University Press, 1984), p. 532.

42 Hegel, *Phenomenology*, p. 479.

43 Ibid., p. 459.

Kenosis is used on both occasions in *The Phenomenology of Spirit* to express an externalization of self which moves consciousness into self-consciousness. This self-consciousness, to become self-consciousness, has to take on form, has to involve itself with representation (*Vorstellung*).

It is exactly at this point – the recognition of the centrality of mediation and mimesis – that the focus of Hegel's account of kenosis differs from the christocentric accounts of the seventeenth and nineteenth century Lutherans. This, in turn, is because of the emphatically trinitarian understanding in Hegel of both Christ's kenosis and the movement of the Spirit towards the integration of knowing and being. Christ is one moment, one figure in a trinitarian narrative. He alone is not the saviour, his death is not in some isolated way the summation of our salvation. '[T]hree moments constitute Spirit ...: essence, being-for-self which is the otherness of essence and for which essence is, and being-for-self, or knowledge of itself *in the* "other".'[44] This Hegel relates to a Lutheran emphasis upon the Word. 'It is the word which, when uttered, leaves behind, externalized and emptied, him who uttered it, but which is as immediately heard, and only this hearing of its own self is the existence of the Word.'[45] This pictures a perichoretic Trinity: 'Thus the distinctions made are immediately resolved as soon as they are made, and are made as soon as they are resolved, and what is true and actual is precisely this immanent circular movement'.[46]

We need to elucidate this further in order to best appreciate its implications – both for an understanding of Hegel's theological thinking and the future kenoticists. Three theological points can be made. First, incarnation completes creation.[47] It reveals the spiritualization of Nature because it reveals the dynamic whereby the infinite spirit in its abstraction and alienation enters into living and necessary conversation with the finite spirit. This raises problems about the freedom of God to create out of nothing, which we shall examine further in relation to Balthasar's emphasis upon the *diastasis* between creator and creation. Hegel's doctrine of kenosis is trinitarian: the Father abandons his abstract distance in an externalization of his Spirit, entering into self-consciousness which, to be self-consciousness, must take on concrete representation. The Son, as this concrete representation of the Father, allows himself to be put to death so that the absolute Spirit, which is the continual movement of consciousness to self-consciousness, might be manifest. 'This death is, therefore, its resurrection as Spirit.'[48] This trinitarian economy parallels creation itself because it was the 'eternal or abstract Spirit' becoming 'other' to itself or entering existence, which created the world.[49] Within

---

44 Ibid., p. 465.
45 Ibid., p. 465.
46 Ibid., p. 465.
47 O'Regan thinks that creation and incarnation are given equal weight, that the body of God in creation is identical to the Body of God in Christ. I am not sure here.
48 Hegel, *Phenomenology*, p. 471. Is there too much emphasis upon pneumatology? O'Regan thinks so. But the Spirit only exists on the basis of creation/incarnation. We could say that there is not enough Spirit in Hegel – that the Spirit simply remains as the movement and the relation between Father and Son, not as a distinct person. See later in this essay.
49 Hegel, *Phenomenology*, p. 467.

this world individual selves do not exist as Spirit because they remain bound to the immediacy of the natural. They must become self-conscious, other to themselves, in order to be spiritual. The fall is therefore inevitable; man 'lost the form of being at one with himself'[50] and began 'this withdrawal into itself or self-centredness'.[51] The withdrawal into oneself is not for Hegel evil in itself, for in the purity of God's trinitarian action there is a withdrawal into God's self. But because human self-reflected 'thought stems from immediacy or is *conditioned* thought, it is not pure knowledge'.[52] The move of the finite Spirit is therefore towards the purity of knowledge, *Gewissen* (certainty). The incarnation is a vital stage on this journey because it is with the incarnation that the truth of universal consciousness is revealed, and the certainty is manifest that human beings strive to attain. 'The dead divine Man or the human God *is in himself* the universal self-consciousness.'[53] This is manifest now in the Spirit of the community. An imitation of Christ is necessary and possible. As Jean Hyppolite glosses, 'The movement that took place in Christ must now be executed in the midst of the community and must become its movement instead of being alien to it.'[54] God empties himself out into the human and the human empties itself out into the divine.

As historians of ideas like Lawrence Dickey and theologians like Cyril O'Regan have pointed out, with certain Romantic modifications all this thinking has a long tradition in the early Church Fathers. In Hegel's subsequent battles against the charges of atheism and panlogism, he emphasized that he was not trying to reduce theology to anthropology, that becoming god-like was not the same as becoming God.[55] Nevertheless, an ontological correspondence does relate God as absolute person to human reflective subjectivity. This is not the individual, the ego, of Descartes and Fichte, in so far as other people enable and create the possibility for that individuality, although it bears marks of a concept of individuality found in and before Descartes, of the human mind moving within the mind of God. As Hegel states: 'not the individual by himself, but together with the consciousness of the community and what he is for this community, is the complete whole of the individual as Spirit'.[56] But the question of ontological identity, the suggestion of the finite dissolving into the infinite and universal consciousness, the absolute negativity involved in what Hegel terms '"I"="I"',[57] like the transposition of religion into speculative philosophy (Hegel's Logic), does provide grounds for complaints of either atheism or the gnosticism of panlogos teaching.

The questions of atheism and gnosticism – the question too of how close Hegel is to traditional, albeit Catholic, positions on the incarnation, the *imago dei*, the Personhood of God, pneumatology and eschatology –

50 Ibid., p. 468.
51 Ibid., p. 468.
52 Ibid., p. 468.
53 Ibid., p. 475.
54 Ibid., p. 567.
55 Ibid., p. 462.
56 Ibid., p. 489.
57 Ibid., p. 487.

revolve around the identity of finite and infinite Spirit. This is the burden of the final section of *The Phenomenology of Spirit*, 'Absolute Spirit'. This section, and the move Hegel makes within it towards his understanding of Logic and Science, determine one of two interpretative directions. The first will emphasize the collapse of the difference between infinite and finite Spirit, on the basis of the previous kenosis or death of God. Absolute Spirit is the new synthesis which collapses all notions of transcendence. As we shall see, this is the line of interpretation followed by the death-of-God theologians and it is an interpretation in line with modernity's obsession with death – this time death as the oblivion of the finite self-consciousness within the universal self-consciousness, the dream of annihilation. The self's absorption into total presence Wyschogrod regards as an aspect of the death event. Difference and alterity is overcome. Time, as history, is viewed as a movement towards its cancellation in eternity,[58] just as all representation and picture-thinking will dissolve into the immediate grasping of the Notion. All is immanent action – a notion on the way to Nietzsche's 'eternal reoccurrence'. The mutual dispossession of the for-itself and the in-itself attains the simple unity of knowing and the dialectic is closed.

The second interpretative direction, on the other hand, will emphasize the necessary continuation of the dialectic. If the realization of the Notion is the realization of the particularity of a thing in its universality; if the 'death of the Mediator as grasped by the Self is the supersession of his objective existence ... [so that] this *particular* being-for-itself has become a universal self-consciousness';[59] then can the dialectic ever be closed? Is living, in its concrete materiality, not itself an abiding in the contradiction of the infinite Spirit and the finite spirit? Does the Spirit keep open a space for the different, the non-identical? If the dialectic continues because life and time continue, then the supersession continues and there remains both alterity and transcendence. The dialectic enables the movement whereby absolute spirit is incarnated in the community. Teleologically this movement may be proceeding towards some eschatological horizon, some final completion of the Word – and such a theme would again be in line with certain Cappadocian teachings. We need to add here that if the movement is eternally open, the closure of the dialectic eternally deferred, that arguably makes Hegel's vision a tragic one. This would be a vision indistinguishable from Hegel's depiction of the Unhappy Consciousness where the Notion of an end, a goal, a synthesis, is unknown. Therefore all movement would be without understanding. Therefore there would be no understanding, possibly no real movement, for the conscious and the self-conscious would simply remain in opposition, in alienation, in contradiction. Can contradiction become paradox or dialectic without a definite end? On the other hand, a closed system means Hegel can endorse, as he wishes to endorse, the holistic aesthetics of comedy.

The difficulty with interpreting Hegel is that in his logic the system proceeds – in fact, can only proceed at all – on the basis that the end, the

58 Ibid., p. 476.
59 Ibid., p. 477.

synthesis, is somehow proleptically available now. He recognizes that 'the community is not yet perfected in this its self-consciousness',[60] yet nevertheless he (a member of that community) can detail this 'last becoming of Spirit'.[61] From some vantage point beyond the phenomenological method Hegel describes the circle of becoming. The question remains, then – a question Jean Hyppolite frames in terms of the Kantian architectonic – does Hegel move illegitimately from the phenomenal to the noumenal, or from the philosophical to the theological?[62] In other words, is this vantage point only available to Hegel *on the basis* of the trinitarian economy of kenosis? Does Hegel begin with faith and move towards knowledge? Is this what he points to in the closing lines of *The Phenomenology of Spirit* by referring the whole philosophical pilgrimage of the work to 'the inwardizing and the Calvary of absolute Spirit'? Or alternatively, does the vantage point come from collapsing an analogical relationship between the divine and the human, founded upon a fundamental *diastasis* between the Being of God and the existence of creation, into a relationship based upon ontological identity, where one can think the thoughts of the other and thus move from the human part to the divine whole?[63]

However we interpret the negativity and sacrifice at the dynamic centre of Hegel's dialectic, the kenotic economy is certainly for Hegel the source of time, self, history, representation (or becoming form), knowledge, self-consciousness and Spirit. Its themes – subjectivity, consciousness, progress, negativity, death-in-life – and its concerns – certainty, absolute knowledge, human history – are those belonging to modernity. But there are older elements here, pointers towards a pre-modern Christian tradition and an approach to a philosophical theology quite at odds, on one interpretation, with modernity's philosophers of religion. 'In his conviction of the complete *self*-manifestation of *God* ... Hegel's thinking does not lack traditional reference points.'[64] Hegel's position remains profoundly ambivalent.

Nevertheless, what is evident in Hegel's presentation of the kenotic act of creation, the kenotic act of incarnation and the kenotic act of coming to identity and knowledge itself, is that the economy underlying the self-emptying is one founded upon lack. God cannot exist in his impassibility and abstractness; he must needs become concrete. Human beings were forced from their immediate consciousness of Nature into self-consciousness. There is a determinism here, but the a priori of that determinism is the-subject-in-lack and that lack is both within God and within ourselves. This economy returns us to the question of God's freedom to act, a question Balthasar's emphasis upon grace will bring into focus. Furthermore, the kenotic economy in Hegel is an erotic economy –

60 Ibid., p. 492.
61 Ibid., p. 491.
62 Hyppolite, *Structure and Genesis*, pp. 451–2.
63 O'Regan, *The Heterodox Hegel*: 'what characterizes the [onto-theological sphere of the immanent divine] is radical anaclasis or openness', p. 99. He believes the synclasis of the logical sphere is hypothetical only. I am wondering if the projected synclasis is a theological rather than philosophical construal.
64 Brito, *Hegel*, p. 257.

force, desire, labour, the movement of the Spirit are correlations of each other. This subject of desire (where 'of' is both subjective and objective genitive) pulls Hegel into the orbit of romantic erotics – Frederick Schlegel, Hölderlin, Novalis and, later, Wagner. The erotic subject then plots its history through Schopenhauer, Nietzsche, Freud, Heidegger, Sartre and Lacan. The modern subject is the subject of desire, the acquiring, possessive subject, the capitalist subject.[65] This subject is male and the female in this economy represents the unimaginable, the un-presentable, the enigmatic, the dark mysterious continent that must be conquered.

If Hegel avoids developing the Unhappy Consciousness of this subject, it is because of Christ and the incarnation of the absolute self-consciousness to which we all aspire. But even so, as with Luther, incarnation is associated firmly with dying. 'Christology only begins through default, condemned as it is to a redoubled reabsorption by its crucifying spiritualization.'[66] 'The entire system seems dominated by a meditation on the death *of Christ*.'[67] The secularization of this subject, subsequently, will only emphasize the death-bound subjectivity we noted earlier. Furthermore, Luther's existential approach to theology is now substantially developed and, along with Schleiermacher's con-temporaneous project, the foundations of liberal Protestantism are laid. It is with the apotheosis of such liberalism and the desiring subject, in the death-of-God theologians, that Hegel's concerns with kenosis will be recapitulated.

According to the flight of history as Thomas J. J. Altizer conceives it, we are the inhabitants of a profound spiritual darkness which has been enshrouding the world since the death of Christ and is now coming towards its final and apocalyptic conclusion.[68] The Word will have its eschatological fulfilment. As the history of religions unfold, Christianity is the final one and Christianity can be the final one because the death of God is the centre of that religion. The distinctiveness of Christianity lies in its commitment, through kenosis, to time and creation. The death of God at the crucifixion is emphatically not simply the death of the Son of God; it is deipassionism – a radical working of the doctrine of kenosis. Altizer builds specifically on Hegelian foundations: 'Hegel is the only thinker who made the kenotic movement of the Incarnation the core and foundation of all his thinking.'[69] In Hegel he finds the total eclipse of the transcendent, sovereign and impassive God and the affirmation of the immanence of the world order, a baptized world order. This is the order of what Altizer calls 'total presence'. On the basis of Hegelian kenosis Altizer recommends us, then, to a Christian atheism.

---

65 For an account of this desiring subjectivity and its abiding influence on twentieth-century French philosophy, see Judith Butler, *Subjects of Desire: Hegelian Reflections in Twentieth-Century France* (New York: Columbia University Press, 1987).
66 Brito, *Hegel*, pp. 138–9.
67 Ibid., p. 141.
68 See his books *History as Apocalypse* (Albany: State University of New York, 1985) and *Genesis and Apocalypse* (Albany: State University of New York, 1990).
69 *The Gospel of Christian Atheism* (Philadelphia: Westminster Press, 1966), p. 29.

Altizer develops this radical kenosis the furthest, followed by the deconstructive theologians Charles Winquist and Mark C. Taylor.[70] These last two thinkers explicitly relate Altizer's 'theology' to the concerns, and philosophical methods, of poststructural nihilism. How accurate their readings of poststructuralism are is a debate we cannot engage with in this essay. But, for example, in Mark C. Taylor's work, the eclipse of the transcendent Word is mapped on to a certain reading of Derrida's critique of the relationship between presence and language (logocentrism), his economy of the endless promotion of differences and deferrals of meaning in language (*différance*) and finally his understanding of the continual need of language to supplement itself (*dissémination*). Thus Taylor can comment that 'writing is a kenotic process; it empties everything of absolute self-identity and complete self-presence'.[71]

In Mark C. Taylor's work Hegel encounters the linguistic turn. Kenosis is Hegel's immanent process of consciousness becoming conscious of itself and always in the process of surpassing itself, reinscribed in terms of textuality. In fact, for Taylor, reality is textuality. But this textuality has none of the allegorical depth and transcendent significance of the Word enfolding all our words – the theme of the kenotic hymn in Philippians. This textuality is all surface, simulacra and façade. As a Christian atheist, Taylor relates this dissemination of the presence of the Word to the eucharist as a celebration of dismemberment, dissemination as distribution and crucifixion of the individual self.[72]

Altizer's total presence, like Mark C. Taylor's linguistic idealism, announces the nihilism of indifference which is the last stage on the road to pure immanence. In Taylor's more performative work we have a vision of the endless, playful erring that fulfils the telos of history as Altizer presents it. Here is total presence – for the writing itself, as it flows along and floats over various ideas and themes, is all there is. The reader constructs and performs and the reading experience of that construction and performance is all the meaning Taylor wishes to promote. Although both atheologians speak of new-found freedoms, particularly freedom from the bondage of a transcendent master God, all value in their worlds is simply local, transient and relative. Liberal humanism – all three thinkers are indebted to the romantic tradition and the theological liberalism of Paul Tillich – has now arrived at the apotheosis of the secular and the superficial. Only the aesthetic, divorced from truth and goodness, remains: Altizer's poetic theology and pastiches of the prophetic, and Taylor's commitment to Dionysian word-play as a form of spiritual exercise.

At a time when the art of taxidermy has declined, the paradoxical necrophobia/necrophilia of which it was a metaphor have found other forms. We have arrived at the end of modernity where kenosis announces

---

70 See Charles Winquist's recent work: *Epiphanies of Darkness: Deconstruction in Theology* (Chicago: University of Chicago Press, 1986) and *Desiring Theology* (University of Chicago Press, 1995). For Mark C. Taylor, see *Deconstructing Theology* (New York: Crossroad, 1982) and *Erring: A Postmodern A/theology* (University of Chicago Press, 1984).
71 *Erring*, p. 118.
72 Ibid., pp. 120, 141–2.

Heidegger's being-towards-death as the only possible authenticity *Dasein* can achieve. This too is an echo of Hegel. For in the final stages consciousness possesses its concept and arrives at that possession by looking back upon its knowledge.[73] Freud plays a variation: the subject of desire is a subject driven towards the *jouissance* of death.[74] But this concentration of theological, philosophical, and psychological thinking on death does not remain simply bound by a negativity at the heart of the modern subject. As the work of Edith Wyschogrod and Zygmunt Bauman has shown,[75] the cultural logic of modernity, with its death-bound subjectivity, leads directly to the Pascheden, Auschwitz and Hiroshima. Modernity's paradox of necrophilia/necrophobia, to which its doctrine of kenosis bears witness, culminates in the technologies that enable its final presentation of annihilation, what Wyschogrod calls 'man-made mass death' and others call 'cleansing'. The objects of interest are scientific data, artefacts, *objets d'art*, worthy of esteem. The objects of no interest are parasites, superfluous, and faceless numbers. Furthermore, what this actualization of death has done is to undermine all of modernity's attempts to make death meaningful, to make it the high and authentic point of living. The aestheticization of death becomes a meaningless, parodic gesture. The realization of the secret inner dream of modernity has brought modernity to a close.

At the end of modernity, therefore, where does the doctrine of kenosis go? Fundamentally, we have to reappropriate what modernity left behind in its own development and exposition of the teaching. I suggest, with reference to the exegesis of Philippians, that what is absent from modernity's concept of kenosis is the role played by theological discourse as response to a reception of, and participation in, the divine. The kenotic trajectory is redemptive and culminates in a resurrection of the body. In the Pauline narrative, being-unto-death does not expunge the greater movement of being-unto-eternal-life. In refiguring the doctrine of kenosis at the end of modernity Hegel is important here. Hegel drew attention to the importance of representation in the kenotic economy. Furthermore, the reading of Hegel by the death-of-God theologians is a particularly selective one. It is Hegel read through Nietzsche's *amor fati* (a version of the immanence announced in Spinoza's *amor intellectus* – which is also a move towards oblivion) and Zarathrustra's pronouncement in the market that God is dead. Hegel rails against those who collapse God into World so that there is too much God – 'God is everything and everything is God' – in the closing pages of his *Encyclopaedia*. He accuses such thinkers of stupidity, falsification, and misconception, forseeing the outcome as 'the secularity of things'.[76] Spinoza is listed among them. Furthermore, Hegel's death of God is not the same as Nietzsche's. Hegel's is more Lutheran and

---

73 *Philosophy of Mind*, tr. A. V. Miller (Oxford: Clarendon Press, 1971), p. 302, on looking back on knowledge. This is linked to Hegel's concept of memory [*Erinnerung*], pp. 219–23.

74 Freud developed his concept of the death-drive in *Beyond the Pleasure Principle* (1920). *The Complete Psychological Works of Sigmund Freud*, vol. xviii, tr. under the editorship of James Strachley (London: Hogarth Press, 1955), pp. 7–64.

75 See Z. Bauman, *Modernity and the Holocaust* (Cambridge: Polity Press, 1989).

76 Hegel, *Philosophy of Mind*, tr. A. V. Miller (Oxford: Clarendon Press, 1971), pp. 304–5.

historically concrete – it is the death of the particular incarnation of God in Jesus Christ. Nietzsche's death of God is a metaphor for the end of any transcendent system of values – Goodness, Reality, Truth, Immortality. God for Nietzsche is the figure *par excellence* of what he terms 'meta-physical comfort'.

For Altizer God is a super-ego, a bigger and more powerful version of ourselves in the sky above – he is overlord. Hegel's God is much closer to Aristotle's *dunamis* and *energeia*, and therefore Aquinas' *actus purus*. Even Feuerbach, as a pupil of Hegel's, distinguished between Hegel's God and his own conception of the divine as a human projection.[77] Fundamentally, for Altizer (as for Nietzsche), God is not trinitarian. It is because of Hegel's insistence upon the trinitarian distinctions that he is not committed (as Altizer and Nietzsche are) to deipassionism. It is also because of the trinitarian distinction that the logic of theology for Hegel retains its insistence upon the transcendent (or, at least, self-transcendent)[78] Christ, who existed before all worlds and returns to unity with the Father.[79] In the movement of that giving and return, that mediation of the infinite and the finite, the Spirit is dispensed into the community. There is, then, an immanent and an economic Trinity and so Hegel believes he avoids the atheism of the pantheist as he avoids the docetism of the panlogist. Altizer does not read Hegel in this way.

Altizer's reading follows a line of Anglo-American antitheological accounts of Hegel; accounts in which 'Hegel is trimmed and important aspects of his vision shelved, misinterpreted, or explained away'.[80] French and German readings of Hegel tend to have a deeper and more positive evaluation of his theological framework. Nietzsche's much greater pre-sence in the thought of Altizer and the death-of-God theologians is evident in talk about being released from bondage to this transcendent God and the new Dionysian life that awaits us all when we move with the flow and pulsations of life. There is an ever greater sense of freedom, these death-of-God theologians argue, as the finite moves towards a greater sense of its particularity and universality. This is a secularized doctrine of atonement and another turn in the Enlightenment dream of human emancipation. But Hegel's concept of necessity means that God has never usurped a position that was not his to begin with. He is as committed to our self-realization as his own. His freedom and ours are co-implicated. There is no scope for a release from bondage to the transcendent in Hegel – this is Nietzsche's reading of Hegel's master–slave dialectic in terms of Christian *ressentiment*. In Hegel, we are bound to God as God is to us – necessity led to the incarnation and death of Christ. It is this necessary relation, which obviates God's own freedom to choose and the traditional teaching of creation *ex nihilo*, that will lead Hegel

---

77 See Lawrence Dickey, 'Hegel on Religion and Philosophy' in *The Cambridge Companion to Hegel*, ed. Frederick C. Beiser (Cambridge University Press, 1993), pp. 301–47.
78 For a discussion of the difference between transcendence and self-transcendence see my 'Sacramentalism or Neopaganism', *Theology* (July, 1991), pp. 279–83.
79 *Philosophy of Mind*, p. 225. God 'has from all eternity begotten a Son, in whom he, as Spirit, is at home with himself'.
80 O'Regan, *The Heterodox Hegel*, p. 86.

into troubled waters. Primarily, there is the impossibility of grace and the Trinity as an economy of gift. All giving (and all reception) takes place within immanent economies of exchange. Secondly, there is a compromised transcendence, a univocity in which part and whole, human and divine, share a common ontological foundation. Kenosis operates here – and this is where he differs from Balthasar or, more recently, Jean-Luc Marion[81] – within, not beyond, the philosophical project (metaphysics understood as onto-theology).[82] And with this lies the danger of presenting far too much God, like Spinoza. Hegel is, then, certainly not orthodox, but he is not apostate either. His work stands ambivalently in two historical epochs – the traditional past (late antiquity and medieval) and modernity's present. To refigure kenosis at the end of modernity we have to develop the Hegel who drew upon the pre-modern. That will lead us to Balthasar and to poststructural thinkers of kenosis – Emmanuel Levinas, Jacques Derrida, Julia Kristeva, Luce Irigaray and Hélène Cixous.

Balthasar's kenotic economy

Kenosis is not simply at the centre of Balthasar's theology. Its economy is both the condition for the possibility of theo-logic itself and its very form (*Gestalt*).

> There is only one way to approach the trinitarian life in God: on the basis of what is manifest in God's kenosis in the theology of the covenant – and thence in the theology of the Cross – we must feel our way back into the mystery of the absolute. (TD III, 301; ThD 4, 324)

> This primal kenosis [*Ur-Kenose*] makes possible all other kenotic movements of God into the world; they are simply its consequences. (TD III, 308; ThD 4, 331)[83]

It is significant that despite being aware of the patristic articulations of the doctrine of kenosis, Balthasar receives and handles the concerns and categories bequeathed to him directly from the Lutheran debates and the theology of Karl Barth. His is a theology of reception and a profound theology of time. He cannot simply return to pre-modernity, that has disappeared. He has to work with and upon that which presents itself to

---

81 Marion develops a *theologia crucis* which rests upon 'une kénose de l'image' which transgresses 'des principes esthetique' in his recent work *La Croisée du visible* (Paris: La Difference, 1991). See also Jean-Yves Lacoste's essay, 'Jalons pour un traitement kénotique de la question de l'homme' in *Experience et Absolu* (Paris: Presses Universitaires de France, 1994).

82 Balthasar wishes to keep metaphysics. In fact, he wants to view the Christian as the guardian of a proper metaphysics of eros, but he distinguishes this metaphysical thinking from the metaphysics which conflates Being with total presence and 'systems of identity' (H III.1/2, 978; GL 5, 651).

83 See the essay of Gardner and Moss (Chapter 3) for further discussion of Balthasar's adoption of *Urkenosis* in his account of trinitarian difference and its presence to and in the world.

him through the Spirit now. God's action in the world is no longer identical to what went on before the entrenchment of secularism. All things are contingent and pass away, that is important for Balthasar. And so while rereading patristic texts, he constructs his doctrine of kenosis in discussion with the German Protestant concerns, shaped by modernity, with the cross, Christ and the distinction between the economic and the immanent Trinity. When Balthasar discusses Catholicism it is nearly always with reference to pre-modern writers and modern French theologians. No doubt, there is a certain politics here. Balthasar, the Swiss, writes in German, weaving back into the German Protestant language the Catholic, pre-modern strains which the French have kept alive. In pushing beyond modernity but through it, then, Balthasar forces Protestantism to question whether it is not itself a product of modernity and therefore passing away.

Balthasar's fundamental sparring partner is Hegel. The similarities to, and differences from, Hegel's teaching on kenosis are profound. They are similar in so far as kenosis opens the possibility and determines the nature and form of their logics. They are different in so far as Balthasar's is a theo-logic and Hegel's a metaphysical logic. Upon this difference hangs the significance of Balthasar's kenotic economy at the end of modernity and at the end of metaphysics. Theologically, what will distinguish their kenotic economies is the attention each pays to the resurrection. For, as a number of Catholic theologians have observed, Hegel theoretically has an account of the resurrection, but it is practically absent from his logic for, like Luther, 'he only perceives the Resurrection as a function of the Cross'.[84]

Nevertheless, these same Catholic theologians consider dialogue with Hegelian theology important, for like Catholicism it announces a *sacramentum mundi*.[85] Albert Chapelle, a foremost expositor of Hegel's philosophical theology, concludes an article entitled '*Absolu et l'Historie: pensée hegelienne et theologies catholique*' with these words:

> Our confession of the Catholic faith enables us to declare the truth in Hegel [*en sa vérité Hegel*]. The eucharistic Word reconciles the philosophy with his texts, and we with him, at the simple cost of our discourse.[86]

Despite Hegel's emphasis upon the community, the eucharist – that place where the eternal giving of the gift of God's presence is actualized in the temporal – is a specific moment in the economy of salvation which Hegel undervalues, as he undervalues the place of the Church. For Balthasar, on the other hand, the eucharist itself is a final moment in the kenotic economy, the resurrection moment when Christ, in his offering of himself to the Father, *is* the giving of thanks (*eucharistia*). It is this Christology,

84 Brito, *Hegel*, p. 12.
85 The Catholic theologians in particular are Emilio Brito, Albert Chapelle and André Leonard, *La foi chez Hegel* (Paris: Desclee, 1970).
86 *Hegel et la théologie contemporaine: l'absolu dans l'histoire?*, ed. Louis Rumf, André Bieler *et al.* (Paris: Delauchaux & Niestle, 1977), p. 218.

inseparable from a more developed understanding of the Trinity, this resurrection and this ecclesiology which reverses Hegel's sublation of faith by knowledge, the *aufhebung* of *pistis* into *gnosis*. And so the dialectical movement of the Spirit (which is the translation of a premodern pneumatology into modernity's secular concerns with its own manufacturing and consumption) is transfigured.

At the end of *The Glory of the Lord*, vol. V, Balthasar views this transfiguration of metaphysics as the Christian task and responsibility for today. Hegel's logic leads to man becoming 'the slave of what he sought to master: matter and the machine' (H III.1/2, 989; GL 5, 653). This slavery, the logic of modernity's project, has brought about our contemporary darkness. But the mission of Christ continues, constantly opening up a future in which human beings can receive, obey and configure God's glory. To what place do we move, then, with Balthasar's work when we move beyond modernity?

To answer that question requires examining the kenotic economy as he describes it, pointing up the specific ways in which he transforms the movement of the Spirit in Hegel.[87] Our task here is made easier by the number of long and explicit discussions in Balthasar's work of Hegel's philosophical theology. Principle among these discussions are the sections on Hegel in *The Glory of the Lord* vol. V (H III.1/2, 904–21; GL 5, 572–90), *Theodrama* vol. I (TD 1, 50–64; ThD 1, 54–75) and *Theologik* III (TL III, 34–41). In these discussions Balthasar points out both why Hegel is important and why he must be superseded. He is important because even though Catholicism goes much further, no one before him more profoundly experienced and pondered Christian revelation in dramatic categories (TD I, 61; ThD 1, 66). He must be superseded because his thinking does not arise from and return to the Scriptures (as Balthasar's thinking does). He sums this up pithily: 'Hegel's great project has produced an all-embracing doctrine of the Spirit with a Christological centre, but it is not a biblical doctrine about the Holy Spirit' (TL III, 41).

For Balthasar, like Hegel, understands the relationship between *processio* and *missio* – that only certain things can be thought and done in any particular *Zeitgeist*; that he has a specific vocation (Balthasar draws attention to Hegel's sense of personal mission in H III.1/2, 904; GL 5, 572); and that the divine life and the shaping of the world through love comes about by individuals becoming organs for the infinite life so that each gives form to the Spirit. Nevertheless Balthasar emphasizes Hegel's cavalier disregard of biblical foundations.

There are four main biblical criticisms that Balthasar lodges against Hegel: first, Hegel's dismissive contempt for the Jewish transcendent God whose glory (*kabod*) is sublime, not simply beautiful (H III.1/2, 911–13, 916; GL 5, 580–1, 585);[88] secondly, the question of God's freedom as

---

87 There are significant discussions of Balthasar's modifications of Hegel's philosophical theology in Brito, *Hegel*, pp. 82–7, 323–31, 368–72, 377–80.

88 Balthasar's aesthetics owe something to Kant here, the sublime being that which transcends the beautiful for Kant because it disrupts the unity of the beautiful, thus creating pain in its pleasure and signalling that which is unpresentable. Hegel's notion of beauty as all-encompassing reduces aesthetics to a Greek sense of

creator with respect to creation (TL III, 36); thirdly, the soteriological significance of the resurrection and ascension (TD I, 60; ThD 1, 65); finally, Hegel's judgement on all forms of historical Christianity, the *ecclesia* and its sacramental life (H III.1/2, 914–5; GL 5, 582–3). Each of these criticisms underlines a basic fault in Hegel's theological thinking – his inadequate understanding of the Trinity. In rejecting the Jewish transcendent God, he collapses the difference between the Father and the Son. In rejecting the importance of the Church, he collapses the Son into the Spirit and Holy Spirit into world Spirit. 'Consequently Hegel's Christology is styled a spiritual Christology [*Geistchristologie*] only in a quite general, that is philosophical, sense' (TL III, 39). The condition leading to these collapses – that which makes possible Hegel's notion of self-mediating identity – Balthasar locates in the univocity of Spirit and Being in Hegel; that is, Hegel's *analogia entis* (H III.1/2, 919; GL 5, 588).

The *analogia entis* as conceived by Suárez – although already evident in Duns Scotus' notion of a neutral Being pervading all distinctions and the Averroist appeals, against Aquinas, to God as First Principle (H III.1/2, 377–80; GL 5, 16–19)[89] – is the watermark of modernity's marriage with metaphysics. In his exposition of kenosis, then, Balthasar has to reinscribe analogy within a theo-logic that denies a metaphysics of presence. In denying such a metaphysics, he also denies the structures of the world as perceived by human beings on the basis of the analogical relationship between part and whole; he denies the foundationalism that so characterizes modernity's project; he emphasizes the groundlessness (*etwas unvorstellbar Über-Grundloses*), and therefore freedom, of God's grace (TD III, 314; ThD 4, 338). Balthasar does this by making Christology the condition for the possibility of analogy (and therefore knowledge):

> because the order of creation is orientated to the order of the Incarnation, it is structured in view of the Incarnation: it contains images [*Bilder*], analogies as it were, dispositions, which in a true sense are the presuppositions for the Incarnation. (KB 177; B 163)

Christ is the form (*Gestalt*) of God's transcendent glory; the form from which all other forms take their measure and by which all other forms are ordered. God's Word is Christ's form as archetype (*Urbild*) for the Church and primal form (*Urgestalt*) in and of itself as it issues from the darkness of God (H I, 204–5; GL 1, 212). Only in Christ is it possible then to understand the nature of the analogy of being: 'the divine Son who becomes man is the concrete *analogia entis*' (TD II.1, 243; ThD 2, 267) which realizes itself in 'the eucharistic movement back and forth from the Father' (TD II.1, 243; ThD 2, 268).

---

proportion and the golden mean. Hegel's aesthetics create self-contained objects – aesthetics is stripped of its erstwhile relationship to truth and goodness (in Plato, for example). See also Noel Dermot O'Donoghue's 'Do we get beyond Plato?' in *The Beauty of Christ*, eds. B. McGregor OP and Thomas Norris (Edinburgh: T. & T. Clark, 1994).

89 See also Eric Alliez, *Capital Times*, tr. Georges Van Den Abbeele (Minneapolis: University of Minnesota Press, 1996), pp. 196–238.

What this emphasis does is to reassert a theology of the hiatus, the *diastasis* between God and creation, theology and anthropology, which Balthasar saw missing from Hegel's treatment of kenosis (and over-extenuated in Karl Barth's).[90] Balthasar sees Heidegger's ontological difference as pointing the way beyond modernity here, returning us to something closer to Aquinas's *distinctio realis*. The theological difference between God and the world supersedes ontological difference. This will become important later when we examine the category of difference as conceived by certain poststructuralists. For Balthasar, hiatus stands opposed to the monism of Suárez' understanding of the analogy of being. For him 'the *analogia entis* (the irreducible "otherness" of created nature) excludes any kind of fusion' (TD III, 357; ThD 4, 383). It is the lack of fusion in this *analogia* which fosters the dramatic interplay between creator and creation. It is the refusal to close the circle between Being and essence (the existent) so that one's gaze can 'seek to penetrate beyond the Ontological Difference ... to the distinction between God and world, in which God is the sole sufficient ground for both Being and the existent in its possession of form' (H III.1/2, 954; GL 5, 624). Such an understanding of *analogia entis* introduces an ineliminable aporia, an irradicable secondariness, a following after, which is the hallmark of human figuration ultimately understood as discipleship. We are made 'in the image of'. The hierarchy, the Lordship and obedience necessitated by this secondariness, Balthasar will expound with relation to several binaries (though not oppositions): woman and man, Mary and Christ, the Bride and the Bridegroom, the Body and the Head. Hiatus fosters desire by opening the space for creativity, the stage for action, the yearning for unity; it fosters a spiritual *dunamis*, a theological *kinesis*, which is kenotic. There cannot be true kenosis without hiatus, without true difference.

Furthermore, the condition for the possibility of this hiatus between creator and creation, and this kenosis, is a hiatus and kenosis within God himself. As with the early Fathers he quotes (Cyril, Gregory of Nyssa, Hilary, Chrysostom) kenosis is a trinitarian event. Laconically, Balthasar writes: 'the Son's *missio* is his *processio* extended [through desire, *verlangert*] in 'economic' mode; but whereas in his *processio* he moves towards the Father in receptivity and gratitude, in his *missio* ... he moves away from Him and towards the world' (TD III, 332; ThD 4, 356). In his essay on Balthasar's theology of drama (Chapter 4), Quash will investigate further the connection between the subject-in-performance and Balthasar's theology of mission. Here I wish to elucidate this account of trinitarian processions with reference to a prayer Balthasar composed which describes the self-emptying love within the Trinity from which creation and incarnation proceed.

> You, Father, give your entire being as God to the Son; you are Father
> only inasmuch as you give yourself; you, Son, receive everything
> from the Father and before Him you want nothing other than one
> receiving and giving back, the one representing, glorifying the

---

90 For Balthasar's insights into and criticisms of Karl Barth's *analogia fidei*, see his book
    B., pp. 86–167.

Father in loving obedience; you, Spirit, are the unity of these two mutually meeting, self-givings, their We as a new I that royally, divinely rules them both.[91]

Kenosis, then, is not the act of the Son (as with Luther and the Lutheran kenoticists of the seventeenth and nineteenth centuries). Such a Christology Balthasar would view as christomonistic. Kenosis is the disposition of love within the trinitarian community. It is a community constituted by differences which desire the other. For the Father surrenders himself utterly to the Son who is 'the infinitely Other *of the Father*' (TD III, 302; ThD 4, 325), making all subsequent separation (and suffering) possible. The Son's response to this is eternal thanksgiving (*eucharistia*). The Spirit maintains and embraces the infinite distance between Father and Son, opening the love that fills that distance to creation. 'Here we see both God's infinite power and powerlessness; he cannot be God in any other way but in this "kenosis" within the Godhead itself' (TD III, 303; ThD 4, 325). The 'generation' of the Son makes possible the creation of the world. The circulation of divine desire is the *processio*. Obedience to that desire to abandon oneself is the nature of one's calling or *missio* – for the going out or *missio* is always the act of love towards the other. Both *processio* and *missio* exemplify kenosis and this kenosis is the operation which enjoins the immanent Trinity to the incarnation. Thus there arises an analogy of natures between the form of God and the form of a servant. All incarnation is kenotic; all Word becoming flesh, all acts of representation, are kenotic. This will have significant consequences for our understanding of *homo symbolicus*. For the moment it is important to grasp that kenosis always made possible the sacrifice of Jesus Christ on the cross; for Christ was sacrificed before the foundations of the world in his utter givenness to the Father. The cross is not then an event that can be isolated and made the fulcrum for all theological understanding. Not only is the event of crucifixion, the death of God, part of a trajectory moving from incarnation to resurrection (and Pentecost). It is the outworking of a soteriological economy inaugurated with creation: 'all the world's darkness is only permitted because of the antecedent *idea, offer* and *mission* of the Lamb, which undergird it and make it possible' (TD III, 335; ThD 4, 360). Creation is made possible by intra-trinitarian difference. Creation is completed in the incarnation just as the incarnation is completed in the eucharist. God becomes form and he, the Son, becomes the transcendental signifier, the name above all names.

For we who are made 'in the image of', kenosis is a mode of living the eternal life of God which sin destroys. Our kenotic action is not identical to Christ's kenotic action with reference to the Father. Ours is a secondary 'Yes' of consent (summed up in Mary) made possible on the basis of Christ's primary self-offering ('*Kenosis* of the Church', ST IV, 119–32; ExT 4, 125–38). We live analogously and kenosis is both the condition of this living and our understanding of it. With this notion of difference, of an unassimilable alterity, the teaching of kenosis moves beyond modernity's concern with epistemology (Kant), metaphysics (Hegel) and

91 *The Von Balthasar Reader*, pp. 428–9.

phenomenological existentialism (Heidegger). Kenosis is the form, character and praxis of a theo-logic that lies outside of, and illuminates, all human logics.

We return to the doctrine of kenosis as it was expounded in pre-modernity, by the early Church, in the work of Origen, Athanasius and Cyril among the Alexandrians, Gregory of Nyssa among the Cappa-docians and Hilary of Poitiers. Beset as it was by the dangers of subordinationism, modalism and deipassionism, the kenosis of Christ was depicted then in terms of a trinitarian procession,[92] what Maximus the Confessor called 'an eternal movement of love'.[93] With Palamas a distinction was drawn between God in himself – who was unknowable and inaccessibly concealed in mystery – and those divine energies or operations whereby he is manifested and gives himself to us. Thus Palamas wishes to speak of a 'divine power and energy common to the nature in three'.[94] This force or energy whereby there is communication and the gift of God was understood as the operation of love within the Trinity, the abandoning of one to the other; and salvation issued from a participation within this intra-trinitarian procession. It is a participation made possible through the incarnation of Christ, the revelation of the true image of God possessed by all. We are saved and deified through the economy of love. The distinctive nature of love is to give, a continual act of self-abandonment; and it is this abandonment in love which char-acterizes kenosis. To paraphrase Karl Barth's understanding of kenosis, God's freedom to love is a self-giving not a giving up.[95] The doctrine of kenosis outlines, then, the giving of the gift of life – a giving that cannot be given if the giving is not part of an economy that includes reception. It is this giving-in-through-and-beyond-reception that *is* the kenotic economy: grace. It is a pneumatic economy, for the new dimension which Christ has opened up, the Spirit maintains and presents 'at our disposal as a new, open space' (ST III, 153; ExT 3, 169).

This kenotic presentation of the Trinity – *missio* issuing from *processio* – is the basis for Balthasar's theological aesthetics, concerned as it is with 'seeing the form': the form of God, the form of revelation, the form of faith

---

92 See Origen, *De Princip.*, 1, II, 8 and Nestorius, *Liber Heraclides*, 1, I, 61.

93 Quoted by Vladimir Lossky, *Mystical Theology in the Eastern Church* (London: James Clarke, 1957), p. 60. P. T. Forsyth's analysis of kenosis (which he understands as part of a dialectic that embraces the plerosis of self-fulfilment of Christ) does draw upon the notion that divine love is the dynamic of action. 'Love alone has any key to those renunciations which do not mean suicide but the finding of the Soul' (*The Person and Place of Jesus Christ* (London, 1909), p. 320). This analysis, in the first decade of the present century, did not fully provide a trinitarian basis for the operation of this love while observing that the kenotic act 'was the most condensed expression of holy love' (p. 316). Forsyth's main focus remains a psychological account of the reduction in divine qualities – the effects, that is, of Christ's eternal knowledge becoming 'discursive, successive, and progressive' (pp. 310–11). For further theological developments of the doctrine of kenosis in British theology, see Hugh Ross Mackintosh, *The Doctrine of the Person of Jesus Christ* (London, 1912) and, more recently, the work of Donald MacKinnon and Rowan Williams.

94 Lossky, *Mystical Theology*, p. 70. For an extensive analysis of Palamas' distinctive contribution to trinitarian thought see Rowan Williams, 'The Philosophical Structures of Palamism', *Eastern Churches Review*, IX: 1–2 (1977), pp. 27–44.

95 *Church Dogmatics* IV/1, p. 184.

and the mediation of those forms. Kenosis is a theological economy of representation – where representation covers both the vicarious representation of Christ dying *pro nobis*[96] and the creative mimesis. Christ the Word descends into all the eloquence, rhetoric, mimesis and endless deferral of meaning in human signs. He is erased by them and through them on Good Friday before sinking down into the silence and the absence of Holy Saturday. But for Balthasar it is in this descent into hell, 'the dying away into silence ... that we have to understand precisely his non-speaking as his final revelation, his utmost word' (MP 79). Through the cross, judgement falls on all eloquence, rhetoric, mimesis and the endless deferral of meaning in signs. Representation experiences its crisis. And a new word appears, 'his utmost word', on the far side of the death's profound *passio*. Only in and through the cross, the death of God, is there redemption and an ability to 'see the form'.

'Seeing the Form [*Schau der Gestalt*]' is the subtitle to the first volume of *The Glory of the Lord*. In that volume Balthasar begins to describe the relationship which exists between *pistis* and *gnosis*, faith and knowledge, in a way which refigures Hegel on the basis of his christological refocusing of *analogia entis*. Faith cannot operate without love (or hope) for Balthasar. Faith, understood as trustful self-abandonment in obedience, is intrinsic to the kenotic economy of desire in the Trinity. He writes: 'the Spirit is not so much a divine object of faith as the divine medium of the gift of faith made to the Father in the Son' (ST III, 107; ExT 3, 118). Our faith is the human response to God's faith, a response of obedience which enables our participation in God's triunal and kenotic love.[97] Through and with and in this faith, the 'light of grace comes to the aid of natural ability: it strengthens and deepens the power of sight' (H I, 169; GL 1, 175). We see and know differently because the realm of signs surrounding us is read through the hermeneutic of God's poured-out love:

> a synthesizing power to penetrate phenomena, a power that derives from God and is capable of interpreting phenomena so that they disclose what God wishes to reveal of his own depths in them. (ST III, 38; ExT 3, 42)

In this epistemology of faith, opinion or view [*Ansicht*] is transformed into true sight [*Sicht*]; the images [*Abbilden*] of the world become true pictures [*Urbilden*] of God. Balthasar's *analogia entis* draws close to Barth's *analogia fidei* at this point. But this *analogia fidei* cannot dispense with a relationship between creator and creature, a creator who gives and maintains the existence of creation, who is, in his ontological difference, absolute Being. The transfiguration of images of the world [*Abbilden*] into true pictures of God [*Urbilden*] parallels the transfiguration of the human form of Christ into the glory of God and human *autarkia* into human *theosis*: 'For now the "prototype" [*Urbild*] (the eternal Son, enjoying Sonship with the Father)

---

96 See Balthasar's essay 'On Vicarious Representation', in ST IV, 401–9; ExT 4, 415–22.
97 See Kristeva's definition of faith in *In the Beginning Was Love: Psychoanalysis and Faith*, tr. Arthur Goldhammer (New York: Columbia University Press, 1988), p. 24: 'faith could be described, perhaps rather simplistically, as what can only be called a primary identification with a loving and protective agency'.

has indwelt [*eingebildet*] the copy [*Abbild*] and stamped his divine form [*Form*] upon it once and for all' (TD III, 355; ThD 4, 381).

This theological notion of representation has further corollaries. One can see the form of God not only in the works of human beings – the music of Mozart, the paintings of Christ-clowns by Rouault – but in the style of the lives of those who have given themselves over to imitating Him. The life of Elisabeth of Dijon 'became a sacrament' (ED 63). She fulfilled an office and a charism. The track of her becoming, her vocation, announces a doctrine, a teaching, carved out in, through and upon her body. 'Her mission was to approach, by way of contemplation, the source of all grace, and so to be a conduit of its flow to the Church' (ED 53). Adrienne von Speyr 'was charged with considering in a Christian way, the sphere of pure *agapē*, through this incarnational process, the sphere of *eros*'.[98] With Thérèse of Lisieux 'it is not so much her writings as her life itself which is her doctrine' (Th 24; Th xxi). '[S]he stands in exactly the same relationship towards her own being as a writer does towards his novel or a sculptor to his statue' (Th 47; Th 17). The form again reveals the glory of God for those who can read it. By extension, the style of a theological discourse betrays the extent to which the theologian is obedient to the call upon his life. For the theologian's task is not only to expound the form of God, it is to be abandoned unto God so that the form of God may be impressed upon the discourse itself, the doing of theology itself. Kenosis operates here as the condition for the possibility of theological method. The passion of Christ has therefore effected an ontological shift, but this 'primal form can never be adequately and exhaustively reproduced by any rational construction [*Gebilde*]' (H I, 205; GL 1, 212).

Without faith as kenotic, self-abandoning love we are simply left in the strident darkness of clashing empty symbols. 'In this amorphous condition, sin forms what one can call the second "chaos" (generated by human liberty)' (MP 173). This is the hell Christ descended into on Holy Saturday and from which the redemption of form and representation will issue on Easter Sunday. Christ descends into the hiatus, the aporia, the margins. It is precisely here that non-speaking becomes 'his final revelation' (MP 79). Death is the autistic state where meaning dissolves into the seas of the chaotic as Christ descends into the depths of the abyss (ST IV, 387–400; ExT 4, 401–14; Balthasar discusses various accounts of *descensus*).

But this God who can separate himself from himself, the basis of a trinitarian distinction between the Father and the Son, brings into this abyss a boundary, a limit. 'God himself has proven to be Almighty who is able to safeguard his identity in nonidentity' (ST IV, 399; ExT 4, 413). That new identity rises to the world again and so a new discourse announces itself which is theological:

> In the presence of the hiatus, the 'logic' of theology can in no way rest on the (unbroken) continuity of human (and scientific) logic, but only on that theo-'logic' established by God himself in the hiatus of the 'death of God'. (MP 79)

98 *First Glance at Adrienne von Speyr*, p. 94.

This is the death of the sign – its silencing, its judgement – which only faith in the transcendent meaning of a love which frames the text can read aright. Language too must experience its passion; that is the central intuition of the economy of representation, the movement towards naming, which the doctrine of kenosis expresses. In the words of Emmanuel Levinas, language 'expresses the gratuity of sacrifice'.[99] In experiencing its passion, it experiences its redemption and this because the Spirit recapitulates always the entire economy of salvation, expressing 'the pneumatic unity of Cross and Resurrection' (TD III, 360; ThD 4, 386). As a further corollary, 'Hell is a *product* of the Redemption' (MP 174).[100] Passion is understood here as ambivalent – the word ties together the twin themes of love and suffering, crucifixion and exaltation. We must always recall that what is poured out is love, a love that in giving itself suffers and through that suffering is able to name. What persists when the continuity of human discourse and reasoning comes to its end or reaches its edge, is the economy of love:

> the continuity is the absolute love of God of man, manifesting itself actively on both sides of the hiatus (and so in the hiatus itself), and his triune Love in its own intrinsic reality as the condition of possibility for such a love for man. (MP 79)

Balthasar concludes: 'Everything turns on his inner-trinitarian Love' (MP 81).

Balthasar at the end of modernity

With Balthasar's understanding of *distema* and *analogia entis* as they relate to kenosis, pneumatology is pushed beyond what he calls 'Romantic notions of "organism" [*Organizismus*]' (TD III, 389; ThD 4, 417). With this his work sidesteps modernity's concerns with evolution, progress, the immanent synthesis of part and whole – summed up in Hegel's understanding of Logic. What we have termed a theology of hiatus might also be called – considering the concern at the end of modernity with re-establishing the category of difference – a theology of difference. It is difference which Balthasar reasserts above and beyond the immanence of Hegel's Trinity. The relationship of the Father to the Son in Hegel is that of the other-for-the-same, not the other for itself as unassimilable to the same. Hence necessity, rather than freedom, characterizes Hegel's kenotic economy. Balthasar announces a second difference in the immanent Trinity, the difference of the Spirit which safeguards the freedom of the Son's givenness to the Father and mediates this obedience to the Father even when the Father and the Son are furthest from each other – on Good Friday and Holy Saturday.[101] This freedom within the Godhead

---

99 *Otherwise than Being or Beyond Essence*, tr. Alphonso Lingis (Le Hague: Martinus Nijhoff, 1981), p. 120.
100 Balthasar develops this in the section '*Hölle und Trinität*', pp. 314–29, TL II, explicitly examining his theology with relation to Luther's.
101 Gardner and Moss attend to the logic of this suggestion of a 'second difference' and its elision of time and space in the divine life (see Chapter 3).

provides the condition for our own freedom of response – and hence distinguishes, in a way Hegel could not, between the Church as those who have responded and the world which remains disobediently set against the love of God focused upon its own narcissistic behaviour. One could say, from Balthasar's point of view, that in Hegel there is too little Spirit rather than too much. 'The sheer mutual love of the Father and the Son amounts first to a binary ... Hegel, the philosopher of spirit has definitely neglected the Holy Spirit' (TL III, 40). Hegel's immanent Trinity consists of two persons and a relationship, not a community of three-in-one. The Spirit is not the Holy Spirit because the Spirit is not a person.

This second difference can be established because Balthasar's theology issues from a view of the human subject that is not at all Hegelian or in line with the reification of consciousness which marks subjectivity in modernity. Subjectivity for Balthasar again takes its form from the personhood of God and is linked to the fulfilment of mission and calling. The subject as a monad in and for itself is a *Geistsubjekt* for Balthasar, not a person (TD II.2, 186–202; ThD 3, 203–20). A person is figured by their mission or vocation in God. The person acts within the larger fields of sociality and ecclesiology. S/he is dialogical, created to love, and there-fore always coming into an identity, that is, a form (*Gestalt*), as the mission continues and unfolds. There is no room in Balthasar's exaltation of obedience and abandonment for the egoism of modernity. In fact, such egoism is specifically related to death, while becoming a person is a continual process and a participation in the eternal life of God. Hence Balthasar does not get preoccupied with the contents of Jesus' con-sciousness in the way earlier kenoticists did. Since the mission of Christ has no conceivable beginning and Jesus possesses full awareness of his Sonship, his life of obedience is not a question of relinquishing certain divine predicates (TD II.2, 175–85; ThD 3, 191–202). The Son receives his identity through a *missio* which is the economic extension of his *processio*. In the same way, the Spirit receives an identity through a distinct vocation which is manifest in the Spirit's role at the annunciation (prior to, in fact, inaugurating the incarnation), the baptism of Jesus and, sub-sequently, in mediating Christ to the Church. In this way Balthasar emphasizes, as Gregory of Nyssa before him, the personhood of the Spirit. In fact, Balthasar's theology centres upon a *Geistchristologie*, which is why his engagement with Hegel and kenosis is so important to him.

> Christian truth is trinitarian in as much as Jesus Christ, the incarnate
> Son of the Father, is incarnated by the Holy Spirit and is 'the truth'
> through His life as the revealing Word. (TL III, 18)

This *Geistchristologie* demands the third divine hypostasis, the second difference. Balthasar devotes his third and final volume of *Theologik* to the person of the Spirit because the Spirit as 'the indispensable interpreter of the trinitarian truth' (TL III, 20) is the condition for the possibility of theological discourse, of the theologians own acts of representation.

If the personhood of the Spirit is so categorical, it may also be the point where Balthasar's theology is most vulnerable. If Christ is incarnate *'vom Geist'* then two theological problems present themselves. The first problem is related to the Western espousal of the *filioque*. That is, the Spirit's independent activity can militate against his proceeding from the Father and the Son. Balthasar discusses this difficulty with reference to what he terms 'trinitarian inversion': the Spirit seems to come before the Son and be above the Son in the incarnation but this is 'ultimately only the projection [*Umlegung*] of the immanent Trinity onto the "economic" plane' (TD II.2, 175; ThD 3, 191). Whether this answers the difficulty is another matter. In its move away from reading the immanent Trinity from the economic Trinity (as in the work of Barth, Rahner and Moltmann), it suggests that we have knowledge of the Trinity independent of the economy of salvation. The second theological problem is the relationship between the Spirit and Mary. On occasions it is Mary who supplies the second difference, not the Spirit (who is reduced to a relation between Father and Son). The mediating role of the Spirit is taken over by Mary. It is Mary, for example, who provides the participating link in the soteriological chain; the purity of Mary's faith provides the possibility for the new covenant (TD III, 328–37; ThD 4, 352–61). In this she both stands for the Church and in a strict sense is more than the Church, the possibility for the Church (TL III, 289). With Mary, there is introduced a third difference, not in the immanent life of the Godhead (which is the concern of the *Theologik* and hence little space is given over in that work to the marian doctrine), but in the economic life with respect to creation. In his essay '*Kenosis* of the Church', Balthasar points to the dangers of this interpretation:

> Only a gnosticizing sophology can wipe away the boundaries and interpolate Mary as a kind of fourth hypostasis of the Trinity. Healthy Catholic theology will protect itself from such a logic. (ST IV, 126; ExT 4, 132)

For Balthasar, Mary announces the ontological difference between Being and existence which is the position of being human and 'made in the image of' and the Spirit presents the theological difference between God and creation. Mary keeps open the possibility of response, the Spirit keeps open the condition for the possibility of the marian openness. What needs further consideration here is the relationship between ontological and theological difference. How is the necessary *diastasis* between God and the world maintained?

Like Hegel, Balthasar's Trinity is a movement in love, but as a consequence of the Spirit's second difference and the freedom vouchsafed to each of the persons because of that difference, the economy of love is not founded in lack. It is not deficiency which propels the Father into a representation of himself, but the excessive givenness of the Son; there is only a Father because there is the self-offering of the Son. Neither is the economy of love a process of continual dying, 'History as the Golgotha of the Spirit (Hegel)' (H III.1/2, 952; GL 5, 623). The kenotic economy here is an economy of eternal Being,

> God-given Being [which] is both fullness and poverty at the same time: fullness as Being without limit, poverty modelled ultimately

[*urbildlich*] on God Himself because He knows no holding on to Himself, poverty in the act of Being which is given out, which as gift delivers itself without defence. (H III.1/2, 956; GL 5, 626–7)

The kenotic economy is an economy of life through death, eternal resurrection through eternal crucifixion, an eternal giving of thanks through an eternal brokenness. In a way this theologically refigures the erotic tradition in which death is equated with orgasm. Balthasar writes: 'By means of the Eucharist, he distributes his death, spilling it as life into the womb of the Church' (TD III, 335; ThD 4, 359). In this refiguration *eros* (the ascending desire) becomes *agapē* (the descending gift). The resurrection is not the result of the cross; death is not an event at all in Christ. Through the way Christ 'lived out [*voll auslebte*] this death' (TD III, 122; ThD 4, 132), death itself is understood to be betwixt natural and unnatural (TD III, 111; ThD 4, 120). Death is swallowed up in the trinitarian circulation of love. The descent of the cross, and more profound descent into the silence of Holy Saturday, folds death into the fabric of eternal life. This eternal life is proleptically dramatized and participated in through baptism and, following baptism, the eucharist. Patristic and medieval theologies read the flow of water and blood from the dead body of Christ as baptism and the eucharist; the ruptured fluids heralded a new birth. Revisiting such readings, modernity's necrophobia/necrophilia is transcended in Balthasar's theology. The vocation of the Church is to realize daily the resurrected body, which is an open, frangible body – the crucified body that is both eternally wounded and exalted. By sinking to its knees and acknowledging (Phil. 2.10), through living the ecstatic life by means of dispossession and poverty, the Church participates in 'the infinite poverty of the fullness of Being and ... the God who does not hold on to Himself' (H III.1/2, 957; GL 5, 627). It actualizes the eternal circulation of the gift, a circulation it neither began nor can end. Incarnation, once again, is seen to achieve its fulfilment in *eucharistia*.

Poststructural kenosis: Kristeva and the transcorporal body

Beyond the metaphysics of presence (as distinct from the 'metaphysics' of the saints)[102] and death-bound subjectivity is the rainbow of God's glory. Prior to the reification, and mortification of the scientific object, there is Being itself (H III.1/2, 943; GL 5, 613) – absolute Being as absolute love. Eclipsing the totality and beauty of the ordered *theios kosmos*, the architectonics of Kantian reasoning and Enlightenment Titanism, is the groundless sublime, the God who is otherwise. A trinitarian theology of difference which makes possible the giving-in-receiving of the gift, announces a mode of living excessive to the narcissism and the possessive logic of a debased *eros*. These are the themes – figured in and through

---

102 His account of the metaphysics of the saints – something Balthasar believes Christian theologians must emulate and develop – is found in H III.1/2 407–91; GL 5, 48–140. He aims to demonstrate in this account how 'speculative idealism seems to have been anticipated by a pious idealism' (p. 484/132).

kenosis – which place Balthasar at the end of modernity in a cultural space shared with several poststructuralists.[103]

The poststructural analysis of kenosis focuses on the ethics of discourse, relating this both to an uneliminable difference between self and other and an economy (or aneconomy, since this word suggests that which overflows and ruptures all constructed and controlled economies) of excess. The employment of the term kenosis is frequent. Emmanuel Levinas provides the most explicit theological account of God's humbling of himself in an identification with human suffering in his essay 'Judaism and Kenosis'. He develops his messianism, a *Heilsgeschichte* in which Judaism announces a continuous creation and calls human beings to be faithful to the Torah. The divine presence is worked out in this world to the extent that human beings are faithful. In a Kantian move, the ethics of human activity are sanctified and, in a Hegelian move, God is understood to need this activity. Our prayer and faithfulness to the Torah are necessary 'in order to be able to associate himself [God] with the worlds'.[104] God's kenosis is realized in and through human kenosis.[105] This develops Levinas' more strictly philosophical project of the self as hostage to and substitute for the other. The emptying of oneself to receive the other,[106] based in a never-to-be satisfied desire for the other, becomes the condition of signification itself. For in the economy of the sign also, what is said (*le dit*) exceeds its significance and portrays (while it also betrays) the transcendental Saying (*le Dire*).

This account of kenosis and discourse has been influential on Jacques Derrida, Luce Irigaray, Hélène Cixous and Julia Kristeva – each of whom, in their own ways, examines the relationship between kenotic ethics and the metaphysics of difference as they are embodied in writing, in textuality. In 'Sauf le nom (post scriptum)', a recent essay by Derrida on writing, deconstruction and the negative theology of Angelus Silesius, negative theology itself is described as the 'kenosis of discourse'.[107] He speaks of the passion in negative theology to locate a place 'over there, toward the name, toward the beyond of the name in the name'.[108] In so far as negative theology comments constantly on its impossibility, performing endlessly a desertification of 'God' and 'being', acting as a critique of its own reference and plenitude of meaning, it is a wounded writing. Kenosis is language in crisis. Language which performs this crisis opens a space, a crack, an aporia within which a love can circulate which maintains the alterity of the other because it installs 'a movement or moment of

---

103 Though I do not investigate here the work of Jean-François Lyotard or Jean-Luc Nancy, Lyotard's and Nancy's return to, defence and development of Kant's notion of the sublime and the unpresentable share much with Balthasar's aesthetics. For an account of Lyotard's and Nancy's work on the sublime and in relation to theology, see my *Theology and Contemporary Critical Theory* (London: Macmillan, 1996. Second edition, 1999), pp. 115–23.

104 *In the Time of Nations*, tr. Michael B. Smith (London: Athlone Press, 1994), p. 129.

105 Compare this with Balthasar's essay '*Kenosis* of the Church?' in ST IV, 119–32; ExT 4, 125–38.

106 *Otherwise than Being*, p. 117.

107 *On the Name*, ed. Thomas Dutoit, tr. David Wood *et al.* (Stanford University Press, 1995), p. 50.

108 Ibid., p. 59.

deprivation, an asceticism or provisional kenosis'.[109] For Hélène Cixous this kenosis is not simply in and of language, it is in and of the reception of language; it pertains, that is, to the operation of reading as well as the operation of writing. For Cixous kenosis describes the ex-propriation of the reading subject in relation to the text. Reading is an act of submission. She herself reflects upon the ethical and metaphysical implications of reading whilst examining her responses to the Brazilian novelist Clarice Lispector. Through reading and writing, a transfiguration of the self through a proper distance emerges in which the other voice, the other imaginary, is confronted and respected. The discipline and ascesis of moving towards this proper distance is 'a relentless process of de-selfing, de-egoization' which acknowledges and respects the 'enigma', the 'mystery', the 'inexplicable' and the 'unavowable'.[110] 'It's at the end, at the moment one has attained the period of relinquishing, of adoration … that miracles happen.'[111] The end of modernity announces the limits of secularity, and Balthasar's writing resonates with this new re-enchantment of the world.[112]

Nevertheless, despite the theological importance Balthasar gives to individual style and its relation to divine form [*Gestalt*], despite also his theological concern with representation, divine [*Urbild*] and human [*Abbild*], despite also the way his work draws upon a vast literary corpus – nothing less than the Western literary canon as it has emerged in several different languages – Balthasar gives scant attention to *homo symbolicus* as such. Though he recognized that, since we are not the object of God's action, we must in some way 'participate in uttering [*mitzusprechen*] God's Word' (TD III, 296; ThD 4, 318) and so, consequently, the Church's 'representative [*stellvertretend*] being, acting and suffering is founded on Christ's representative being, acting and suffering' (TD III, 395; ThD 4, 423) – nevertheless, he does not examine the nature of mimesis which relates various forms of representation (vicarious, mirroring or partici-patory), being, action and suffering as such. And even though his own theological style shows a profound awareness of the textual – note his word-plays, like the Christic association he unfolds between '*vergeben*' (to be given), '*vergebens*' (for nothing, in vain), '*Vergebung*' (forgiveness) and '*Vergeblichkeit*' (futility) – his appreciation of literary texts is more on the level of themes and narratives rather than their language. There is a sophisticated, imaginative and awesome analysis of analogy from a theological perspective, but nothing on the nature of the analogical as such, on the theological and anthropological significance of rhetoric. This is partly a question of theological method. As Gardner and Moss show

---

109 Ibid., p. 74.
110 '*Coming to Writing' and Other Essays*, ed. Deborah Jenson, tr. Sarah Cornell *et al.* (Cambridge, MA: Harvard University Press, 1991), p. 156.
111 '*Coming to Writing*', p. 117. For a more developed picture see my 'Words of Life: Postmodern plenitude and the work of Hélène Cixous' in *The Way* 36:3 (July, 1996), 225–35.
112 It is the sociologist Zygmunt Bauman who views postmodernism as a re-enchantment of the world, overturning the dis-enchantment of the world that Weber understood to be the effect of technologicalization. See the Introduction to his *Intimations of Postmodernity* (London: Routledge, 1992), pp. vii–xxviii.

(Chapter 3), Balthasar's work is a performance: to read is to engage in receiving and to participate, liturgically, in an action that may have salvific consequences. He is unable then to step outside of the theological and present a strictly philosophical (and therefore anthropological) account of language. Nevertheless, some account of his own discourse is necessary and that means some reflection upon what it is to represent when one is 'made in the image of'. How are our words, gestures, sign-giving – the textuality of life – related to the Word of God and the Spirit as Writer?

The closest Balthasar comes to a discussion of theological discourse is in his section 'The mediation of the form', in the first volume of *The Glory of the Lord*. It is significant that he recognizes that in the revelation of the Son of God,

> his form in various ways became intertwined with the interrelated forms of his immediate and more distant historical context and with the given forms of the world of nature and of salvation history. (H I, 506; GL 1, 527)

For what this passage affirms is a recognition of the intratextual nature of mundane existence when viewed in Christ. Human beings live within an allegory: to the extent that we are obedient, our lives are continually caught up in the process of being formed, receiving a name; these lives being formed are contexualized by other forms (natural, cultural and historical); furthermore we are manufacturers of forms. We have to learn how to read all these forms that constitute the particularity of our existence. We have to learn to see them *as* forms and not objects containing a meaning closed within themselves and independent of Christ.

Balthasar's doctrine of perception implies a doctrine of *ecstasis* (H III.1/2, 581; GL 5, 604). As forms all these things refer beyond themselves – to 'Christ, who, through his existence that fills all things, compels history and cosmos to bear a witness that is beyond their will to expression' (H III.1/2, 510; GL 5, 531). This is why there is no true knowledge outside faith. The spiritual adheres not only to the letter of Scripture, the eucharistic elements, the figure of the sacraments and the proclamation of the Word, but to the cosmos and 'man's shaping powers [*im Menschen die Antwort dergestaltenden*]' (H III.1/2, 579; GL 5, 602). Only by reading the facticity of the world in Christ's incarnation is the trinitarian love of God made concrete and visible. And yet, Balthasar does not explicitly examine the systems of signification employed by human beings responding to the formless and ineffable God through their shaping powers (H III.1/2, 579; GL 5, 602).

As we saw in the exegesis of the kenotic hymn in Philippians, the linguisticality of God (in Christ) and human beings (in their response to that Word), indeed the linguisticality of the Church, is prominent. It is precisely with linguisticality, the textuality of living, that poststructural accounts of kenosis have been concerned. It is with reference to these accounts that we cannot only develop Balthasar's own position but also locate the theologian with respect to contemporary philosophical, anthropological and psychological concerns. The existential has always played an important part in Balthasar's theological account of what it is to be human, open to the transcendent, creative and artistic. This existentialism may be the liberal weak point in Balthasar's conservative theology. 'A non-existential theology, therefore, remains unworthy of belief because it is not capable of making anything really visible' (H III.1/2, 579; GL 5, 602). Nevertheless, Balthasar's work breathes in a certain rarefied atmosphere, a post-resurrection perspective. It is as if his work was composed on the frosted heights of Thomas Mann's own magic mountain or, to use a term Quash will develop further in Chapter 4, in epic mode. The social, the political and the physical orders of being proceed somewhere in the plains at the foot of the escarpment. This need not be. Balthasar's own gaze may be fixed on the transcendental categories of the good, the beautiful and the true, but his work endorses no gnosticism and warrants no docetic concentration upon the spiritual. His theology sacralizes, through Christ, the historical and concrete, giving back soul to the historical and concrete.[113] The concrete and historical take on a certain permeability while remaining quite emphatically material, corporeal. As he himself describes it, through Christ mundane reality is delivered from self-glorification (H I, 566; GL 1, 589) – that is, empiricism, naïve realism, positivism. In bringing Balthasar's work into an examination of post-structural concerns with textuality, I am, then, simply extending and applying it. That is, I am reading, on the basis of faith, the watermark of God's glory in the experience of being 'made in the image of'. Theology precedes and makes possible an anthropology which emphasizes the nature of the symbolic worlds we construct. This is how Augustine comes to relate the Trinity to his concept of personhood, theology to psychology, in *De Trinitate*. We are going to make a similar move, for what is at stake in the ineradicable correlation between *homo symbolicus*, kenosis and an anthropology grounded upon the mission of Christ, can be seen more clearly by developing Balthasar's understanding of God's kenotic love through an examination of Kristeva's phenomenology of desire. Most particularly, we need to examine her work on the relationship of love to language, the order of the symbolic to the abject.

We can legitimately develop Balthasar's work through Kristeva's because they share so much. Let me briefly point to four fundamental parallels. First, there is a common appeal to the primacy of love as an anthropological root. Balthasar develops this through his notion of the *imago dei* and divine *eros*, based upon his work on, among others, Gregory of Nyssa. Kristeva develops this from the attention given by psychoanalysis to sexual desire and, more specifically, Freud's discussion of narcissism and the Oedipal triangle. Secondly, for both of them the relationship of mother and child acts as the locus for a metaphysical analysis of living towards transcendence. Balthasar begins his exploration of the wonder of Being and the awareness of our radical contingency in

---

113 Balthasar is returning the soul back to materialism in a way Walter Benjamin endorsed towards the end of his *The Origin of German Tragic Drama*, tr. John Osborne (London: New Left Books, 1977), p. 230. For Benjamin, materialism without this soul was Satanic.

association with their relationship. Kristeva explores the nature of the unfathomable and the mystery of identity beginning with the mother-child unity. Thirdly, they share an understanding of selfhood as caught up in and constituted by wider economies of desire than simply the intentions of an 'I'. For Balthasar the significance of human *eros* (man/woman, mother/child, self/neighbour) is located in the larger economy of divine *eros* and so self-autonomy is always fissured: one moves towards a realization of personhood in following Christ and obeys the call to intra-trinitarian participation. Here an *anthropologia crucis* is sketched, which can only enter the condition of an *anthropologia resurrectionis* through entering the divine performance of redemption. Nevertheless, the condition of *anthropologia crucis* is the existential condition for the possibility of entering this economy of resurrection life. For Kristeva, the ability to love oneself aright is dependent upon loving others. The ego is not the *ego cogito* of Enlightenment reasoning, but the *ego affectus est* of Bernard of Clairvaux. The self is always in process, always part of an ongoing performance, always being displaced, because it is always constituted only in relation to being affected by that which is other. Finally, Kristeva herself recognizes the connections between her own semanalysis – the analysis of the semiotic traces rippling the symbolic surface of a text – of amatory discourse, kenotic abandonment and Christ's passion. In her short book, *In the Beginning was Love*, she writes:

> Christ's Passion brings into play even more primitive layers of the psyche; it thus reveals a fundamental depression (a narcissistic wound or reversed hatred) that conditions access to human language. The sadness of young children just prior to their acqui-sition of language has often been observed; this is when they must renounce forever the maternal paradise in which every demand is immediately gratified. The child must abandon its mother and be abandoned by her in order to be accepted by the father and begin talking ... [L]anguage begins in mourning ... The 'scandal of the cross', the *logos tou stavron* or language of the cross ... is embodied, I think, not only in the psychic and physical suffering which irrigates our lives ... but even more profoundly in the essential alienation that conditions our access to language, in the mourning that accompanies the dawn of psychic life.

She goes on to conclude in a way that returns us from Lacanian psy-chology to Balthasar:

> Christ abandoned, Christ in hell, is of course the sign that God shares the condition of the sinner. But He also tells the story of that necessary melancholy beyond which we humans may just possibly discover the other, now in the symbolic interlocutor rather than nutritive breast.[114]

In what follows the theological implications of this astonishing passage will be drawn out in relation to Balthasar's depiction of Christ's kenotic

114 *In the Beginning*, pp. 40–1.

love and the aphasia of Holy Saturday, and the descent towards the name
and beyond the figurative in Paul's letter to the Philippians. For what
Kristeva presents us with is an account of the inseparability of a
morphology of selfhood from a theory of representation on the basis of
kenosis. We recall that there is a concern with the morphology of selfhood
in Paul's *carmen Christi* – with the move towards one's true identity *post
mortem*. For Kristeva, our initial entrance and any subsequent entrance
into language is an experience of kenosis. But unlike the economies of
lack and negation which characterized Hegelian kenosis – and characterize also the psychological economies of Freud and Lacan, founded as
they are upon a similar notion of progress through negation and rejection
(*Verneinung* and *Verwerfung*), the symbolics of castration – Kristeva's
emphasis is upon resurrection. 'I see symbolic castration less as asceticism
than as an expansion – through asceticism – toward an endless poiesis ...
my own path to vitality.'[115] This growth, this movement beyond the death-
drive, comes in and through the advent of language which Kristeva is all
too aware parallels the Advent of the Word. This advent of language, and
this constitution of personhood, is initially situated within the nexus of
relations which comprise the Oedipal triangle and the movement from
the imaginary to the symbolic order through the mirror-stage.

The mirror-stage is associated now with the work of Jacques Lacan –
though Lacan developed the notion from Henri Wallon, who was
probably developing Freud's meditation on primary narcissism. The
stage describes the effects of that scene when the child confronts its image
in a mirror. Before this stage, the child occupies an imaginary phase in
which it experiences, produces and stores up various images of itself and
its body through mobilizing any number of identifications it makes of the
world around it.[116] This imaginary level, closely associated for Kristeva
with the rhythms, pulsations and drives of the psychobiological, provides
the foundation for the subject of enunciation, the entry into discourse. It
remains present in the discourse itself as the semiotic as distinct from (but
not polarized to) the semantic.

> I therefore distinguish between the *semiotic*, which consists of drive-
> related and affective *meaning* organized according to primary
> processes whose sensory aspects are often nonverbal (sound and
> melody, rhythm, colour, odors, and so forth), and on the one hand,
> *linguistic signification* that is manifested in linguistic signs and their
> logico-syntactic organization.'[117]

In the mirror-stage the child comes upon an imaaged, but unified
conception of itself, which at first it takes as being itself and later realizes

---

115 *New Maladies*, p. 90. Both Irigaray and Cixous have continued in their own work
    to stress the difference between feminine economies of desire – emphasizing
    extravagant giving and excess – and masculine economies of desire – charac-
    terized by lack and anal retention. For a concise expression of this theme see
    Cixous' essay '"The egg and the chicken": love is not having' in *Reading with
    Clarice Lispector*, tr. Verene Andermatt Conley (Hemel Hempstead: Harvester
    Wheatsheaf, 1990), pp. 98–122.
116 *New Maladies*, pp. 103–4.
117 Ibid., p. 104.

is separate from itself. This realization that the unified 'I' is not the real 'I' develops into the realization that it needs the images, the substituting representations of itself, if it is to be and to have any conception of itself as a subject. With the mirror-stage, then, the child enters into the symbolic order. It recognizes both its own need for symbols and at the same time its own separation from full identity because of the uncrossable bar between the symbolic and the real (S/s). It is at this stage that Kristeva places the child's descent into depression. The realization of separation is a profound realization of loss – a loss which is continually sublimated by the employment of symbols or language. Semanalysis is, for Kristeva, the inquiry into the relationship between that which is sublimated – which she terms the semiotic – and that which is being symbolized. This fundamental sense of loss, which Kristeva associates with the passion of Christ and which I am describing as a kenotic economy, Kristeva terms abjection. 'Abjection,' she writes, 'or the journey to the end of the night.'[118]

The economy of abjection outlines the logic of separation which begins earlier and then informs Lacan's mirror-stage. *Anthropologia crucis* is a condition established primordially in the individual's life with separation from the body of the mother, the abjection of the mother, and the move towards the law of the father. For the father governs the creation of firm identities in the realm of the symbolic. This separation from the body of the mother Kristeva views as a separation from the semiotic *chora*. This has to occur prior to the move through the thetic or image stage and the arrival at the semantic concern with the proper name. Abjection institutes an exclusion which marks a beginning and a boundary. On one level, abjection marks the beginning of the social order by defining that which is forever external, distinct and threatening its domain. On another level, abjection marks the initiation into subjectivity as the I discovers what is not-I, what is other (both the semiotic body of the mother and the imaginary father). On a final level, abjection marks entrance into the symbolic order – what we necessarily leave out and remains silent in order for us to construct. In all these cases, abjection constitutes the possibility for the autonomy of the order – social, subjective, symbolic – while haunting such order by identifying the boundaries of its frailty, its instability, its ephemerality. As such, abjection constitutes what Kristeva calls 'the margin of a floating structure'.[119]

The effect of this separation Kristeva discerns in the melancholia which affects children just prior to entrance into language, prior, that is, to entering the realm of the symbolic. The separation which institutes primary narcissism also creates a space. The child as presubject enters an emptiness which will lead to the entry into the symbolic order at the mirror-stage. Kristeva locates, in this emptiness and the separation which precedes it, a primary identification with what she terms the 'imaginary father' – that is, the loving father/husband of the mother. These are troubled waters in the clinical studies of Kristeva's work, for the 'imaginary', loving Father prepares the subject for desiring the phallus,

118 *Powers of Horror*, tr. Leon Roudiez (New York: Columbia University Press, 1988), p. 58.
119 Ibid., p. 69.

which is the dynamic for entry into the symbolic order and the Oedipus complex. For our purposes, this haunting by the 'imaginary' father – whatever the coherence of the idea in Kristeva's work and her dialogue with Freud and Lacan – is another example of how Kristeva's morphology of the self parallels the doctrine of kenosis in the *carmen Christi*. Frequently Kristeva likens the operations of this imaginary father – the entry of the third party that comes from outside, or above, the dyad of mother–child – to the Christian God. The triune economy of love is explicitly compared with Christian *agapē*.[120] It is not maleness as such that the imaginary father figure installs. Another woman might play this loving role in the life of any particular family. This pre-oedipal father is open to either sex. And as Kelly Oliver remarks in her commentary upon Kristeva's work: 'The irrepresentable that makes representation possible is represented ... by the imaginary father ... It is only in the context of 'his' love that the Symbolic can become meaningful.'[121] This making meaningful of the symbolic through agapaic love, Kristeva weaves into the psychic process of identification, where (in one form of identification) there is a recognition and participation of one subject in another. The eucharist figures large in such discussions. In fact, Kristeva's construal of the meaningful sign, the affected representation, the effective symbol, is transubstantiation. As the eucharist is a participation in eternal life and fosters resurrection, so does involvement with language. The eucharist, as an emblem of the kenotic economy, is always both a giving of life and a sacrifice, a loss, an act of violence.[122]

The melancholy moment before entering language is a moment in which meaning is lost. It is not only in children learning to speak that this occurs, and so Kristeva's work is not limited to the psychology of child development. The loss of meaning, and its consequent relinquishing of desire, is found paradigmatically in depressive states of all kinds but is constantly having to be negotiated as the self-in-process grows in and through its misidentifications with others: in all transference and countertransference. This loss, this use of symbolic substitutions, and the dialectic of demand and desire that all representations participate in, place the self always in process, always searching for a place to belong to, always experiencing a certain dispossession.

What is important, in terms of Kristeva's semanalysis, is that representation remains infected by that which is abjected.[123] The semiotic drives operate dialectically within and upon the symbolic, so that 'writing causes the subject who ventures into it to confront an archaic authority'.[124] What this means is that the melancholy moment where meaning is lost is rediscovered and performed in every act of representing. Some acts of

---

120 *New Maladies*, pp. 121–3, 179–80.
121 *Reading Kristeva: Unravelling the Double-Bind* (Bloomington: Indiana University Press, 1993), pp. 63–4.
122 *New Maladies*, p. 183.
123 Semanalysis treats three interrelated forms of representation: 'representations of words (close to the linguistic signifier), representations of things (close to the linguistic signified) and representations of affects (labile, psychic traces subject to the primary processes of displacement and condensation)' (*In the Beginning*, p. 4).
124 *Powers of Horror*, p. 75.

representation appeal to that suppressed melancholy more than others. Hence, when discussing Holbein's *Dead Christ* in *Black Sun*, Kristeva writes: 'very much like personal behaviour, artistic *style* imposes itself as a means of countervailing the loss of other and of meaning'.[125] The death of Christ becomes a portrayal of a paradox: representing the erasure of beauty, transcendence and form; presenting ironically an icon being iconoclastic. The experience of depression, of descent into emptiness, is endemic to the economy of representation, as it is also to the self-in-process – both of which are constantly searching for, but can never attain, stable identity. Such stability, the stability of a proper name not infected by the body of the mother, the semiotic *chora*, remains forever futural and eschatological, and yet constitutive of the present as hope and promise. Holbein's presentation of Christ in the tomb, then, leads us 'to the ultimate edge of belief, to the threshold of non-meaning'.[126] Non-meaning causes frigidity and paralysis. According to Irenaeus, throughout this time in the tomb Jesus looked upon chaos.[127]

We saw with Balthasar that 'the death of Jesus, like his Incarnation, was a function of his living, eternal love' (ST IV, 398; ExT 4, 412). Similarly, for Kristeva, the logic of separation, the necessary recognition of *diastema* (with attending plurality and heterogeneity), which provides the possibility for the ongoing configuration of self-in-relation-to-others in and through language, is part of a more general economy of love. Loss must lead to a renewal; death to resurrection. The psychologist's work is installed here where the movement breaks down, where the dead body of the mother is buried within and brings death to the soul, silence and autism to the speaking subject. Resurrection comes with becoming reconciled to the loss, the attachment to the mother, and searching for new identifications in and through discourse with the ideal and loving father. This Kristeva depicts in terms of the love of the mother for and by the father. Participation in and desire for complete reconciliation with this love functions as the Utopian horizon which makes psychological healing possible. Without this love there is only abjection and melancholy; the material world is without meaning because it cannot signify at all.

This concern to re-establish the primacy of a transcendental love is yet another reason why Christianity haunts Kristeva's own analyses and why her work can be paralleled with Balthasar's. She asks what psychoanalysis is, 'if not an infinite quest for rebirths through the experience of love'.[128] Psychoanalysis probes not the genesis (for we are born into a love always already in operation) but the *dunamis* of love. This is the economy of desire which, for Kristeva, we enter with that primordial separation from the mother. We are born to love because we are born divided. As Kristeva writes, elliptically: 'Love is a death sentence which causes me to be.'[129] The ego issues then from an economy of love and death (as separation) already in operation. Since this issuing is inseparable from entering the

---

125 *Black Sun*, tr. Leon Roudiez (New York: Columbia University Press, 1989), p. 129.
126 Ibid., p. 135.
127 Adv. Haer. IV c. 22. n. 1.
128 *Tales of Love*, tr. Leon Roudiez (New York: Columbia University Press, 1987), p. 1.
129 Ibid., p. 36.

symbolic order, it is the economy of love which infects the symbolic order with its desire for identification with the Other. All discourse, then, is amatory discourse: 'The speaking subject is a loving subject.'[130] All representation is a kenotic act of love towards the other; all representation involves transference – being caught up in the economy of giving signs. Kristeva, taking up Lacan's structuralist understanding of language, views metaphor as the condensation of this love present in discourse, and desire for the other as the operation of displacement or metonymy. '[W]riting serves as a resurrection.'[131] As she herself concludes, in a way which returns us to theology: 'the literary experience stands revealed as an essentially amorous experience, unstabilizing the same through its identification with the other. In this it emulates theology, which, in the same field, has strengthened love into faith.'

These two elements of Kristeva's semanalysis – the relation between abjection, the symbolic and descent into non-meaning (the logic of separation) on the one hand, and the relation between representation and transcendental economy of love (the logic of identification) on the other – parallel the doctrine of kenosis in Paul's *carmen Christi* and Balthasar's analysis of Holy Saturday. Kristeva's work, I wish to argue, roots a theological examination of the doctrine in an anthropology which relates the fundamental experience of human existence as one of dispossession (or in Schleiermacher's term, 'absolute dependence') to our nature as the creators of signs and symbols. We are makers of images because we are 'made in the image of'. Of course, while pointing to a triunal economy in Kristeva, a distinction must be made between this and Balthasar's trinitarian theology. It is a distinction between the way difference is understood and championed in Kristeva's work (as in that of Levinas, Derrida, Irigaray and Cixous) and theological difference. Heidegger's ontological difference is the site for both their meeting and their departure from each other. Theological difference, trinitarian difference, is other than ontological difference, while being the condition for the possibility of ontological difference in Balthasar. But ontological difference characterizes the human situation – summed up in Mary's open womb – and one could say that it is this difference which post-structuralism teaches us about.

The kenotic economy becomes the very root of sign production and therefore theological discourse. In fact, the Bible as a place where this economy is most evident is privileged by Kristeva.[132] Of course, it could be argued that what Kristeva presents us with is a demythologized, psychoanalytic reading of the Christian faith. This would, in fact, identify her work as continuing the project of modernity. And there are emphases in her work which support the view that psychoanalysis 'explains' the religious phenomena – codes of practice, liturgies, symbols, narratives – which make up Christianity. There are other, more recent emphases, which recognize parallels between the work of the analyst and the work of the priest (and between the work of the psychoanalytical theorist and

130 Ibid., p. 170.
131 *New Maladies*, p. 181.
132 *Tales*, p. 279.

the theologian). Karl Jaspers was among the first to suggest that psychoanalysts replace the traditional priest and sacramental confession, but Kristeva does not seem to wish to secularize a religious praxis. As a therapist, she works for the resurrection of the subject, through bringing that subject into a participation, in love, in the economy of the Word. She does this by fostering desire and vitality on the far side of depression and descent into a death-like asymbolia. She accepts that theologians have resolved many of the 'maladies of the soul' by 'granting their subjects a single object in which to delight – that is, God (as Saint Augustine said, *res qua fruendum est)*', but recognizes that 'If God no longer exists, the unconscious must reassemble the fragments of hysterical heterogeneity and its masks.'[133] Therapy seems to function, then, as establishing subjects within a kenotic economy of love and its representation at a time when theology no longer has cultural dominance and when God, for many, can no longer be believed in. That is, therapy helps those who are outside faith, outside communities of those practising faith, those who are left washed up on the beach after the wave of secularism has crashed on Dover Beach and ebbed away.

Furthermore, Kristeva is aware that psychoanalysis cannot become a metanarrative, a master discourse that can explain away religious discourse which is also founded upon establishing persons in the economy of love. '[P]sychoanalysis . . . is an art – I admit, an artifice – that may allow the men and women of our modern, sleek, lofty, costly, and profitable cities to preserve a life for themselves.'[134] Psychoanalysis is an artifice, 'an imaginary discourse that serves as truth',[135] for assisting modernity's *ego* in its search for a lost soul, for facilitating a transposition from necrophilia to resurrection life. Kristeva's own theory of the dialectical relationship between the semiotic and the symbolic would, in fact does, militate against placing psychological discourse above theological discourse, giving symbolic priority to one form of language. To make such a claim 'creates the danger of transforming psychoanalysis not only into an ideology but also into a religion'.[136] Certainly, Kristeva's reflections upon her Catholicism have caused embarrassment among several of her admirers and critics.[137] But if Kristeva is right, then, on the basis of the theological account of kenosis, we can understand each act of signification (speaking or writing) and each act of performing that act (reading, liturgical practice) as a move in love, a kenotic giving towards an ineffable Word, a name above all names, a name which gathers up all our naming and within which we too are named (*en tō onomati Jesou*). If she is right that this

---

133 See 'The semiotics of biblical abomination' in *Powers of Horror*, pp. 90–112 and 'Reading the Bible' in *New Maladies*, pp. 115–26. 'The Bible is a text that thrusts its words into my losses' (*New Maladies*, p. 119). This remarkable essay argues for psychoanalysis as 'post-Catholic' and demonstrates the analyst's continuing dependence upon biblical reference, logic and love.
134 *New Maladies*, p. 76.
135 Ibid., p. 44.
136 Ibid., p. 123.
137 *In the Beginning*, p. xi. Kelly Oliver, *Reading Kristeva*, has spoken of Kristeva's 'nostalgic relation to Christianity' and how her work 'privileges and recreates the Christian imaginary' (p. 128).

descent to the marginalized is also a movement towards the recovery of the lost semiotic body of the mother, then Christianity must possibly refigure its doctrine of the Trinity in terms of sexual difference. But that is another essay.

Transcorporality

The Godhead, who makes us in his image, circumscribes all human creativity. This creativity receives its transcendental meaning (truth, beauty, goodness) only in its relation to him. We are makers because we are made 'in the image of' and our making, in so far as it configures God's own making, is salvific. To be salvific, to participate in the economy of salvation opened and perfected by Christ, the form of God's glory, our making cannot be in our name. Our making cannot, like the builders of the Tower of Babel, make a name for ourselves. Our making cannot reify our own autonomy, like the stuffed animals of taxidermy. Such making is only death and idolatry. Our making must be in and through an abandonment that will instigate the crisis of our representations. Our making has to experience its passion, its descent into the silent hiatus. 'The simplicity of God "judges" all human thoughts that strive upwards of themselves to attain the utmost, and requires of them something that they can accomplish only in self-denial' (H III.2/2, 13; GL 7, 15–16). This crisis and passion is, in fact, the condition of all human making – Derrida's '*Kenosis* of discourse' – but we can only understand this crisis and passion aright if they are read in terms of a theology of kenosis. The endless differing and deferral of meaning, read philosophically, will only return us to the tragic vision of Hegel's Unhappy Consciousness. To be redeemed, the chaotic and febrile semiosis has to be bounded by the trinitarian operation. To this extent, kenosis in Levinas, Derrida, Irigaray, Cixous and Kristeva requires the theological framework they allude to and employ metaphorically in order for the 'resurrection', the 'eschatology', the 'Utopia' of which they speak, to be possible.

Balthasar's work explicitly announces this – metaphysics is only possible on theological conditions. The trinodal economies found in Kristeva (and Levinas and Derrida)[138] require a theological reading, require the difference they speak of to be a theological difference. Without it, these post-structural economies of the sign simply point towards the aporia of alterity without end – Hegel's Unhappy Consciousness, the tragic vision. With this reading, then, all accounts of meaning and sign-giving are coherent in terms of the incarnation. The incarnation of the Word reveals the ineradicable theological nature of all our wording. The intratextuality of human existence is grounded in the groundlessness of the divine. As such, all discourse is theological discourse. The subject of theology, on the basis of the relationship between kenotic Christology and representation, is the economy of the gift or, more accurately, the economy of giving, receiving and responding. This economy of the

---

138 For a discussion of these trinodal economies in Levinas and Derrida see my *Barth, Derrida and the Language of Theology* (Cambridge University Press, 1995), pp. 164–70, 247–8.

gift, which is inseparable from the exchange and economy of signs, is the very crux of the incarnational problematic, the crux of the question concerning mediation. Read theologically, discourse is always a meditation upon, as it is also an operation within, the divine–human exchange. Derrida has recently observed that a gift is never pure.[139] There is no pure giving of the gift; its recognition and reception as gift involves it within an exchange and economy. Nevertheless, there is what he calls 'continuity with respect to [the] difference' between gift-giver and gift-receiver.'

What is Christian theology about for Balthasar? It is about the play, the irresolvable dialectical play, between presentation and representation, between divine disclosure and reception. It is about the economy of grace, an economy inseparable from our own attempts to grapple with and grasp the meaning of that grace. It is not only a meditation upon grace (then it would place itself above grace); rather, it is a meditation from grace and within grace. As such, discourse read theologically is a means of grace; of incorporation into that which is given. If Derrida is correct and the gift cannot be given without obligation, then our human condition before the Godhead (as conscious recipients of grace, made conscious, that is, by faith) is one of being under obligation (there are echoes here of Levinas' recent exploration of ethics and Derrida's recent exploration of negotiation as it issues in and through intratextuality)[140] and God's grace cannot operate without prior and eternal covenant. The question then emerges as to who or what maintains the continuity in difference, the *sine qua non* of any exchange, in a theological investigation of the divine and human kenosis. If the incarnation provides the primary example, then God becoming form in Christ provides the ontological possibility for such a continuity. The continuing noetic possibility is the work of the Spirit of Christ through the Church's *eucharistia*. The Trinity is the condition for a transcorporality which is the hallmark of human existence.

Kristeva provides Balthasar with an anthropological account of transcorporality; Balthasar provides Kristeva with the Catholic theology which acts in the silent white margins of her own texts. The human *eros* is made part of a wider economy of desire – the desires of other people which propel my desire and the divine *eros* drawing me out in love, worship and obedience, pouring me into a trinitarian kenosis. Kristeva demonstrates how language is motivated by and abides within desire. Discourse, then, is always an amatory discourse proceeding through a never-to-be-entangled interplay of human and divine desire. It is a desire which both affirms and requires representation and yet denies and puts representation into crisis. Its enfleshment, its incarnation, is both its prison and its possibility of freedom. To employ one of Kristeva's definitions of psychoanalytic discourse, theology is a 'discourse[s] of love directed to an impossible other'.[141] It is both a meditation and a mediation; a coming to

139 *Given Time: I Counterfeit Money*, tr. Peggy Kamuf (University of Chicago Press, 1992), chapter 2.
140 For Levinas' understanding of the ethic of being under obligation, see *Otherwise than Being*, pp. 9–11. For negotiation in Derrida see his essay 'En ce moment même dans cet ouvrage me voici' in *Psyché* (Paris: Galilee, 1987), pp. 159–202.
141 *In the Beginning*, p. 7.

understanding and a participation; knowledge as love. We gain access to God and God to us through a transferential discourse. It has been recognized by many theologians (Karl Barth, George Lindbeck and Nicholas Lash most recently) that theology is a second-order reflection and redescription upon the faithful practice of the Church. Hans Frei sums up this observation: theology 'is an enquiry into the logic of the Christian community's language – the rules, largely implicit rather than explicit, that is exhibited in its use of worship and Christian life, as well as in the confessions of Christian beliefs'.[142] These rules constitute the cultural linguistics of the Christian religion. What this essay outlines is an expansion, by detailing the economy, of that 'logic of the Christian community's language', placing it within what Balthasar would call the theo-logic of trinitarian love. As such, Christian theology is not secondary and epiphenamenal, but participatory, a sacramental operation. It is a body of work at play within the language of the Christian community. Our physical bodies are mediated to us through our relation to other physical bodies and the mediation of those relationships through the body of the signs. Thus we are mapped on to a social and political body. The meaning of these signs is mediated to us through the body of Christ, eucharistic and ecclesial, so that we are incorporated into that spiritual body. Transcorporality is the hallmark of a theological anthropology.

We noted, when discussing Paul's *carmen Christi*, that we can either view the images, forms and deferrals of meanings, the textuality of this world, as caught between two aporia – incarnation and death or we can view the textuality of this world as a hiatus within the economy of love within the Trinity. The textuality of this world is a product of the *diastasis* stamped upon the human creativity because we are made 'in the image of'. As the creature is made, so the creature makes. Discourse issues from this *diastasis*, this space created by the love that gives and the love that responds, where giving and responding are two sides of the same act of abandonment. Space emerges in our abandonment to another; a womb from which the Word of God and the word of being human are both birthed; a name in which I too am named. Discourse, read theologically, is constitutive of personhood *en tō onomati Christo*. Here the I am is named; and the *I am* is God in me, and me (I in the accusative) in God. Practising theology, engaging in theological discourse as writer and reader (and any reader rewrites just as any writer reads), becomes an act of faith (and faithfulness). It is an ongoing liturgical act, a sacramental and soteriological process in which knowledge of God is inhabited rather than possessed.

Put briefly, what is suggested by transcorporality is that *en Christō* it is by our sign-giving and receiving, by our wording and reading, that we are redeemed. Every particular body participates in the universal form because it participates in the eschatological reordering of creation through Christ. As Christians, then, we are caught up not in a knowledge but a knowing of God, a revelation of God about God, that issues from the movement of his intra-trinitarian love. Epistemology and ontology as conceived in modernity by Kant and Hegel fall as metaphysical idols

---

142 *Types of Christian Theology* (New Haven: Yale University Press, 1992), p. 20.

before the economy of God's love. We are not brought to know without also being brought to understand that we are known. We do not grasp the truth without being grasped by what is true. Our knowledge of God is, then, both active and passive, a knowing as a being known; a form of incorporation coupled with the realization that we are incorporated. The kenotic economy is the narrative of transcorporality. It narrates a story of coming to know through coming to love – love given, love endured.

The age of angels

Balthasar is a maker of myths. He is a Dante composing a *divina commedia* for the late twentieth century. At the end of modernity he has recreated the kenotic myth as an allegorical reading of the world. Through this myth the world and our place in it are rewritten. He leads us out of the arid deserts and catacombs of modernity and into a new theological vision, pertinent because in a certain resonance with another culture. For post-structural textuality also, bodies and matter have changed. No longer are bodies discrete entities, limited by their own attributes. No longer is matter simply positivist data. Bodies are always multiple, never the same in any moment, always mapped on to other bodies, participating in other bodies, part of a continuing ex- and inter-change. For Balthasar, all things exist within the floating margins of a divine allegory.

At the end of modernity, taxidermy has become unfashionable. As an art, it is passing away. There are other more prominent cultural metaphors, symbolic expressions of contemporary cultural values – like the return of angels. Angels turn up everywhere; they are paradigmatically transcorporal according to Aquinas.[143] The British Library records 436 recent title entries for 'angel' and 321 recent title entries for 'angels/angel's/angels'. Angels appear in fiction (recently, in Britain, in A. S. Byatt's *Angels and Insects*, Jill Paton Walsh's *Knowledge of Angels*, Sara Maitland's *Angel and Me*), in film (Wim Wender's 1994 *In weiter Ferne, so nah!*), in philosophy (Michel Serre's 1995 book *Angels*), as gilded *putti* suspended by wires from the ceilings of religious bookshops and as tropes in popular songs by Robbie Williams and Céline Dion. For Irigaray, they

> open up the closed nature of the world, identity, action and history ... They destroy the monstrous elements that might prohibit the possibility of a new age, and herald a new birth, a new dawn ... They represent another incarnation, another *parousia* of the body.[144]

Angels stand on the near edge of her Utopia (a new way of being embodied, of being divine through being sexuate). For Balthasar also, angels 'make visible the social character of the Kingdom of Heaven, into which the cosmos is to be transformed' (H I, 649; GL 1, 675). They teach us how to bear witness to what is other and glorious, how to worship, how to live ecstatically. Is all this contemporary promotion of angels gnostic

---

143 *Summa Theologia*, Part 1, Q.51, Art. 1–3.
144 *An Ethics of Sexual Difference*, tr. Carolyn Burke and Gillian C. Gill (London: Athlone Press, 1993), pp. 15–16.

fantasy, or mystical yearning, or the gathering of an eschatological host as time bends towards another millennium? Who can say? Upon whose authority? Ours is simply the shepherd's lot: gathered in the darkness and guarding those we have been given to guard (while they guard us), we wait with expectation for the sky to burst into flame and song.

3

Something like Time;
Something like the Sexes
– an essay in reception

LUCY GARDNER   DAVID MOSS

Introduction

An ever deeper experience of [the] fundamental structure of analogy, and reflection upon it, may be regarded as the secret law and hidden stimulus of the development of Christian thought.

J. Splett and L. B. Puntel

The reception *of* Balthasar's theology provokes an invitation to which this essay is but one response; and this in the double sense of the genitive. For to remark upon the reception of Balthasar's theology involves marking both the complex reception of his work by ecclesial and academic publics;[1] and also, critically, the nature of Balthasar's theology as precisely a logic and performance of reception. No doubt this latter consideration should provoke a scholarly investigation into the 'tributaries of influence'[2] on Balthasar's thought; but more fundamentally, it should direct our attention to the very configuration of the *theme of reception* at the heart of Balthasar's theology. A figuration imitative of creaturely existence itself, which is to say the *receptivity* and *ek-stasis* of the creature in its distance (*diastasis*) from God.[3]

---

1 Something of the ambiguity of the ecclesial reception of Balthasar's work can be discerned in Joseph Cardinal Ratzinger's 'Homily at the Funeral Liturgy of Hans Urs von Balthasar' in *Hans Urs von Balthasar: His Life and Work*, ed. D. L. Schindler (San Francisco: Communio Books, 1991). See also M. Kehl and W. Löser's comments in *The Von Balthasar Reader* (Edinburgh: T. & T. Clark, 1982), pp. 4–6.

2 The phrase is that of Edward Oakes SJ in a chapter title to his introduction to Balthasar's theology, *Pattern of Redemption* (New York: Continuum Publishing, 1994).

3 Raymond Gawronski SJ comments in his *Word and Silence – Hans Urs von Balthasar and the Spiritual Encounter between East and West* (Edinburgh: T. & T. Clark, 1995): 'If for Balthasar there were one word to characterise the correct stance of the creature to the Creator, it might well be *Empfänglichkeit*' (p. 14).

To pursue this question here is neither accidental nor without political implication, for the mystery to which Balthasar never ceased to draw attention was the handing over of the Son to the world. A handing over which demands from the creature an *imitatio* of the Son's perfect 'receptivity' (*Empfänglichkeit*) in which his very being consists. A costly receptivity leading from and to *kenosis*, and yet a receptivity which can, in turn, only be received; a receptivity which occurs not only as the handing over of the Son to the world, but also in the Father's handing over of all to the Son.

We glimpse here already the knotting of several themes at the centre of Balthasar's thought: (i) in the notion of *empfangen*, and the repeated doubling turns taken through its three main meanings – to receive; to conceive (a child); and to give a welcome – we discover a continual movement and undecidability which present receptivity as requiring an 'always already' having been received. And what this 'always already' amounts to, as we shall discover, is a questioning of our ability to tell time in any serial or chronological sense. And (ii), in that this handing over always involves 'a profanation in its innermost essence'[4] – for the mystery *appears* before the temple and so in the courts and under the law of the *polis* – it invokes the trauma of a politics, of a gathering. For the *polis* is fundamentally the place of gathering, the place for the ordering of relations between a subject and its others.[5]

Thus, in these two brief strokes, we are brought to recognize that not only does receptivity receive a thoroughly theological grounding in Balthasar's work, but also, and unavoidably, it provokes – indeed prepares – the question of a *sexual politics* in this 'our time': perhaps the time of the 'End of Modernity'?

Hasty reactions to this proposition should be avoided, though, for the question here concerns not a particular politics – a series of decisions, actions or ends (although this can never be entirely suspended) – but, in Balthasar's theology, the representation of the *gathering* of *Mensch*[6] in creation.

In a determinative observation for this essay, Balthasar writes:

> The basis of the biblical religion is the *diastasis*, the distance, between God and the creature that is the elementary presupposition that makes it possible for man to understand and appreciate the unity that grace brings about.[7]

---

4 ExT 3, 462.
5 Conflated in this suggestion is the twofold idea of (i) politics as 'designating the domain or practice of human behaviour which normativizes the relations between a subject and its others' and (ii) the political 'as the instance that gathers or founds such a practice as a practice' (see Richard Beardsworth, *Derrida and the Political* (London: Routledge, 1996), p. 158). We shall have cause to reflect upon both aspects of this account in our argument.
6 *Der Mensch*, that is, the human being. The translation of this key term into English (human being/man) serves only to add to the confusions of Balthasar's text. We have elected simply to transfer the word into English in the attempt to represent the manner in which the human being can both attract a masculine identity and yet remain ostensibly 'unsexed' and generic.
7 ExT 3, 173.

To speak of this representation, this understanding, then, is to attempt to articulate the differencing of creation (or better, creation as a differencing, a *diastasis*) in relation to the drama of redemption. It involves representing or laying out the theological difficulty that arises from the interleaving of the 'orders' of creation and redemption.[8] Thus the question: in the difference of the world from God, which is constitutive of world itself, how can this 'achieved' gathering of the *Mensch* in the *logos* of God be represented in a non-effacement of this 'original' difference – of world from God? Balthasar asks how God can

> gather back into himself the whole freedom of his creatures including all the consequences of such freedom, including, that is rebellion and self damnation, can gather it up and bear it up. And still remain God?[9]

In formulaic terms, the answer to which this essay attends, in its circling enquiry, can be expressed thus: grace prepares nature to receive grace. And this, of course, invokes the analogical nature of thought of the God–world relationship. Which is to say, thought directed towards a conjecture on and participation in the *identity-in-difference* of world with God. A thinking that would seek to link up (gather and represent) the whole order of the divine *logos* in a way which neither transposes our *logos* into heaven nor substitutes for this an alogic or illogic of pure and simple erasure.

Thus, and to complete this brief résumé of the various themes of this essay, the labour of analogy is an endeavour, a mode of thought, patient of reception. It involves the seeking of some sort of convergence, some 'similarity within a greater dissimilarity', within the experience of recognition and discernment which are irrevocably temporal. Analogy provides us with no eternal measure of the divine; rather, in the words of Ghislain Lafont, the labour of analogy

> very strongly challenges human autonomy and implies at the level of the word as well as at that of liberty, a renouncing of self-sufficiency and an openness to that which does not come from the self.[10]

In this compressed introduction, then, the strands of *this* reception of Balthasar's work have been set out and drawn together in an initial bonding. Reception, *diastasis*, sexual difference, time and analogy: all these themes continually play in Balthasar's texts. But how?

The secret law of analogy

There can be little doubt that reading Balthasar's work is to read an intensely 'compacted thinking', which is to say that part of the remarkable

8 This issue is helpfully set out in Fr David Burrell's article 'Incarnation and Creation: the Hidden Dimension' in *Modern Theology* 12:2 (1996), pp. 211–20.
9 *Elucidations*, tr. John Riches (London: SPCK, 1975), pp. 50–1.
10 Ghislain Lafont, *God, Time, and Being* (Massachusetts: St Bede's Publications, 1992), p. 107.

achievement of his great theological *œuvre* is precisely the repeated rehearsal of fundamental theological (and metaphysical) commitments in ever new configurations which seek to illuminate the same mystery. Thus, if one were to speak of the 'systematic impulse' in Balthasar's work, we should recognize that this does not reside in any riveting of 'parts' on to an empty frame, nor in any correlation of God to his creature, but rather in the 'ever more deeply plumbed repetition' yielding a formidable density of the same mystery: the *kenosis* of the Son prefigured in the *Urkenosis* of the Father.

Down the many paths of thought that Balthasar opens (and at times closes) we are invited to discern (to receive) *Das Ganze im Fragment*[11] – a locution which constrains us to acknowledge not only the arrival of fullness and plenitude in the fragment, but also the presence of the whole in pieces. In this undecidability, intimating the trembling of loss and retrieval, of a dispersion and gathering which always belong together, we touch what is always at stake in Balthasar's theology: the dramatic encounter between God and the creature in the excessive, wanton love of the former.

However, if this encounter provokes a crisis of unheard-of dimensions, and for Balthasar it most certainly does, it is nevertheless a crisis that is to be negotiated by participation in its own secret law. For thought, this is the law of analogy: the trembling receptivity of the creature guaranteed a similarity to its ever more dissimilar Creator. Thus, in the luminous observation with which we have headed this chapter, J. Splett and L. B. Puntel have observed that

> An ever deeper experience of [the] fundamental structure of analogy, and reflection on it, may be regarded as the secret law and hidden stimulus of the development of Christian thought.[12]

And this is no more true than in the case of Balthasar, for whom the abidingly valuable aspect of the notion of analogy remains the magnetizing of thought to the staging of *kenosis*. A greater receiving in response to a still greater dispossession, as discovered in 'the New Rhythm' of the Word made flesh (TD II.1, 376; ThD 2, 411). For this teaches that God is not only the Other – an other who would remain endlessly encodable in the dialectics of identity – but also, and more so, the 'non-Other' (the *non-aliud* of Nicholas of Cusa). The God whose *esse* can only be said at the crossing place of identity and difference which is itself exchanged in and for another differencing – a second differencing.[13]

How, though, in the 'concrete mediation' of the Word become flesh – the event that provokes this impossible thought – are we to speak of this

11 *Das Ganze im Fragment* – 'the whole in the fragment' or even 'the whole in pieces' – was the title of a book published by Balthasar in 1963, translated as *Man in History: A Theological Study* (London: Sheed & Ward, 1968).
12 *Sacramentum Mundi* vol. 1. ed. Karl Rahner *et al.* (London: Burns & Oates, 1968), 'Analogy of Being', p. 24.
13 For a brilliant rehearsal of what this logic may entail see John Milbank's essay 'The Second Difference' in *The Word Made Strange* (Oxford: Blackwell, 1997), pp. 171–93.

reality, the question we raised earlier in terms of the interleaving of the orders of creation and redemption? Balthasar's answer is determinative for the entirety of his thought:

> The Word of God in Jesus Christ becomes (a) bodily *Mensch* in Jesus Christ, and because *Mensch* exists in the three-fold rhythm that has been described, where *Menschsein* [that is: human being, human existence] includes an either-or, Jesus Christ can only step in at one pole, in order from there to fulfil the other. This becomes particularly acute in the man–woman tension: on the basis of the natural, relative 'superordination' of the man (alongside the equal value of both persons), the Word of God with his absolute 'superordination' can only step into the human in the form of the man and so form the woman to himself (Eph. 5:27).... From this a new rhythm already allows itself to open onto the first tension, that between spirit and body. (TD II.1, 376–7; ThD 2, 409)

Here and everywhere in Balthasar's theology it is sexual difference – the difference between the sexes and the differencing of sexes – that brings into view (engenders) the encounter between God and creature. Thus, for Balthasar, the thought of analogy (of the possibility for telling the linkages between God and world according to Being as gift) will never slip free from the corporality of gendered and engendered life. Moreover, if the thought of revelation – of a revealing in a concealing – has repeatedly remained shackled to a specular economy of the gaze and auditory economy of the ear – to 'see' and 'hear' the Word – then in Balthasar's colossal deployment of sexual difference the linkages that analogy would tell intimates the flesh become thoughtful.

To follow Balthasar here is to reckon with no mere parallel or similitude between ontological and sexual difference, but the cleaving of Being to birth, to life, in all our attempts to tell of the Word made flesh. For Balthasar, we shall claim, sexual difference is the *chiasm* of creation. Which is to say the crossing place, the threshold, which indicates no horizon or limit of the world to God (in which the world can settle into a relation with its Other, God), but rather is the world *as threshold*. Creation is the site for the gift of life which knows itself only in its differencing to and from God. For it is only ever the *sexed body* that stirs into a life that is gifted. It is this recognition that brings Balthasar's thought into a proximity not so much with the inheritance of *Lebensphilosophie* as with the thought of sexual difference and, by this token, we suggest, with the thought of Luce Irigaray.[14]

---

14 Can a genealogy be drawn here to justify this juxtaposition: the Belgian 'feminist' theorist Luce Irigaray and the 'conservative' theologian Hans Urs von Balthasar? For sure, there are themes common to both, and Irigaray's explicit and controversial meditations on the Christian tradition (which we shall have cause to consider especially with regard to her work *Marine Lover*) encourage a reading-in-relation which few theologians have been prepared to consider. However, in our assessment it is perhaps in the proximity that both bear to the thought of Martin Heidegger that their deepest affinity is to be found. That is to say, we would hazard an 'elective affinity' to the question of and decision upon sexual difference in this

It is, then, the cleaving of Being to birth – of differences ontological to sexual – that magnetizes the thought of Balthasar to that of Irigaray, and both (though in no simple way or correlation) to the thought of transcendence and the divine. It is for this reason that a remark by Irigaray in her essay 'Sexual Difference' will initiate in this essay a more deconstructive reading of Balthasar's texts than commentators have thus far been minded to develop.

Irigaray remarks (with unmistakable Heideggerian resonance):

Sexual difference is probably the issue in our time which could be 'our' salvation if we thought it through.[15]

and (which will be determinative for our argument):

In order to make it possible to think through, and live, this difference, we must reconsider the whole problematic of *space* and *time*.[16]

The argument
These remarks set the scene for the argument of this essay, an argument that will be developed across four volumes of Balthasar's *Theo-Drama* (TD II.1 to IV; ThD 2–5).[17]

In the first section ('Sexual difference as *diastasis*'), Balthasar's two accounts of the fundamental *Grundbestimmung* (ground determination or transcendental) of human existence, the 'polarity' between man and woman, will be rigorously analysed in order to reveal how the undecidability of sexual difference in TD II.1 (ThD 2) becomes in TD II.2

---

age. In Balthasar's brilliant portrait of Heidegger's work in the fifth volume of *The Glory of the Lord*, it is Heidegger's inheritance that Christianity is called upon to make 'its own' if it is to understand and complete 'the philosophical task of modernity'; while in her homage, her mourning work (*Trauerspiel*) to Heidegger, begun on the day she learned of his death in 1976, the radicality of Irigaray's commitment to think the oblivion of Being (Heidegger's *Seinsvergessenheit*) is manifestly evident. Both Balthasar's and Irigaray's thought inclines towards that ecstasy that Heidegger seeks to reawaken as *reception* – the *Es gibt*, 'There is/It gives'. This inclination, though, is troubled in both Irigaray and Balthasar by their suspicion of a still deeper forgetting in Heidegger. For Irigaray, even if the Heideggerian site of reception moves from sexless *Dasein* to the event of language, she is still left wondering if this home built by man is built in oblivion of that upon which words hang, ring, and are borne – the air. What she calls, in short, the 'material–matricial support'. While for Balthasar, a delight in Heidegger's renewal of the theme of glory, that is of our wonder at Being, becomes a lament at his failure to see that precisely because Being gives and so is giving (and gift), it is Being that is given, given first by God. And this lesson, this rapture, arrives not in anxiety and displacement but in the mother's smile that awakens the child upon its entrance into the world. Again, the child rests, is cushioned and borne upon a 'material–matricial support'. For both Irigaray and Balthasar it is the bearing (perhaps the carrying to term) of Being that has been forgotten in Heidegger's thought.

15 *An Ethics of Sexual Difference*, tr. Carolyn Burke and Gillian C. Gill (London: Athlone Press, 1993), p. 5.
16 Ibid., p. 7.
17 At the time of writing, ThD 5 – the translation of TD IV – has not yet appeared in English.

(ThD 3) the securing of sexual difference in woman and as woman. In Balthasar's second account, woman is doubled, duplicated, in order to become the place or space in which man can stand in creation and grasp himself as standing in relation to God.

The consequences of this logic (the violence of a pre-decision 'imposed' upon the fluidity of creation) yield the demand for another account which refuses this valorization of a creaturely difference. It is this other account that traverses Balthasar's argument and finds focus in the 'temporal clue' given in the encounter between Mary and Christ, which we explore in our second section ('The ecstasies of time').

Our case is neither that Balthasar's gestures towards the 'equality' of the sexes hide a more sinister intent, nor that at the last gasp an ineluctably patriarchal logic is in fact redeemed. The issue is altogether more complex and has to do with the fact that what Balthasar looks to secure in creation as a preparation for redemption is precisely that which unravels in the light of his intuition concerning Mary's *fiat*, her 'Yes' to the offer of salvation.

Balthasar's intuition here invokes a *deconstruction* of a particular en-coding of time and space in which sexual difference is fixed.[18] It is this that opens on to the thought of the differencing of difference as the measure or configuration of creation with redemption, and indeed sanctification. This, we suggest, constitutes the 'reflective substance', the thought, of analogy – of the abiding demand to think in and from *within* our reception of God's gift of salvation within creation, and not from without it.

Thus, the third section of our argument ('The order of thought') presents a reconstructive outline of Balthasar's figuration of analogy which resides nowhere and everywhere in his texts and which we pick up in TD III (ThD 4) and in particular with reference to accounts of trinitarian

18 Our reference to *deconstruction* suggests a brief mention of the thought of Jacques Derrida here. To be sure, Derrida's work offers no earthly consolation to Christian theology, even at the end of modernity (a point trenchantly, if a little excessively, made by Vassilis Lambropoulos in his *The Rise of Eurocentrism: Anatomy of Interpretation* (Princeton University Press, 1993); see pp. 234f.). However, Derrida's diagnosis of its structural diseases is another matter. In this essay we deploy a series of *motifs* – notably undecidability, *aporia*, representation, doubling, differencing and withdrawal – which are central to Derrida's work, as well as engaging with the issues of temporality and sexual difference to which Derrida's thought repeatedly returns. To our minds, rigorous treatment of the genealogical significance of his work for or towards Christian theology is a labour which still remains for the future. John D. Caputo has done valuable service in his recent book *The Prayers and Tears of Jacques Derrida – Religion without Religion* (Bloomington/Indianapolis: Indiana University Press, 1997), but in this, as in so much theological appropriation of Derrida's work, a familiarity with the theological grammar of the Great Tradition is lacking. As a result, his re-visioning of traditional Christianity amounts to an account shorn of its proper christological offence in something not far short of neo-liberalism. Derrida's work has attracted our attention by virtue of what we would call his *patience*, his preparedness to dwell with difficulty. It would, no doubt, be too easy to suggest that it is the same patience that touches everywhere in Balthasar's work. Needless to say, this entire problematic – the very significance of *problematics* (and never only a general problematic) at the end of modernity – continues to demand attention in the theological reception of the thought of both these thinkers.

differencing. What this amounts to – and herein, we would want to claim, lies Balthasar's most central and startling insight – is an account of the *analogia entis* from which the experience of creaturely becoming and generation are no longer systematically excluded in an atemporal order of reflection. We can speak, analogically of course, of something like time and of something like the sexes in God.

And so, following on from Graham Ward's consideration of Balthasar's account of the event of *meaning* as figured in the Christian *motifs* of kenosis and resurrection, this essay proceeds to Balthasar's unfolding of the significance of *time* and the manner of its signing in thought 'after Christ'. Ben Quash, in his turn (Chapter 4), will take up this theme of the sign of temporality in an exploration of Balthasar's attempts to represent time and the Christian story in the guise of a *Theodramatik*.

Balthasar has been accused of offering metaphor in place of metaphysics, picture in the place of argument. Philosophically the charge is naïve in itself, but more substantially it fails to broach with any rigour the fundamental grammar of Balthasar's theology. This grammar, as many commentators have been quick to point out, is determined by a fundamental commitment to the analogical knowledge of being as precisely reflection upon the event of the absolute *identity-in-difference* of world and God. To interpret this event has, in the tradition from Plato to Aquinas, led to the idea of the communication of being or participation, where the language or utterance of this event is analogy. It is our contention that Balthasar, in a remarkable binding together of 'something like time' with 'something like the sexes' in God, offers not a God beyond metaphysics[19] but rather a God freed from any ancient binary creaturely marking which would seek to marshal the multiple differences of creation against an absolute oppositional limit. Balthasar does not offer metaphor in place of metaphysics; but rather, beyond modernity's 'philosophy of subjectivity', and so as no antique retrieval, he offers theology 'a retraining into the lost primordial articulations[20] of human thought'. (H III.1/2, 568; GL 5, 222)

Sexual Difference as *Diastasis*

Woman is still the place, the whole of the place in which she cannot take possession of herself as such.

Luce Irigaray

The couplings of sexual difference – an initial indication
In a preliminary anthropology, entitled '*Mensch* and nature' and formulated as it were[21] 'before Christ', Balthasar identifies three inseparable

---

19 See J. L. Marion's important work *God Beyond Being*, tr. T. A. Carlson (University of Chicago Press, 1991).

20 *Urartikulationen* – a typical neologism making use of the prefix *Ur* which will become the focus of particular attention in the attempt to think the nature of God's 'anteriority' and the senses in which an *Urkenosis* can be attributed to the Father.

21 This 'as it were' is no idle qualification, but serves already to mark the difficulty of the telling of time, both in the telling of creation (and particularly here the sexual differentiation of the *Mensch*) and also in the telling of Christ and the events of salvation. This 'difficulty' will be the main focus of the next two sections.

'polarities' of human existence: (i) between body and soul, (ii) between man and woman, and (iii) individual and community (TD II.1, 325; ThD 2, 355). These he also describes as *Grundbestimmungen* – 'Ground-determinations' or, importantly, 'transcendentals' (TD II.2, 260; ThD 3, 283). Together they form a 'threefold transcendence'.

It is in the suspension of these 'polarities' that the *Mensch* is suspended between heaven and earth as an enigma or riddle to itself. It is against these 'transcendentals' (but also always with and in them) that the *Mensch* steps out and stands out. They are the 'constants' of human identity, the 'borders' which the *Mensch* is always overstepping, the condition or state of his *ek-stasis*:

> But if the *Mensch* finally becomes a question to himself in this stepping out, then he nevertheless always takes his constants with him: he is spirit and body, he is man and woman, he is individual and community. These constants belong to his nature, his being,[22] which precisely does not mean that they solve his riddle for him: rather, they deepen it and render it more urgent. In all three dimensions he appears to be built polarly, constrained to a perpetual transition, in order always to seek his completion and rest in the other pole; and he is precisely thus directed beyond his whole polar structure. He is incessantly crossing the border, but is thus precisely defined most exactly through the border which is brutally held before him by death without any respect for his threefold transcendence. (TD II.1, 325; ThD 2, 355)

The second of these transcendentals or polarities – that of man and woman – has a critical part to play in this threefold transcendence, for it is in some sense the centre of the three. As well as being one of the three, it is that within which all three are gathered, such that body–soul and individual–community can meet:

> The tensions [body–soul] which have just been displayed repeat and deepen themselves when one crosses over to the genderly [*geschlechtlichen*] differentiation of human-nature in [*or* into] man and woman; moreover, this also draws with itself the third tension, that between individual and community, into play in advance …

22 Here, *Wesen* – being, essence, existence, nature – in contrast to and as complement of *Natur* – nature. The distinctions between *Seiende* (being – almost always in relation to *Sein*), *Dasein* and *Wesen* are difficult to draw and maintain in English; this difficulty is compounded by Balthasar's apparently inconsistent (and therefore not always 'technical') use, which can render it hard to identify whether (and if so when) *Wesen* might be used in an explicitly existential key. That Balthasar's thought occurs in proximity to Heidegger's – and in particular his thinking of the relationship of *Dasein* to the difference between *Sein* and *das Seiende* (Being and being) – is a persistent theme of our argument, but it is not one which we can trace in all its similarities and differences of vocabulary, provoked in part by Balthasar's wide range of reference. In all that follows, we have tried to convey the sense of individual quotations, rather than preserve any consistency of English vocabulary for the word *Wesen*, but note its presence in the original text. Similarly, we take care to draw attention to the use of the terms *Sein*, *das Seiende*, *Dasein* and their cognates.

[for] the relationship between man and woman represents the 'paradigmatic case' of the thorough-going communal character of human being. (TD II.1, 334; ThD 2, 365)

The centrality of this second polarity of human being is also signified in the potentially double reference of the term *geschlechtlich*. This is derived immediately from *Geschlecht*, which can be translated equally as 'gender' and 'species'. Thus, the differentiation of human nature *into* man and woman is the differentiation of *gender*, 'sexual difference'; but the differentiation of human nature *in* (that is, *as*) man and woman is also the differentiation of this *species* from all others. The *Mensch*, as *Mensch*, 'is' these two: 'he' is man and woman. This is not to suggest that human being is the only one of God's creatures to be sexually differentiated, but rather to point towards the *Mensch*'s recognition of itself as sexually differentiated (in its sexual differentiation) as of primary significance.

But there is another critical role which sexual difference is asked to perform in Balthasar's theology. It is also presented as *analogical* to the difference between the world and God – a difference we shall name *theological difference*. Properly speaking, this role only first comes into view with the exposition of sexual difference 'after' Christ in TD II.2 (ThD 3). Nevertheless, foundations are laid for its introduction in the claim made upon a 'meta-cosmic dimension' of this polarity in the preliminary anthropological sketch of TD II.1 (ThD 2).

Balthasar claims that 'no metaphysical polarity can enter to explain human sexual difference' (TD II.1, 337; ThD 2, 368). And yet, he also suggests that the unavoidable suspension or hovering of this difference is directly dependent upon the hovering, undecidable character of the relationship between the cosmos and the *theion*. Balthasar thus draws a link between sexual difference and at least the ontological difference (Being–being) and hints towards a link between sexual difference and theological difference (God–world). That theological difference is to be granted its measure in sexual difference is also suggested in a remarkable image quoted from Hamann:

in order to measure the scope [of the self], we must press into the lap [*or* womb] of the godhead, which [that is, the lap or womb] alone can define and solve the whole mystery of our existence [*Wesen*]. (TD II.1, 341; ThD 2, 372)

This section, therefore, concentrates on Balthasar's two accounts of sexual difference – that 'before' Christ (in a preliminary anthropological sketch, TD II.1, ThD 2) and that 'after' Christ (in a phenomenological introduction to Balthasar's mariology and his account of life in Christ, TD II.2, ThD 3). In attention to the development of the second account from the first, we trace the fixing of sexual difference – in the over-determination of woman as essentially second and dual, and ultimately as body – as a difference in which the God–creature differential is to be secured. This fixing of sexual difference, however, appears set likewise to over-determine theological difference itself, and so render impossible the reception of God's gift of salvation (for which it appears intended to prepare) before ever that gift can appear on the world's stage. *At the same time*, of course, it is precisely that (impossible) arrival of God's gift in the God–*Mensch* (Christ) which forces the original over-determination of woman. In this we uncover a relentless, elisory logic which at every intensifying turn threatens to undo all and everything it would secure – including itself. In his essay (Chapter 4), Quash traces the effects of this elisory logic in Balthasar's account of the Church and the human relation to God as life lived in Christ.

The undecidability of sexual difference in outline

The title to the outline of sexual difference provided in the preliminary anthropological sketch of TD I.1 (ThD 2) – *Mann und Frau* – turns from talk of the *Mensch* to introduce man and woman together. Balthasar returns almost immediately, however, to a time when the first *Mensch* is alone.

In the beginning, before the creation of woman, the first *Mensch*, Adam, is with God, but he is *lonely* in this priority. This loneliness is not good (TD II.1, 334; ThD 2, 365). Woman is therefore introduced as his companion and helpmate. Thus, in Balthasar's retrospection, man mourns woman before her arrival. The implied, greater tragedy, then, is that before Eve's creation, the first *Mensch* cannot even know his own loneliness or recognize his 'loss'.

But as this attempt at description reveals, the identification of the first *Mensch* before woman's arrival remains problematic. Sexual difference runs so deep in human being that Balthasar will not countenance any neutral, universal *Mensch* beyond, before or apart from sexual difference. The original Adam is not an original bisexual or androgynous being, awaiting its devolvement into two. Adam is not a 'universal' *Mensch* (TD II.2, 334–5; ThD 3, 365–6).

Nevertheless Balthasar is also careful not to describe Adam-before-woman as *Mann*. He remarks upon the confusion of *Mensch* and *Mann* in Origen's *homo* (TD II.1, 339; ThD 2, 370) and, following the biblical texts, names Adam as 'man' only with the arrival of 'woman'. It is as if Balthasar would present gender as arriving with woman. At the same time, there is an identity between Adam-before-Eve and Adam-with-Eve which appears to permit the identification of Adam-before-Eve as 'man', even if only retrospectively. This in turn repeatedly permits and reflects an almost unnoticed elision between *Mann* and *Mensch* – an elision veiled by the grammatical gender of *Mensch*.[23]

Moreover, this observation of man's chronological – that is, temporal and in a sense temporary – natural, relative priority tends towards an assertion of his persistent logical primacy.[24] But here we encounter another structural difficulty in the attempt to locate and define sexual difference. For the man's 'first' would appear to be dependent upon the

23 We have already noted this above: 'He' is both man and woman!
24 This logic is reflected in Balthasar's translation of *isha* by the neologism *Männin*, literally 'man-ess'; but at the same point in his text, woman's (apparently paradoxical) tendency to assume the whole of humanity, to swallow man, is also reflected in the second interpretation of *isha* as *Mensch* and man's diminution in the translation of *ish* as *Männischen* – literally 'little man' (*almost* a homophone for *Mensch*).

woman's 'second'. Before and without woman as second, man cannot be first. And yet this seems to be precisely what this sketch seeks to secure – before the arrival of woman.[25]

Despite, and probably partly because of, this difficulty, a certain fluidity and undecidability pervade Balthasar's first characterization of sexual difference. He firmly resists the temptation to locate sexuality solely in the body as opposed to the spirit. Adam without Eve is not a sexless, spiritual *Mensch*, nor can any *Mensch* escape sexuality by flight into a sexless 'reason' or 'spirit':

> The Adam of Genesis misses his companion amongst the animals, not because of the exchange of spirit to spirit, but rather as his 'opposite' [*Gegenüber*] in whom the bodily could encounter him in a spiritual manner and the spiritual in a bodily. (TD II.1, 335; ThD 2, 366)

For all that he is blessed with the communication of spirit to spirit (in his relation to God) and of body to body (in his relation to the animals), without his companion Adam (the first, incomplete *Mensch*) misses the communication between body and spirit so characteristic of his being. He is without bodily–spiritual encounter and exchange. Before and apart from woman, Adam, the *Mensch*, can only long for this exchange and with it his proper transcendence and ecstasy. He is suspended alone between heaven and earth, with no one to interpret or embody to or for him his embrace of these two. Awaiting woman, this 'man' awaits a certain *chiasmus*, in awaiting the one who can interpret and embody, and indeed first allow, the meeting and exchange of body and spirit which occurs in the *Mensch*.

But there is another cause for the indeterminacy of sexual difference. For Balthasar, any account of the essence of human nature, whether by way of phenomenology or otherwise, is hampered by the fact that it must be constructed from a standpoint which is not only after the beginning, but also after the fall:

> Given that the supralapsarian state of human nature cannot be reconstructed from its present situation: to what image[26] of the *Mensch* are we to hold ourselves, in order to define his being [*Wesen*]? (TD II.1, 343; ThD 2, 374)

This difficulty is particularly problematic in the attempt to discern the significance of sexual difference and human sexuality. For sin and the fall have changed the *Mensch*'s finitude into mortality by introducing death to the world, (Rom. 5.12; Wis. 2.24). This in turn affects the other pole of the *Mensch*'s finitude, his birth or origin – human procreation, generation and begetting. Death and begetting, as the limits of postlapsarian human

---

25 The temporality of this aporetic structure will receive further analysis in our next section, 'The ecstasies of time'.
26 The German word here is *Bild* – picture, image; this is the term which Balthasar repeatedly uses in his various inflections of the image doctrine. Of particular interest here is his persistent return to the thought of Christ as the image.

existence, and so also its heart, are in some sense 'reciprocal'.[27] Sexuality – human differentiation into two sexes – is especially implicated in this intimate coupling of begetting and death. This means that the question as to the nature of human sexuality and generation in the supralapsarian state remains an insoluble *aporia* from a postlapsarian viewpoint.

Nevertheless, Balthasar attempts a sketch of this *aporia*. Tracing various responses to this difficulty, he pursues most closely the line of 'Greek doctrine', expressed quintessentially in Gregory of Nyssa's suggestion that human sexuality was created with a view to the fall. The 'solution' lies in conjecturing an unidentifiable 'middle' between 'lower' and 'higher' understandings of human sexuality. This involves a separation between 'the fruitful encounter[28] of man and woman in personal giving over' (which remains and always already was 'erotic') 'and their sexual[29] union' (TD II.1, 349; ThD 2, 381). At the same time, it forbids a denouncing of the sexual union as only happening in the postlapsarian state and so in and of itself sinful. It likewise forbids – and this in apparent contradiction to Balthasar's treatment of sexual difference as a transcendental – a reification of the sexual union as a moment of transcendence *par excellence*.

Balthasar similarly refuses any identification of either the sexual or the feminine with the bodily. Although woman introduces gender to the *Mensch*, she is not herself to be equated with gender.[30] The polarities of sexual difference and spirit–body do not coincide (fall together) in marking the same difference twice. They are two different differences, running through each other, not so much in any sense of quartering something (human-being) or of creating four different sites, but rather as differences within difference; as, that is, the differencing of difference.

Sexual difference 'before Christ', like human being itself, is characterized as an undecidable oscillation or suspension, a 'gaping wound', 'an insoluble between', an enigma awaiting its fulfilment in Christ. That which is so central to human nature

> cannot be constructed out of itself. It plays its play between earth and heaven, where there is no marrying (Matt. 22:30) but the marriage of the lamb is celebrated. (TD II.1, 350; ThD 2, 382)

As we have shown, this indeterminacy does not prevent Balthasar from taking the decision to refuse certain decisions. Sexuality is not to be located only in the body; nor is the feminine to be identified as either

---

27 See TD II.1, 342–4; ThD 2, 374–6 for Balthasar's tracing of this theme through (amongst others) Augustine, Fichte, Hegel and Schopenhauer.
28 *Begegnung* – coming up against, encounter. The place of encounter in Balthasar's construction of sexual difference will receive particular attention below.
29 Here, again, *geschlechtlichen* – sexual *or* of the species.
30 It is important to note that here the consideration is of the explicit statements and logic of the text. These concerns, of course, reveal that there is a danger of making such identifications – and this not only in the thought and texts of those with whom Balthasar would converse. Moreover, as we shall see, this double ban also introduces the possibility of the identification of sexuality with the feminine. It will form a critical part of our argument that contrary to such explicit statements of intent, woman and the feminine do become inextricably associated with the sexual and most particularly the bodily in the logic of Balthasar's text.

bodily or especially sexual. He is also adamant that the feminine is not to be devalued: before ever man is first, or woman is second, man and woman are *equal*. At the close of Balthasar's first account of sexual difference, these firm denials provoke two questions: (i) can this thought, in its assertion of and dependence upon man's primacy, fulfil its own demands for equality between the sexes? and (ii) can woman and the feminine escape identification with sexuality and the body if, as we shall suggest, Balthasar locates sexual difference in woman?

Sexual difference and the architecture of the **Theo-Drama** – the christological timing and placing of sexual difference

The second section of the Christology of Balthasar's *Theo-Drama* – 'Christ's person and mission' – addresses and is addressed by two of the determinative, transcendental polarities of human existence: the relationship between body and soul is reflected upon in the treatment of Christ's *Person*, and that between individual and community in consideration of his *following*. The central transcendental polarity – *Geschlechterdifferenz*, that which, following the English translators, we have named 'sexual difference' – is, however, in Balthasar's own words, 'left out of view' (see TD II.2, 260; ThD 3, 283). This is reserved for the Mariology which ensues, in a treatment which, we suggest, amounts to a second outlining of sexual difference, constructed this time as it were 'after' and therefore also 'in' Christ. This repetition has an important párt to play in the structure of Balthasar's *Theo-Drama* and therefore in his theological triptych as a whole.

Having introduced Christ and described his task of opening up the acting area, *der Spielraum* – the playing room or space – in which all other characters of the *Theo-Drama* are to receive their role,[31] Balthasar turns to consider the place which other characters can (and must) assume in the drama. His consideration begins with a correction of the omission of sexual difference from his Christology as he turns to view this third transcendental ground-determination as it is to be found in Mary, the first 'theological person in Christ'.

At least, this is what Balthasar appears to prepare. However, in a move which repeats the previous attempt to secure man's first before woman's second, this second attempt to locate and describe sexual difference is apparently made before and apart from Mary. Here sexual difference is fixed as a distance between the sexes which can become the measure of each. In this, sexual difference becomes structurally ambiguous: it occurs 'after' and yet also ostensibly 'within' Balthasar's Christology; it is supposed also to be viewed 'in' his mariology; and yet it would appear to be established 'before' that mariology. Now this might indicate another sense in which all crosses in sexual difference – sexual difference would here be seen as the *chiasmus*, the exchange between Christology and Mariology, such that the latter can only ever come to be from within the former. But at the same time, this might also be to present the distance of sexual difference as a space or a bridge between Christ and Mary which can be both (a) established before and apart from Mary's (woman's)

31 See especially TD II.2, 37–9; ThD 3, 41–3.

entrance, in consideration of Christ (man) 'alone', as the place in which woman will come to be (and thus allow man to come to be), but also (b) only constructed as it were 'in' Mary (woman), read precisely as space.

Coming after Christ and before Mary, but remaining within Christology, sexual difference attempts to open up a spacing and a timing of difference *from* Christ which appears to find no room *in* Christ. Similarly, sexual difference appears to be introduced in order to space woman, in order to provide her place, and yet (as we shall argue in greater detail below) it seems that it can only make woman this place. The task of sexual difference is to prepare a place from which we can be saved, for soteriologically the significance of sexual difference is to be found in the reading of Mary as the type of the Church. Sexual difference is already structurally destined to mark a distance between – between Christ and Mary – a between which occurs both within Christ and in Mary. It is, then, a problematic, *aporetic* spacing. That sexual difference is also already destined to mark a very particular timing – the timing of preparation, and a preparation for time – will be the main focus of our next section.

Thus, despite Balthasar's warning that it must not be bracketed out of Christology, sexual difference can appear to happen in another space and time. At the same time, this 'other' space and time – of sexual difference, perhaps of woman – has been bracketed *into* that Christology. At the very heart of Balthasar's Christology, there is a fraught attempt to tell the possibility of its beginning. The elisions of this attempt are potentially traumatic for woman, for she will appear destined to become the *topos* of sexual difference, since in the brief subsection entitled 'Woman as answer', Balthasar attempts his 'phenomenology'[32] of sexual difference in a description of woman.

Sexual difference, then, is, structurally speaking at the very least, a space and a time between Christ and Mary, between Christ and the Church, analogous always to the difference, the *diastasis*, of creature from Creator. And, since sexual difference is here introduced and located *in* woman, she, too, is between Christ (man) and Mary (woman), between creature and Creator. But she, like sexual difference, *is* also the between; she is made to contain these differences. In this she threatens to assume, or even consume, Christ's place as the Gatherer of Differences. Similarly, in her oscillation between two poles, she becomes the *Mensch par excellence* (again *Christ's topos*). And yet, also in this, she reveals the *Mensch*'s *aporia*: for she appears to be one of the two poles and the oscillation between them; 'her' – the *Mensch*'s – oscillation is thus reduced to the oscillation between one pole and oscillation itself, the closed, fruitless, spinning circle of the difference of one alone from difference itself, in place of the differencing difference of two. Pursuit of this logic will demand a closer reading of Balthasar's texts.

Sexual difference and methodology: the displacement of biography by phenomenology
In terms of the architecture of Balthasar's theological triptych, the role played by this second account of sexual difference is pivotal. It is one of

---

32 See below for an account of our choice and use of this term.

the purposes of this essay to argue that the unfolding of this account is also crucial to the very thought of this structure. The burden which sexual difference will be made to carry will perhaps become too much for it to bear, as it is unveiled as a, if not the, determinative moment for Balthasar's thought. At the same time, this determination has itself already been pre-determined in the opening pages of his great trilogy, in which sexual difference is presented as the thought of the end of modernity.[33] Despite being in some sense inevitable, however, this exposition of sexual differ-ence also comes as something of a surprise.

After the introduction of Christ, the logic of confession (of, that is, the appropriate response to Christ) would suggest that the telling of persons in Christ should take the form of biography. This Balthasar's text implicitly (and almost explicitly) acknowledges.[34] If, as Balthasar suggests, the life of the Church is to be told in the life of Mary, if Mariology is to follow Christology (whilst nevertheless remaining within Christology), then at this point in the triptych we might expect to receive a biographical account of Mary's life.

We are, however, presented in its stead with an attempt to complete the implicitly christological anthropology of Balthasar's preliminary account of the significance of Christ in a second account of sexual difference. The differences which are to be told in the telling of Mary's life are extracted, as it were, in advance of that telling and presented as the difference to be told in the being of woman: phenomenology, of a sort, has displaced the biography upon which it is dependent. And it is this movement of inversion (for we have here displacement and not replace-ment – phenomenology *before* (instead of after) biography; not pheno-menology *instead* of biography) which firmly establishes sexual difference as a determinative (and over-determined) measure or distance between – between Christ and Mary, between man and woman, but also between Mary and Mary, woman and woman. We suggest, then, that the dense,

---

33 To trace the genealogy of the thought of sexual difference as the thought of the end of modernity through the whole of Balthasar's theology is a task which would prove too great a distraction for our purpose here. However, in another essay, 'Helena's oblivion' (forthcoming), we outline the determinative introduction of this theme – and its coupling with ocular metaphorics and an 'economy of the gaze' – in a close reading of the opening pages of *The Glory of the Lord*. There, Balthasar deploys the *motif* of sexual difference in describing modernity's malaise (that is, its severance and loss of the transcendentals) and in outlining his suggested remedy, particularly as evidenced in his extraordinary comments on Faust's embrace of Helena's wraith and the twentieth century's recommendation of an 'impossible hymen'. In this, sexual difference is most certainly presented as 'the issue' of our age – an issue which could be 'our salvation', if only we thought it through (see Irigaray, *An Ethics of Sexual Difference*, p. 5).

34 Mary has a 'life to be told', a flow and a flux which cannot be reduced to a principle: 'The woman is thus on a double ground 'reducible' to no unambiguity [*Eindeutigkeit* – clarity, singular meaning] ... only the theorising of men attempts to ironise [*or freeze*] this river into a rigid principle. ... If one wishes to speak of a 'principle' at all ... then one must take account of the inner historicity of the woman, which needs the stretch of time in order to become a bearing, nourishing and raising mother from a receiving/conceiving [*empfangenden*] bride. Therefore a concrete Mariology cannot avoid something of a simply narrative part' (TD II.2, 269–71; ThD 3, 293–4).

short sub-section of 'The woman's answer' entitled 'Woman as answer' attempts to stake out a path from Christology to mariology by way of reading an elided phenomenology of *diastasis* in terms of the operation of sexual difference. But first a word as to the ascription 'phenomenology'.

As we have already noted, Balthasar comments elsewhere that

> The basis of the biblical religion is the *diastasis*, the distance between God and the creature, that is the elementary presupposition that makes it possible for man to understand and appreciate the unity that grace brings about.[35]

Dia-stasis, in its etymological constitution, invokes no valorization of an interval, but rather the dynamic movement of that which properly belongs together – a distance which gives unity. For the creature, *diastasis* is simply the fact of creation, the 'magic circle' in which it turns and whose borders are internal to the constitution of its own finitude.[36] The creature does not run up against God as its proper limit, but turns in the horizon of its own presensing.

Balthasar traces a preliminary outline of *diastasis* in his reflections upon sexual difference, as provoked in particular by the Genesis accounts of creation (and in response to other commentaries upon these passages). In repeating these stories, he is working in the spaces they provide, making good their promise, a promise which he interprets in terms of phenomenology:

> The beginning of the Bible gives free-room for a phenomenology of the *Geschlechtlichen*,[37] which is first viewed in the sober framework of *creatureliness*. (TD II.1, 337; ThD 2, 368)

Jacques Derrida remarks, in his essay 'Violence and metaphysics – an essay on the thought of Emmanuel Levinas', 'In phenomenology there is never a constitution of horizons, but horizons of constitution',[38] and it is precisely in this sense that we wish to speak here of the phenomenology of *diastasis*. For the work of phenomenology, at least in its Husserlian and Heideggerian form, is a work of unfolding, explicating and laying out the implicit fore-structures which make the explicit possible. It should not be a determination of horizons, but rather a learning of the horizons of presensing which are caught sight of in the *Vor-griff* of fore-sight. And what for Balthasar is caught sight of in Adam's infinitely lonely sighting of the world is precisely Eve.

---

35 ET 3, 173. The importance of distance and difference in this regard is recognized by Irigaray. See Luce Irigaray, *Marine Lover of Friedrich Nietzsche*, tr. Gillian C. Gill (New York: Columbia University Press, 1991), p. 171: 'According to Christianity, God is found only in Distance, the relationship to the Father only takes place at a remove and in the respect for separation. God – the Different, who is encountered only through death and resurrection.'

36 See, e.g., PT 29.

37 Again, to do with the sexual *or* to do with the species.

38 *Writing and Difference*, tr. Alan Bass (London: Routledge & Kegan Paul, 1978), p. 120.

It is in his account of this operation of sexual difference – the relationship which Balthasar claims as 'ultimate'[39] – that we wish to show that the differences crucial to any phenomenology are reduced to a synchronic cross-sectional slice that purports to establish the operation of creation as *diastasis*, conceived not so much as graceful unity but as a fixed distance or measure. This, in other words, is to suggest that in the movement of Balthasar's text, we appear to be given no time – no time for the between of Christology and Mariology, no time in which to pass from Christology to Mariology. In this sense the section entitled 'Woman as answer' must be read as aporetic – an impossible passage which still has to happen. But to return to the text.

Woman – as (over-)determinedly second

First of all, woman is introduced as second, and this severally.

She is 'textually' second because she comes after the man whose appearance interrupts her introduction. The first account of sexual difference attempted to configure the relationships between man and woman and tell them *together*; even there woman was figured as second to Adam's loneliness which interrupted her introduction. But in the second account, man – Adam – is introduced alone before woman. Her absence is re-marked only in the absence of 'a partner for him'. Woman then succeeds man; Eve comes after Adam.

This second account of sexual difference occurs in a section which purports to be devoted to woman (and not to the consideration of man and woman). However, man intervenes several times. Woman is being (re-)introduced after the *Mensch* (man) has been considered without her. Secondly, woman (Mary) is being introduced after Christ (man-*Mensch*). But more than this, this section which claims to be about woman begins with a consideration of *Christ* and his surprising apparent 'femininity' (*weiblichkeit* – womanliness). And again, the second subsection ('Answer, answering glance') of this section ('Woman as answer') begins not with woman but with Adam.

Woman is also chronologically, temporally, historically, accidentally second: in the creation, woman, it would seem, happens on the earth after the man (*Mensch*); Balthasar's text mirrors this 'fact' several times over. In the first account of sexual difference, it becomes clear in the consideration of the *Mensch* as man-and-woman that these two must be together, can only be together, and so must always in some sense be described in their relation to each other. It is only right that woman should be described in her relation to man. But there is here at least an apparently unequal difference, for, as we have already suggested, the very same text introduces and considers the *Mensch* (man) without any reference to woman.

Moreover, in this ascription, woman appears over-determined. For the original *description* of woman as second becomes a *definition* of woman as second. Just as the man's natural, temporal, relative priority tends towards an absolute priority, and in direct proportion to this tendency, so the woman's historical, chronological, natural, temporal secondariness

---

39 See TD II.2, 266, ThD 3, 290.

becomes the logical necessity of that first. She is to be 'essentially', 'logically', 'necessarily' second. This tendency to stabilize the essential fluidity and undecidability of sexual difference was noted in the first account. Woman's introduction as second (but equal) to man in that account of sexual difference is reinforced, if not extended, in the opening section of the second, where Balthasar comments: 'If the Logos proceeds eternally from the Father, is he not then (in respect of the Father) (at least quasi-) feminine?'[40] (TD II.2, 260; ThD 3, 283).

To be woman is to be second, such that to come after or out of (*proceed*) is to be feminine, womanly; a fact which is decided before the second introduction of woman is allowed to happen. It is as if femininity ('womanliness') existed apart from and before woman; woman is second not only to man, but even to her own definition.

Thus, in the redoubling turns of an insistent logic, woman is introduced second, at least twice over. She is also introduced (first) simply as second, but (second) also as second in at least a double sense. She is introduced first, as second (before man's first); she is then introduced second, as second. And in this second introduction, she is made to be second over and over again. This, it would seem, is in order to delineate man as (logically, essentially, necessarily) first, for the preliminary answer to the first half of the opening conundrum of the section 'The woman's answer' reads:

> however the one who originates from the Father is to be designated, as *Mensch* he must be *Mann*, if his Sending[41] is to represent the Origin, the Father, in the world. (TD II.2, 261; ThD 3, 284)

To be first one has to be man. (Indeed, could it be that in order to be *Mensch*, 'one' has to be man – first, singular and male?) In order for man to be first, woman must needs be second. In this, however, woman is in fact second almost before man can be, or even become, first. Moreover, sexual difference, and with it *diastasis*, is thus located as a vulgar difference or fixed distance between two unchanging, un-interchangeable points (man-first :: woman-second) between which there can be no exchange. This fixing of (chrono-)logical order seems set to leave its mark in attempting to concretize all remaining undecidability, including that between world and God (the undecidability proper to *diastasis*) in sexual difference, and so continue woman's increasing over-determination.

Woman as Gegenüber, Gegenwort and Gegenstand

In this second account of sexual difference, as two of its titles make clear, woman's 'second', the man's companion, is also interpreted as 'answer' or 'response': the whole section is entitled 'The woman's answer' (TD II.2, 260–330; ThD 3, 283–360); its first subsection, 'Woman as answer' (TD II.2, 260–1; ThD 3, 283–4). This causes a further difficulty in this phenomenology of woman/sexual difference: woman is not only second, the second *Mensch*; she is 'answer' (and thus perhaps *not* answering *Mensch*).

---

40 Here Balthasar plays again on the term *weiblich* – womanly, feminine.
41 *Sendung* – that is, his mission.

In the first introductory subsection of 'The woman's answer', which bears no separate title, woman, contradictorily, appears to be introduced in order to appear to disappear. This passage is more about Christ and the *Mensch* than it is about woman; moreover, woman is introduced to these as an other, to the extent that she might appear not to be a *Mensch* herself at all. Perhaps it is indeed the case that in order to be *Mensch* one has to be man, male and singular, not woman, female or dual. The emerging definitions of woman and the womanly appear to be remarkably close to not-being.

The second *Mensch*, then, threatens to disappear – from the first *Mensch*'s (man's) view, at least. In a theology in which the metaphorics of sight and vision have such a key part to play, woman is defined first in terms of the auditory – determined as man's answer, his *Antwort*, before ever his word, his *Wort* or question, has been articulated.[42] That which is being examined, then, is not 'The woman's answer' but *man's* answer, the *Mensch*'s answer. Here, rather than belonging together with the man, woman appears to belong *to* him; she belongs to *Mensch* as an object of property, not as a proper subject. This and the following subsection consider the woman *as answer*, woman as the *Mensch*'s answer; and so woman would cease to be *Mensch* or be prevented from ever becoming (or being) *Mensch*.

If, however, woman disappears either from *Mensch* (from, that is, being *Mensch*) or from the *Mensch*'s (man's) view (which perhaps amounts to the same thing), then she can no longer be his answer, she can no longer answer him and so can no longer perform the essential task proper to her. The logic of this text requires woman to give an answer; this in turn would require her to be someone who can answer. But the logic of this text *also* tends to deny woman any ability to answer, to deprive her of any subjectivity. Woman, therefore, can neither have nor give an answer. If there is to be an answer for the *Mensch*, then it must be in woman's being that answer.[43] She is then to be excluded from the *Mensch*, as it were, from the other side as well. Before this phenomenology will consider woman as woman, as, that is, her self, it determines her as answer. This, however, is itself another impossibility, in the light of woman's tendency to not-being (woman, *Mensch* or even at all).

This disappearance or tendency to not-being increases in the subsection 'Answer, answering face', in which Balthasar plays upon the idea of woman as 'over-and-against' (*gegenüber*) man as his *Gegenüber* (his companion, opponent, other, counterpart) in apparently etymological, almost punning turns through an 'Indo-European' *ant*.[44] In this, woman's

---

42 Here again we detect the tendency to an over-determining exclusion from the *Mensch*. The *Mensch* has already been characterized as a riddle to himself, finding no 'solution' or 'answer' even in Christ. And yet here, woman is presented as 'answer'. If she becomes the answer to the *Mensch*'s riddle to himself, then she is no *Mensch*; she will also be that which hardens and petrifies, prevents life and undoes mystery.

43 This eliding identification of woman with answer is grammatically facilitated by the simple fact that, whilst the German word *Wort* (that is, 'word') is a neuter noun, the word for 'answering word' – *Antwort* – is feminine.

44 TD II.2, 261–2; ThD 3, 284–6.

standing over and against man determines her not as subject but as object – *Gegenstand* (that which stands against, next to, opposite). And so woman ceases to be, ceases ever to have been, even a *Mensch*-like thing to disappear, but becomes a word and then a face, a vessel, a delight and even encounter – almost anything but herself, anything but woman. This figure is not man's companion (*Gegenüber*) but his object (*Gegenstand*), *his* possession, a totally other which shares no 'same' with him, with which he can have no exchange – a property in which he will lose all that is proper to him as *Mensch*, and most especially the exchange between the spiritual and the bodily.

Woman as dual and the numbering of time

Woman is also characterized in both of Balthasar's accounts of sexual difference as *dual*. She is a double principle. It is in this way that she can be *both* woman *and* answer; both bride and mother. Thus, first and second are transcribed into singular and double; the one-two of time is read as a one-two of number. At the same time, woman is in some sense separated from herself, in order to open up a space within her in which man can come to be, in which singularity can be contained. This is also read as the enclosing of a line in a circle, but then again as the cleaving of a circle by a line.

In the second account of sexual difference, woman's duality comes most to the fore in terms of her fruitfulness: woman receives a fruitfulness from man and returns a fruit to him. The fruit which she returns both is and is not himself; both is and is not herself. It is always also more than this – a third (and not always a child) which hovers on the margins of this construction of two. Woman then is the fruit-bearing principle *and* the fruit (a duality). But she is also not the fruit:

> Insofar as it is the essential [*wesentliche*] task of the woman to take up the fruitfulness of the man into her own fruitfulness and so unite the fruitfulness of each in herself, she is, in the creaturely realm, the actual principle of fruit-bearing. This means, to speak in the greatest generality,[45] that the woman does not only give back to the man what she has received from him, but rather [returns to him] something new, in which his gift is indeed integrated, but which steps against him [*entgegentritt* – encounters] in an unhoped-for renewed form. (TD II.2, 263; ThD 3, 286)

This in turn Balthasar also interprets as a certain duality:

> The woman thus gives him a double answer: a 'personal' [answer] and [an answer] which goes out of and beyond the I-Thou relationship, ... which one can name *gattungshaft* [*i.e.* 'of the species']. (TD II.2, 263; ThD 3, 286)

Here again, in this duality, we see the crossing of sexual difference and the specificity of human being, dependent upon this identification of woman.

45 *Allgemeinheit* – also 'universality' and so unavoidably carrying associations with 'catholicity'.

Woman as **Begegnung** – *the impossible, necessary exchange*

In the first subsection of 'Woman as answer' (of, that is, the second account of sexual difference), entitled 'Answer, answering face', Balthasar returns to the Genesis accounts of creation and again begins not with woman, but with Adam, defining woman second and as second before introducing woman. Balthasar's explicit purpose in this introduction is to provide the *Mensch*, that is, the man, with the possibility of exchange and communication between body and spirit. Such an exchange can only occur between the man and the woman with whom he belongs in their 'original encounter' (*Begegnung* – their coming up against each other).

Balthasar would make a claim upon a substantial unity between man and woman, but in a contradictory logic exposes only their absolute separation, the rending of human being; and this because he has begun with man without woman. Rather than effecting the possibility of this exchange, becoming as it were its condition of possibility, woman serves only to mark its impossibility. For the interval between man and woman – the phenomenon which should here be open to view – is erased. In encountering woman, or even 'in woman', man is meant to see himself; but this requires him first to see or to meet woman. But woman is always only disappearing. In woman, man cannot meet woman; and if he cannot meet her, then he cannot see himself.

Here sexual difference has been constructed in such a way that it holds man and woman either so close together (no difference between *Mensch* and *Mensch*) or so far apart (insufficient similarity between *Mensch* and thing, or even *Unding*) that there can be no exchange between them. The phenomenology which was designed to show how man and woman belong together can only show that they are apart by absolutizing their differencing into a fixed difference or distance (*diastasis* misread) – a distance of belonging *to*. In woman, man encounters only himself. There is no room in this phenomenology for the coming together of two, perhaps not least because it is always told from the point of view of one.

This impasse is confirmed in Balthasar's text. For he makes the most remarkable claim: 'In this sense, woman, as answer and answering face, is not only a delightful encounter' (TD II.2, 262; see ThD 2, 285),[46] that is *Begegnung* – a delightful coming up against. But if she is not *only* this, then she must also *be* this. In order that encounter might be represented as possible, woman is here conceived of as encounter. In woman man should encounter, not woman, but himself. Already then this encounter is not that between man and woman. But since woman is encounter – and therefore perhaps not woman – man cannot encounter woman in order to encounter himself, but encounters nothing other than encounter itself.

In this description, then, woman must again disappear and become something else – a something not proper to her, but a something which has become man's property. A something tending always towards event and disappearance. Woman construed as 'not only a delightful encounter,

---

46 The important and grammatically difficult reference *Begegnung* is simply omitted in the English translation.

but rather the man's called-for help, shelter, home, the vessel of fulfilment specifically conformed to him' (TD II.2, 262, ThD 3, 285) belongs to man, and so cannot belong together with him. And this even though she is emerging (or disappearing) as his *limit*.

Woman – as disappearing, self-effacing space and limit

As the last and the first word to respond to man's call, woman not only brings man into view, into his own view; she would also appear to mark and define his limits. Apart from the creation of woman, the first man, the first Adam, is incomplete, and his own place in creation remains insecure:

> It is only when God has modelled the woman from his side that nature (finally!) opens itself to him with a counter-word which measures up to him, to his. (TD II.2, 261; ThD 3, 284)

Man's arrival in Balthasar's text has necessarily been delayed until woman's introduction. For it is only their introduction (to each other) which opens nature for man (the subject) and provides him with a place in which to be, a place in which he can come to himself, in which he can recognize, identify himself. Woman's spectral presence, her disappearing appearance, then, serves to provide a faint outline, an edge which has only an inside, an impossible 'envelope'.[47] As that which stands against the man, she is his limit. Without her he has no place to be; apart from in her, apart from in her difference, the man cannot know himself as 'same'.

In order to space (and time) man as 'first' by her being 'second', rather than being required simply to appear, to present a presence, woman is in fact required to appear in order to disappear. Man's limits can only appear, can only be felt or seen, in woman's self-effacement. She is asked to give, to be an answer – and yet her voice is never heard, never recorded (neither in Balthasar's text, nor, at the points he considers, in the Genesis texts). Her answer, she as answer, has no 'content', but becomes the limiting event of answering, of meeting a call; she, as encounter, offers nothing to be encountered, except encounter itself. Woman spaces man, not so much by providing him with a pre-formed space into which he can enter, but by forming his substance (by giving him form) and limiting him as a shimmering, glistening, disappearing horizon.

In these phenomenological reductions, in this spacing of 'first' and 'second' and its fixing of *diastasis*, movement (exchange) is fixed and so rendered impossible. And this, we suggest, is the problem of the telling of time – a problem to which we shall turn in our next section. But first we shall pursue this phenomenology's concretizing logic of self-effacement a little further in order to outline its significance.

The elisions of woman

Woman is intended to be another, a second, *Mensch*, and yet she is repeatedly excluded from the *Mensch* – from human being – and

47 This is a recurrent description of woman's function in Irigaray's readings. See, e.g. *An Ethics of Sexual Difference*, pp. 10–11.

ultimately from being at all, in a series of elisions. We gather these together from what has so far been considered.

The introduction of woman to the *Mensch*, when the *Mensch* has been considered without her, opens the question as to whether the *Mensch* has in fact been man all along. In this, it is man who is elided with *Mensch* and woman who is thus excluded from the *Mensch*.

At the same time, and no doubt in some sort of compensation for the exclusion, woman is also represented as the *Mensch par excellence*. Here she is elided with the *Mensch* to whom she is supposed to be introduced.

In suggesting that with the arrival of woman nature at last and first of all provides an answer to or for the *Mensch*, Balthasar also approaches the equation of woman with *nature*, against which he himself warns: woman is not her own answer to man, she is not even 'man's' answer to himself (although she is *his* answer), she is *nature*'s answer to man. (And in so far as – and only if – she is God's creation, then she is also *God*'s answer to man.)

And yet again, in this elision (of woman and nature) another threatens, for if here it is woman who opens nature to man, or even to the *Mensch*, if she gives him form, then this task has already been identified in the *Theo-Drama* as Christ's.

But this elisory logic harbours yet another elision. Woman is equated with (non-personal) *things*: she 'is' vessel, answer, face. She is also re-quired to be 'event': encounter, oscillation. In order to enable the neces-sary exchange for which she is introduced, she becomes not only one with and in whom the *Mensch*/man can exchange, nor even only the exchange itself, but in some way she becomes interchangeable; she is *that which is exchanged*, or even *exchangeability itself*. And so she always threatens to prove exchange impossible. In these approaches, she approaches being no thing. She is locked into a necessity of self-effacement, to the extent that she approaches not-being: she appears in order to disappear; she 'is' towards nothing and not-being, almost an *Unding* always undoing the text. Woman threatens to elide with nothing (and so everything – and thus all things with nothing).

In all of this, another elision seems immanent. For this self-effacing work is remarkably close to the Spirit's,[48] such that we could perhaps suggest that woman and Spirit approach elision with each other in so far as they approach elision with elision itself, and precisely thus with 'femininity'.[49]

---

48 Yves Congar, in his study *I Believe in the Holy Spirit*, vol. 1, tr. David Smith (London: Geoffrey Chapman, 1983), suggests that there is a 'deep bond that exists between the Virgin Mary and the Holy Spirit' (p. 163). But it is the extraordinary remark of the Jesuit theologian John O'Donnell (echoing the reflections of Vladimir Lossky's *The Mystical Tradition of the Eastern Church*) which suggests here the bond of self-effacing withdrawal, perhaps even elision: 'In the bestowal of the divine gift of deification ... the Holy Spirit annihilates herself, so to speak, losing herself in the work of sanctifying the human person (John O'Donnell, *The Mystery of the Triune God* (London: Sheed & Ward, 1988), p. 75.)

49 The brevity of this adumbration should in no way disguise the colossal implications of the task it sets us. Our concern has been with specific texts within Balthasar's *œuvre*, but the implications of this deconstructive reading suggest a subterranean logic which has repeatedly ordered the Christian tradition into precise and

From sexual difference to theological difference

The specifically *theo*-logical significance of sexual difference hinted at in the first account is drawn out in the particularly short and dense subsection of 'Woman as answer' entitled 'Feminine creature',[50] which follows Balthasar's treatment of woman as answer and answering face. In this subsection, he turns from the intramundane to the meta-cosmic dimension of sexual difference in the relationship between God and creature, for from all that has been said of the relationship between man and woman, 'an analogical inference allows itself to be drawn for the relationship between God and creature' (TD II.2, 264; ThD 3, 288).

And this because the creature is to be seen as secondary, answering, 'feminine' with respect to God. At the same time, however, the difference between these two relationships is asserted: every equation of God with Adam is forbidden, on the basis of *trinitarian* relationships:

> In particular, according to Christian Dogmatics, God the Father does not need to be rid of his fruitfulness, he begets the Son not in order to have a vessel for his richness,[51] but rather out of the superabundant fullness of his love, which is pressed into self-communication by nothing external to it, just as the answer, the Son, does not come to the Father as 'Help', but as equally full encounter and indeed the fruit of their love, the Spirit, proceeds out of their union – simultaneously [*or* immediately] as their nature [*Wesen*], their product, their witness and their womb [*or* lap] – but not as something self-interpreting, which can ground new generations. (TD II.2, 264; ThD 3, 287)

The analogy, as always, is only one of proportion in so far as it is of *dis*proportion: creaturehood is feminine, just as women are feminine, in the same sense that women are feminine. And yet, in so far as Godhead could ever be understood as masculine, it is *not* in the same sense that men are masculine, and this is not least because God is three and in some sense *both* 'masculine' and 'feminine' in his relationships with himself.[52] Nevertheless, every creaturely spirit has a 'certain natural mission' – in analogy to the sexual relations *and* to christological mission – to stand

---

predetermined articulations. The issue here is not with sweeping denouncements of patriarchy and 'patriarchal religion', but with a patient attention to the far-reaching nature of the configurations and determinations which allow any in/ equality of the sexes to come to the fore as a question in the first place. The significance of sexual difference in and for Christianity has never been superficial.

50 In rendering these texts in English, we have not sought to distinguish between *Weib* and *Frau*, which both mean 'woman'. Balthasar usually uses the word *Frau*, but here the logic of his text turns upon the proximity of the thought of *Weib* to that of *weiblich* and *weiblichkeit* (feminine and femininity, respectively).

51 Not, then, out of any need or lack.

52 Here, contrary to Balthasar's essentializing attempts to portray woman, sexual difference is again revealed as a question of relation: masculine and feminine can only be determined in the relationships of 'persons' to each other.

ready and open for the taking up (the receiving) of the seed (semen) of the divine Word.

Sexual difference, then, marks two horizons of difference: that of the intramundane within human being (a creaturely difference, turning always on the ontological difference) and that of the supramundane (metacosmic) between God and creature (the difference of creation, theological difference). However, as becomes clear at the beginning of the next subsection, 'Widening of the question', it marks each of these differently. These two horizons Balthasar names 'aspect'; they are two aspects which come together in Jesus Christ. It is only in the union of these two 'aspects' (two aspects of one differencing? two aspects of 'sexual differentiation'?) in Jesus Christ that woman's christological place or placing becomes visible, *as a third*:

> First there where [*or* only because] the intramundane aspect (man-woman) and the supramundane (God-world) aspect unite themselves in the God-*Mensch* Jesus Christ, is the christological place [*or* placing] of (the) woman within sight [*or* foreseeable; conceivable] as something third. (TD II.2, 264–5; ThD 3, 288)[53]

This constitutes a significant *theo*-logical and *christo*-logical statement. For, if sexual difference is the link between these two horizons of difference, the link between creaturely and theological difference, then this is not a difference, not a linking site, in which one person – however divine, however universal, however social – can stand alone. As sexual difference, the link itself must be a relationship between two – the relationship of a man and a woman. A logic in which *Christ alone* spans these two horizons will not be sufficient to its task. However, before concluding this section by considering Christ's significance for the determination of sexual difference, we shall pursue the theme of analogy a little further.

Sexual difference: the analogy of analogy

Balthasar proceeds to provide an outline of this 'christological placing' which has been prepared for the one who will have to share with Christ the linking between creaturely difference and the difference of creation, theological difference. Since Christ is an individual *Mensch*, the christological woman will have to be a 'particular someone', in order to have an individual relationship to Christ. At the same time, she will also need to have a social aspect, in order to represent the whole of creation which the Son is to redeem. Thus the christological woman is to be dual in a new sense; she will be Mary *and* Church, such that

> these two aspects will, like the human and divine sides of Jesus Christ himself, be neither simply identical, nor separated from each other (corresponding to the unconfused and undivided of Chalcedon). (TD II.2, 265; ThD 3, 288)

---

53 Here Balthasar's reference is unclear: the christological placing of woman appears as a third – a third what? – aspect (of what?); place (for woman?); a third christological place; a third to God and world; or to God and Christ?

Here, in Mary–Church's relationship to Christ, we catch sight of *analogical participation*. Christ's bride (the christological woman) carries within herself *something like* – something analogous to, but not identical with – the union of the two natures in Christ, by virtue of her being his bride, by virtue of her correspondence to and with him. The Second Eve's marriage to the Second Adam (Mary–Church's marriage to Christ) is her marriage to and union with the relationship between the divine and human natures in Christ – a *conubium* of the *admirabile commercium;*[54] perhaps a *communicatio idiomatum* of sorts. Married to a miraculous, wonderful exchange, Mary–Church comes to participate in that exchange, but in a new way. For in Christ, two natures (divine, human) are held together as one, in one person. In Mary–Church one person (Woman, Second Eve) is held apart in two aspects, redoubling (in a 'non-identical repetition') the union of two 'aspects' in the person of Jesus Christ.

This participation in participation and exchange of exchange – this linking of two horizons of difference in sexual difference – is the analogy of analogy. For, sexual difference is held to be an analogy of the relationship between God and creature, but this relationship is itself analogical. And so this identification does not operate in such a way as to allow a reading which assigns the creaturely difference to Mary (Church) and the difference of creation (theological difference) to Christ. Sexual difference does not mark a spacing between these two differences in marking the spaces between Christ and Mary (Church). Sexual difference does not mark a spacing. Sexual difference is here a differencing: the differencing between Mary and Christ as the difference of exchange and participation, without confusion and without division.

But here perhaps the threat which Mariology will always pose to Christology begins to emerge. In Balthasar's theology, Jesus Christ is to be understood as 'the concrete analogy of being';[55] this is the significance of his being the union not only of God and *Mensch* but also of an intra-mundane with a supramundane difference (man–woman with God–world: see above quotation). And yet, at the same time, sexual difference is (also?) that in which these two differences meet. To what extent can Christ and sexual difference be coincident? Or, to put this another way, can either Christ or Mary be made to contain sexual difference?[56]

But there is another tendency harboured within these (near-) identifications. If sexual difference is to be read as the analogy of analogy, then it might also be read as in some sense outside analogy, above or beyond it. In the recognition of the importance and the extent of analogy,

---

54 Balthasar's treatment of this doctrine will be one focus of the argument in our next section.

55 Thus, for example, in *A Theology of History*, tr. Ignatius Press (San Francisco: Ignatius Press, 1994), pp. 69–70, Balthasar writes: 'In this sense Christ can be called the concrete analogy of being, *analogia entis*, since he constitutes in himself, in the unity of his divine and human natures, the proportion of every interval between God and man.'

56 Certainly in Balthasar's text, Mariology is contained within Christology, and sexual difference within Mariology. Considered purely spatially, then, these differencings might be represented as concentric circles. But, as we shall argue, this representation is disturbed by the thought of *time*.

there lies an attempt to secure it, and this in something other than itself. If analogy is to be secured in sexual difference, then sexual difference is in effect excluded from analogy – and thus from the properly creaturely relation of *diastasis* – threatening, like woman, always at once to disappear from creation and to engulf it.

The analogical body

This tendency is not without its implications for woman. For Balthasar, sexual difference occurs in woman. Indeed, the sexual difference from man (and sometimes, it seems, from the *Mensch*) is woman. In so far as this identification is successful, then, *woman* becomes the analogy of analogy; she is the end, *the outside of* analogy itself. In a series of (con-) descending differences, between God and world, God and *Mensch*, between man and woman, between *Mensch* and woman, between masculine and feminine, between spiritual and bodily, woman – and in particular woman's body, perhaps even her sheer bodiliness – becomes the limit of analogy.

For, as the man becomes increasingly bodiless, the woman is more and more equated with the body – she *is* a face, a look, a silent answer – the silent opening of two lips.[57] It is *in* this body that man seeks to place himself and the world, in the 'between' opened by woman's duality, not least as mother and bride. But, as we have seen, this logic is always to be frustrated, for it will also demand that, as perfect creature and perfect *Mensch*, woman will be also neither, always tending towards being 'something' uncreate. But if she disappears, then so does man, either after or in her. For man's place has been fixed as between (or in) woman – between mother and bride; emerging from between or in the movement of the two sets of lips of mother and of bride. If either or both of the woman's two pairs of lips[58] are elided into the one-sided markings of an edge on to nothingness, man will disappear in woman's disappearance into woman-nothingness. Woman, or more properly her body, thus becomes only the exteriorization of man's, and so the *Mensch*'s, internal limit; reified as body and bodiliness, Kant's fantasy object; the glittering, seductive, withdrawing, enveloping phenomenon.

And so in a logic of over-determination which is always a decision on a properly prior indeterminacy, all difference becomes figured in the difference not between man and woman but between God and woman, in the (infinite) distance between God and women's bodies. For women's bodies appear to be fixed outside of meaning in order to secure meaning.

---

57 Much depends on woman's 'answer' – and in particular Mary's 'yes'. And yet neither Genesis nor Balthasar records the *speaking* of this answer. Woman herself becomes the silent answer, a silent opening in and through which man can emerge, forced always to have spoken this answer, and yet never in fact heard or listened to. Similarly, the Gospels might well record that which can be interpreted as Mary's consent, but she is not recorded as having said 'yes' – her 'yes-word' is not 'yes' – and yet this difficulty remains untreated, ignored, silenced even. We shall return to this puzzling fact in our conclusion.

58 For an inspired and inspiring attention to the morphology of women's two pairs of lips (the mouth and the vagina) see especially the essay 'Veiled lips' pp. 75–122 in *Marine Lover*.

And this not least because it is the woman (in Mary) who gives God (and not only man) the answer he has been waiting for. Fixed in another economy of interpretation where there is not give and take but only univocal and unequivocal representation and substitution, women's bodies analogize analogy.

Concretization en Christo

We have sought so far to think after two accounts of sexual difference in Balthasar's *Theo-Drama*. The first account presents this difference as something undecidable, indeterminate: a fluid relationship between a first and a second, between 'first' and 'second', between active and passive, between two different forms of fruitfulness. And all this – purportedly at least – within a relationship of equality. This fluidity shares in the fluidity of the relationship between the *cosmos* and the *theion*, to the extent that God can be represented as 'feminine' without comment or remark. In this first account, sexual difference in some way represents in the world the difference – that is, the *diastasis* – of the world from God. Within the fluidity of the relationship between *cosmos* and *theion* and the fluidity (the indeterminacy or undecidability) of the 'first' and 'second' of sexual difference, the *Mensch* hovers or oscillates (*schwebt*) as a riddle to itself.

In the second account of sexual difference, more extensive characterizations of the two partners in this difference are attempted; its *essence* is sought. Here the temporal order of first and second becomes a numerical, arithmetic ordering in which first is 'one' (singular) and second is 'two' (dual). In this essentialization, first becomes itself primariness, or anteriority, and second becomes secondariness, procession. In this, woman is over-determined, not only as second, but as essentially second, even secondariness itself, and in becoming thus necessarily second she threatens to destabilize 'first'. At the same time, man himself is also over-determined as 'first', singular, primary, anterior, perhaps to his even greater peril. Why and how might this have happened?

Between these two accounts, Christ has been introduced, in response to the *Mensch*'s riddle to himself. Balthasar claims that Christ is not introduced as an 'answer' – in the sense of solution – but as a deepening and intensifying of that riddle. And yet this introduction does seem to reduce this riddle, for it requires and effects a calcification, a concretizing, of sexual difference, which has formed such a key part to this riddle, in preparation for itself: from within the oscillation and fluidity of human sexual differentiation – and from within the fluidity of the relationship between *cosmos* and *theion* – a space must be cleared between first and second into which the God–Man (the God–*Mensch*) can enter. And yet, this 'space' is only made in or by Christ's appearance. And so it is in and for Christ that the man's *relative* 'natural' priority becomes *absolute*:

> Because the Word of God becomes (a) bodily *Mensch* in Jesus Christ, and because *Mensch* exists in the three-fold rhythm that has been described, where *Menschsein* (human being/existence) includes an either-or, Jesus Christ can only step in at one pole, in order from there to fulfil the other. This becomes particularly acute

in the man–woman tension: on the basis of the natural, relative 'superordination'[59] of the man (alongside the equal value of both persons), the Word of God with his absolute 'superordination' can only step into the human in the form of the man and so form the woman to himself (Eph. 5:27), that she, stemming from him himself and at the same time led to him by [*or* from] God, might be evenly-[*or* equally-] born as 'flesh from his flesh'. From this a new rhythm already allows itself to open onto the first tension, that between spirit and body. (TD II.1, 376–7; ThD 2, 411)

In the analogy between the man's natural, relative *Überordnung* and Christ's absolute *Überordnung*, the woman's subordination[60] – and with it sexual difference – is fixed: *this* man's *Überordnung* is both relative and absolute; it is for and because of (precisely relative to) this man that the woman becomes absolutely second. And so it is not only in the theorizing of men, but more particularly in their thinking after the arrival of Christ, that woman's flowing current is ironized into a single principle of secondary duality (see TD II.2, 269; ThD 3, 293).

Thus it would appear that the precious freight that sexual difference has to bear cannot allow it to remain unstable, undecided and indeterminate. And so a decision is prematurely forced upon this proper un-decidability and its fluidity is halted and fixed. Ironically, fixing the bearer seems set similarly to fix and concretize the load. But the irrepressible oscillation of life continues and so needs to break through this ossification, shattering with it all that was to have been preserved.

Our tracing of these two views of woman, 'before' and 'after' Christ, has begun to reveal the knot between sexual difference and time in the concretization of the timing of sexual difference as a particular spacing. But Balthasar's treatment of sexual difference does not end here, and so we turn now in our third section to attend to this question of the over-spatialization of time in the attempt to tell the timing of time, and in particular the timing of the preparation for the reception of salvation. It is this consideration of time that will lead us – in time – to a third account of sexual difference, which promises at once to unite and to deconstruct all that has gone before.

59 The German here, *Überordnung*, is something of a neologism along the lines of an 'over or above, a super- (or supra-) ordering'. The English translators' 'priority' fails here in so far as it masks the use of the problematic prefix *über*, meaning beyond, over, above, super, supra, meta and so also frustrates any conveyance of the sense in which that which is *über* is *not* that on the other side of a line or that which begins where its subordinate stops, but is *rather* that which overtakes, exceeds and embraces. Balthasar, as we have already suggested, plays constantly upon this prefix, and not least here, where attention must be paid to the ways in which the man's *Überordnung* to the woman may differ from Christ's *Überordnung* beyond the difference between absolute and relative. These two are, no doubt, analogous – that, surely, is the point – but this does *not* mean that they are the same and only different in degree. A second ambiguity for this word lies in the sense of *Ordnung*, which might refer to an ordering activity or to a being ordered.
60 For the man's *Überordnung* suggests here the woman's correlative *Unterordnung* – first becomes also above, greater; second becomes also below, lesser – a suggestion which repeatedly disturbs Balthasar's text, not least in his frequent denials of the legitimacy of the inference of any implied inferiority.

The ecstasies of time

How shall we arrive at a view of time which, at the same time, respects the density of matter, the dissuasive power of the word, the possibility of a future as well as the wounds which culture has inflicted upon itself?

Ghislain Lafont

The question at stake

We have argued that for Balthasar the *diastasis* of the creature from God is fundamentally grasped or unveiled to the *Mensch* in sexual difference. This 'relationship of sexual complementarity within the God-creature differential' is 'irreducible' (TD II.2, 311; ThD 3, 338). And, moreover,

> [the] creaturely 'being over against God' [*Gottgegenübersein*] can be shown to be an image of the inner-divine trinitarian life ... whereby the opposition [*Gegenüber*] of man and woman receives a new dimension of meaning. (TD II.2, 312–3; ThD 3, 340)

However, we have shown that the pre-understanding of phenomenological reduction which Balthasar commends with regard to explicating this creaturely analogy instigates a methodological passage towards essentiality and violence. For while 'Woman as answer' intends to show the ultimacy of the man–woman encounter – that is, their belonging together as their *Ergänzung* (complementarity) – what it in fact effects is the *aporia* of woman as spectral presence and man's tendency towards unrepresentability. In short, Balthasar's attempt to tell man's and woman's belonging together results in a concealed inversion by which woman's apparent belonging to man (as his 'answer') conceals *man's* actual belonging to woman.

If sexual difference should properly open on to the *diastasis* of the world from God – indeed be, in an aspect, this opening – then what we have discovered in Balthasar's account of this *Grundbestimmung* is a creaturely difference that threatens closure (again, *Ergänzung* in the sense of completion). That is to say, the attempted fabrication of an *identity* between man and himself 'in' woman, in which creaturely transcendence ('his' *ek-stasis*) amounts to an attempt to find himself in woman alone, as the discovery of himself in creation. He seeks in woman the 'sublime' borders of his world – its beginning and end – which would thus become an inviolable, glittering limit from which to measure his relation to God.[61]

The implications of this logic for Balthasar's entire project are considerable when we recognize the centrality of this concept of *diastasis*. As one of his more recent commentators explains:

> [T]his whole issue of distance is fundamentally related to the central theme of Balthasar's vision, analogy. The whole scheme of salvation opposes to cosmic identity the presuppositions of 'the analogy of

---

61 The whole issue of the sublime and sexual difference is treated by Slavoj Zizek in his *Tarrying with the Negative* (Durham: Duke University Press, 1994), Chapter 2.

God-world, the freedom of divine mission, and the Trinity in God.'
Without the analogy proper to him, man is destroyed: his natural
desire for God pulls him out of the world, draws him to deny or
destroy the world in his desire for God, and so loses his created place
as a creature with a God-given distance from God. As witness to
this, beauty is based on analogy, not on identity, and this is true both
for innerwordly aesthetics as well as for the spiritual order.[62]

What comes into view here then is the whole panorama of Balthasar's
theology pared down to its most fundamental articulations: distance,
analogy and beauty. That is to say, the 'space' for there to be any
recognition of the splendour and glory of love (most especially in the cross
and descent of the Son) which will bear us towards God. Is all this to
founder on Balthasar's account of sexual difference?

The **chiasm** *of space and time in sexual difference: two further questions*
Now, no doubt this question claims too much and too quickly; nonetheless it may serve to initiate a reception of Balthasar's argument which
is more critically sensitive to Irigaray's directive that we noted in the
introduction to this essay: that to think through sexual difference involves
a reassessment of the whole problematic of space and time. It is to this
issue that we now turn, in consideration of the fact that if, as we have
claimed, it is part of Balthasar's singular insight to have recognized in
sexual difference an anteriority in and as creation which 'allows' God to
be non-Other, then this is itself configured as a timing of space and
spacing of time which establishes a preparation for the arrival of God. In
considering this chiasm of space and time we shall pursue two questions:

(i) What is the fate of *time* in Balthasar's telling of *diastasis* as sexual
difference? Which is to ask, if the interval between the sexes has in
Balthasar's account been interpreted fundamentally in terms of a
'spacing', if the difference between the sexes is fixed as a valorized
interval, a 'vulgar difference' which in turn measures and fixes *diastasis*,
what are we to understand the *temporality* of this spacing to be? This issue
will lead us to a second urgent question.

(ii) How are we to understand the belonging together of man and
woman in space and time which would enable an apperception of the
ungraspable belonging of the world to God such that God, far from being
'simply the "Other" (the "partner") ... [is] exalted so very high above
[*über*] everything created that he is just as much the "non-Other"' (TD II.1,
392–3; ThD 2, 428)?

How are we to speak of this reality as no dialectical and harmonious
rhythm of contraries, but as an analogical participation in the coming
forth of God? It is this questioning that will thus bring our argument,
following Balthasar, to a 'third' configuration of sexual difference in the
exchange between Christ and Mary. This will provoke an assessment of
the ecstasies of time as a bringing to birth and a subsequent reflection

62 Raymond Gawronski, *Word and Silence*, p. 85.

upon the interleaving of the doctrines of the immaculate conception and the *admirabile commercium*. We shall take each of these questions in turn.

The timing of sexual difference

First, what is the fate of time in Balthasar's telling of *diastasis* as sexual difference? If we belong together in space, then so also in time? In the phenomenology of sexual difference that we have traced, two times – 'first' and 'second' – appear as punctiliar instants in the same time. Balthasar well understands that for sexual difference to be an opening, as opening on to the divine, then exchange (encounter) must, as it were, be the event of creation.[63] The world does not begin or come to an end at a threshold, but *is* a threshold. It is perpetual opening, an exchange, an encounter in which God offers all and in which, most surprisingly of all, we are given a part to play. It is *for* this exchange, in Balthasar's text, that man and woman appear; it is *as a result* of this exchange, in the world, that they are there at all. And yet in the (a)temporal spacing of time that Balthasar establishes in his account of sexual difference, exchange becomes strictly impossible. Space and time are no longer thought of, configured, as belonging together, but rather they are elided. First and second become times which are required to occur not only in the same time or timing, but *at the same time* – an impossibility.

Now, that 'first' only becomes so with the arrival of 'second' is true; indeed we could suggest is the truth of time – of time's timing, as it were. But this does not mean that that which is first only *happens*, only *is*, 'at the same time' as that which is second. It must in some way happen 'before' in order to *become* 'first' with the later arrival of the second. Moreover, although that which is first must have been before, it was not *then* 'first' – it could only become 'first'. What this means is that that which has become first must be continuous with that which was to become first before it became first, but this becoming *effects a change*. This is the effect, the event of the timing of time; it is the differencing of time whose aporetic nature amounts to the fact that time is required in order to have becoming and exchange, and that to recognize becoming and exchange requires the ecstasies of time – of past, present and future. In order for 'first' to be recognized as such there must be an anterior configuration (temporally marked) which is no 'simple' past, but a convoluted anteriority. It is an outside of time dwelling inside time, the passage between which is properly aporetic. This *aporia* should not be dialectically resolved in order to marshal its deconstructive effects; in order, that is, to bring time to order by way of an elision with space as its purported 'other'. It is precisely this gesture – to resolve the *aporia* of time against a difference: the difference of space – that Balthasar attempts to effect in woman. How has this occurred?

Two things are of note here with regard to sexual difference. First, the fact that what Balthasar's move amounts to is a *spatialization* of time; and second, that this move is not unconnected with a general feature of the logic of modernity. To expand on these two points.

---

63 Ultimately of course this exchange yields to a trinitarian logic, to which we shall return in the next section.

The spatialization of time in sexual difference as the difference of anteriority

In the time 'before' sexual difference, the gaze of the lonely *Mensch* travels across an undifferentiated 'empty' landscape. The *Mensch* is infinitely lonely, for the *Mensch* is not only without companion but in a radical and surprising way without God.[64] There is no event of exchange and perhaps we should say that the name of this strange time 'before' time is simply loneliness. The biblical narrative recalls an event of differencing – itself an ambiguous, double remembering. Balthasar describes with persistence and rigour this event of sexual differencing in terms of a 'first' and 'second', and of a doubling of woman. He understands that this first and second belong together, that man and woman belong together and that in this event of their belonging together they belong to God. This is what Balthasar would have us understand is the privilege of sexual difference.

However, they also belong to the *Mensch*, and belong to the *Mensch* in different ways. It is in or rather across the timing of these relationships – of man and woman belonging together; of man and woman belonging to *Mensch*; of man and woman belonging to God – that the *aporias* of time are intensified to an extent that from the midst of this intensification Balthasar seeks to bring relief by attempting to order these exchanges *in* and *at* the same time.

Balthasar achieves this through a two-fold move which folds into one: a retrospective sexing of the *Mensch* by way of a reading of woman as space. It is precisely because woman is understood as space and therefore as containing the difference of sexual differencing that she can become the Other that will resolve the *aporia* of time: the 'pure' event of encounter, the eventing of event. It is only in this way that Balthasar can answer his fear that the *Mensch* will be understood as some sort of androgynous being.

This move is critical for what it effects is the translation of the *anterior differencing* of sexual difference (the site for the coming of life) into an account of the *difference of anteriority* as the 'first' and 'second' of sexual difference. Time becomes the spacing of a line passing like an arrow through its own *aporia* which stakes out 'first' as the completion of a 'before'. The belonging together of man and woman, of first and second, is thus split in order to be reassembled along with the *Mensch* (and God?) at the same time, which means in the same space – in woman. What has been forgotten here is the 'temporal clue' given in sexual difference (which of course Balthasar has seen) which concerns the fact that in the aporetic 'arrival' of time, which is the end of the *Mensch*'s loneliness, there will henceforth always be more than one difference which breaks up any field of the same and other through the disseminating effects of time. The arrival of a difference from 'man' – 'woman' – makes a difference to 'man'. And even in this, one has barely indicated the complexity of biblical accounts which would have us reckon with the different modalities of 'becoming' man and woman in the event of sexual differencing. Perhaps

---

64 The complexity of this theme is taken up with powerful effect in Jacques Pohier's work, *God in Fragments*, tr. John Bowden (London: SCM Press, 1985), pp. 272f.

one could say, because there is time, there is never and nowhere – neither in eternity nor in God – only one difference. There is only ever an anterior differencing which is never the difference of anteriority.

Thus, if we have tracked the logic of woman as space we can now see how this draws with it an encoding of time which amounts to the elision of time in space, in woman. The anterior differencing of sexual difference represented as the difference of anteriority effects the calcification of the manifold exchanges between the sexes into a 'first' difference; and this by way of representing something that is always in the process of becoming as the completed effect of something that has begun.

In this sense, then, we should recognize that what Balthasar's decision upon sexual difference amounts to is precisely a decision taken *against* the time of creaturely existence as the experience of becoming. The timing of time, that which is most proper to time and which at the same time is time's other, is precisely that which allows it to belong together with space and not be collapsed into space. It is only this that will, analogically, allow for the thought of God as precisely *not* circumscribed by a diachronic ordering of first and second which amounts to a creaturely *ratio* by which to measure God from here to there; from our place in creation to its origin. It is only by observing these protocols that we will be patient with the time of becoming – or the becoming of time – which, as we shall argue, is precisely the translation into creation of 'something like time' in God.

Modernity's elision of time as feminine

If our argument would thus far demand raising these issues in any reception of Balthasar's theology, then, we should add, this must occur in proximity to the logic of modernity in general. For it is of note here that Balthasar's logic appears dictated by a general feature of modernity which, as Walter Benjamin pointed out, involves the shift from a Christian eschatological concept of historical time to a modern 'secularised time into space'.[65] As Catherine Pickstock has noted, modernity is marked by an 'overspatialization', by which 'space' is valorized over time and it is precisely under these conditions that we are not merely led to speak of space, but rather 'that space becomes our language, space speaks itself'.[66] We can only note that in this process of homogenization – a process which allows the different and differing temporalities of different communities to be diachronically ordered – lies the considerable power of the political logic of modernity.

Moreover, if we can recognize in Balthasar's argument a gesture of modernity in the spatialization of time, is there also a gendering of modernity as feminine? That is to say, as Christine Buci-Glucksmann argues in her examination of the aesthetics of modernity, 'the feminine as allegory of modernity'. Her elegant argument cannot be rehearsed here other than to suggest that woman-body becomes the interpretative principle of modern allegory in respect of the essence of modernity as 'a

---

65 *Benjamin: Philosophy, Aesthetics, History*, ed. Gary Smith (Chicago University Press, 1989), p. 62.
66 Catherine Pickstock, 'Necrophilia: the middle of modernity. A study of death, signs, and the eucharist' in *Modern Theology* 12:4 (October, 1996), p. 407.

task and *conquest*.[67] To this we could also suggest a homology in support of Buci-Glucksmann's provocative suggestion. For modernity as category plays a peculiarly dual or doubled role as a configuration of historical totalization. Modernity designates both the existence of an epoch in a typology or classification of chronology *and* the contemporaneity of the 'now' in terms of its self-transcending effect in distancing the present from even the most recent past. Modernity, like woman it would seem, is both a space and the spacing of space. And in this modernity gains its effect from the permanent transition of an elided temporality.

The questions that this inevitably raises concern the nature of Balthasar's entire engagement with modernity; an issue whose full dimensions extend way beyond the scope of this essay. This engagement, though, runs like a golden thread throughout his work and in its nuanced and convoluted articulation yields to no easy summary. No doubt in his assessments of 'our time', Balthasar learnt much from the thought of Martin Heidegger;[68] however, and in careful attention to the remarkable opening pages of *The Glory of the Lord* vol. 1 (H I), we would argue for a novelty in Balthasar's interpretation which very precisely links the destiny of Being (in a Heideggerian sense) to the corporality of sexual difference.[69] To think the end of modernity after Balthasar in this sense is not to think a border over which we would gingerly or boldly step into the novelty of the postmodern; but rather to think the 'internal' limits of this historical totalization (modernity) which are precisely an encoding of time and space in which differences – ontological and sexual alike – are secured.

Asking after the 'unity that grace brings'

Our second question (asking after our understanding of the belonging together of man and woman and the ungraspable belonging together of the world to God) concerns that 'unity that grace brings about'; a unity which presages no collapse into identity but rather bears a *belonging together* of man and woman in a manifold differencing of 'first' and 'second'. How are we to represent the belonging together of man and woman in space and time which would enable an apperception of the ungraspable belonging of the world to God such that God is no Other (absolute or otherwise) but, in Cusa's phrase, the non-Other?

Now, what is at issue here is not so much a metaphysical account of the nature of time – although one should readily admit that philosophical commitments are of substantial importance – but the nature of theology (and thereby the thought of sexual difference within this) as *Nachdenken* – a 'thinking after'. Balthasar's theology is indeed a theology 'after' revelation – thought in the light of revelation and never apart from it in some conjectured space of 'pure nature': a positing of sexual difference in some way 'untouched' by revelation. In this sense, then, to ask *after* 'the

---

67 *Baroque Reason: The Aesthetics of Modernity*, tr. Patrick Camiller (London: Sage Publications, 1994), Chapter 5.
68 See especially the concluding section of the fifth volume of *The Glory of the Lord* (H III.1/2): 'Inheritance and the Christian task'.
69 And modernity's simultaneous reification and denuding of both the body and sexual difference. See again the forthcoming essay 'Helena's oblivion'.

unity that grace brings about' involves no directive to theology to excavate a 'third thing' that stands behind any two brought into a unity; rather, its task is to describe retrospectively the timed configuration of that which presents itself as belonging together. Balthasar is acutely aware of the dangers of any theo-logic which would dialectically allow one to fold creation back into its origin. For any creaturely difference cannot (should not) allow us to posit God at the end of an unfolded chain of Being, or descending emanation of energies. As he notes in conclusion to the second volume of the *Theo-Drama*: 'the *Mensch* is . . . in no regard and at no level traceable back to God' (TD II.1, 393; ThD 2, 428).

Nevertheless, it is precisely because of the elision of temporality in Balthasar's diachronic ordering of sexual difference, that the analogical protocols that prevent the representation of God as only ever the Other are threatened: the Other no doubt as sublime 'holy' limit, perhaps even as *mysterium tremendum*, but still 'an other' entangled in creation's difference – the Other marked at the border named 'woman'. As we have already argued, the 'other' of time is not space, and if there is to be discovered in our experience of sexual difference a 'temporal clue' to God's relationship to the world, then it is a clue which is not such as to provide us with a limit or end-point for making complete and satisfying sense of God's relationship with the world.[70]

Asking after the unity of man and woman belonging together

The unity that grace brings is not something apart from the arrival of grace, and so we must understand that the unity of grace and nature is precisely the gift that grace brings. To represent a belonging together proper to the differencing of difference – in other words, in distinction to a placing on an already measured interval – is to ask after that which allows a gathering together of different things that does not collapse into an identity or 'simple' undifferentiated unity. Man and woman are indeed not identical but they belong together in time (and space) – the time (and space) of lived experience. What this suggests is that the ecstasy of

---

70 An immediate response and indeed corrective to Balthasar may suggest itself here. Thus, if his mistake has been to make woman identical with space – a space or envelope to contain everything that is – should we not simply turn to time to make good this imbalance? Evidence of this gesture can be found in an essay by Julia Kristeva entitled 'Women's time'. Here Kristeva argues that 'for time, female subjectivity would seem to provide a specific measure that essentially retains repetition and eternity from among the multiple modalities of time'. In short, woman's time should be set against the linear temporality of masculine ideology. However, paradoxically, in the light of what we have thus far argued, in opposing women's time to historical, linear time, Kristeva ends up by associating the former with space once more. Which is to say that, caught in the entanglements of an oppositional logic, she uncritically replicates the logic of 'spacing' that we have traced in Balthasar's argument. To oppose a male hegemony, woman again becomes space, albeit the space of the infinitely fruitful circle. Now this is not to dismiss much of what Kristeva has to say in this pioneering essay, but it does return us again to Irigaray's insight that in order to think through – moreover live through – this difference, sexual difference, we must 'reconsider the whole problematic of space and time'. See *The Kristeva Reader*, ed. Tori Moi (Oxford: Blackwell, 1986), p. 191.

creaturely temporality – of living in and through time – is precisely that
which allows for the belonging together of man and woman *at the same
time*, and thus where the temporality of this belonging together is brought
into question. To attend to the temporalization of theological thinking
(after-thinking) which recognizes in sexual difference the ground for
representing our relationship to God, will intensify the aporetic structure
of our account. To answer our question of the belonging together of man
and woman in space and time as an apperception of the ungraspable
belonging of the world to God is thus to attend repeatedly to the
analogical nature of our representations as *temporally structured*. (That is,
to invoke another idiom, to think through representations as *performance*.)
Theology does not pass beyond time in a representation of the eternal, for,
as Balthasar writes:

> Problems do not exist in order to be solved; we can never get
> 'behind' Being ... Problems should always become more luminous
> in the light of the great mystery in which we live, move and have
> our being. (GOW 21)

Can we provide an account that begins to free us from a tyranny of
spatialization and opens us ecstatically to the experience of time as the
patience of God expressed in the coming forth of God? Where patience
refers not to that which is temporally or indefinitely postponed, but to
that which, in the light of the incarnation, allows creation to dwell with
God in the light of grace. How can this be represented – the patience of
God in the coming forth of the Word? Is it possible that something like
this is to be discovered in Balthasar's 'third' account of sexual difference
represented in the interleaving of the christological and marian doctrines
of the *admirabile commercium* and the *immaculate conception*?

Mary: the temporal 'between'
We now return to Balthasar's argument in the third volume of his *Theo–
Drama* in order to consider his presentation of a dramatic Mariology in
the context of his account of what it means to become a person in Christ.
And here we shall suggest that Balthasar's dogmatic trajectory begins to
open up a new possibility for thinking through the *chiasm* of creation (as
the coincidence of the timing of place and the placing of time) as it is given
to us in the relationship between Christ and Mary. To understand this, we
must keep before us the endeavour to think of the world as always a
threshold and not as beginning or coming to an end at a threshold – that
is, as a collapsing of time into space. For to think of the world as threshold
(openness to God) is to think of the gifted *chiasm* of time and space
(creation) as the juncture or crossing point where the Word becomes flesh.
And this as no mathematical point, but precisely in *the event of reception*.

    To begin with a preliminary sketch of the structure of Balthasar's
argument. If our argument thus far has considered the section 'Woman as
answer', we now turn to the fourth part of this section: 'Mariology II:
Mary as dramatic character.' It is here that Balthasar outlines his own
'new start' that reveals 'Mary as a genuinely dramatic role in the
theodrama'. Balthasar begins this section with the claim that 'Mary is a

dramatic character above all because her existence lies between all *status* of human nature' (TD II.2, 293; ThD 3, 318).

This is demonstrated in consideration of her being 'between' three pairs of timing: between paradise and fall, between Old and New Covenant, and finally and most fundamental of all, between time and eternity. Balthasar explains that she exists,

> not only between belonging to [*Zugehörigkeit*: belonging-to-ness] the old covenant, to the time of Christ and to that of the Church; rather further reaching between a paradisal (supralapsarian) existence and one such in its fallen state, but also eschatologically between the latter and the final fulfilment. Thus she appears to be nowhere really at home apart from [*außer* – outside of] in her Son who endures and overcomes the same tensions, or finally in a Church that should at least endure them but for the most part does not want to. This synthesis of all *status* in Mary has understandably prepared great difficulties for theology, and a final glimpse on to the 'how' of her being one has not been granted even with the binding formulations which have been arrived at after long, hard work. (TD II.2, 293; ThD 3, 318–9)

Immediately apparent in this outline is the appearance of the temporal ecstasies – of the past, present and future of 'salvation history'; ecstasies which reach their 'greatest tension' in 'the last, eschatological tension between time and eternity'. However, if time emerges as a predominant theme in this section of Balthasar's Mariology, we must not regard this as simply offsetting and thereby correcting the diachronic ordering that determined his account in 'Woman as answer'. If the *epoche* of temporality is lifted and the 'first' and 'second' of sexual difference yield to the flow of salvation history, still this logic continues to order this configuration – which is precisely its intended effect as anterior ground.

The appearance of these *three* pairs, then, in so far as they serve to characterize time, serves to disrupt the telling of time as *two* in its spatialization into two discrete moments – a before and an after. More-over, the description of Mary as oscillating between the 'poles' of each of these comparisons similarly suggests that two will not suffice to tell the passing of time. At the same time, however, each of these comparisons does continue to work with the logic of two – of two poles, or sites, between which Mary can oscillate. Thus, the problem of the telling of time – which is, of course, the creature's riddle – is wrapped in this difficult mariological representation.

Briefly, Mary is apparently located in a state of oscillation *between* the pairs of three temporal comparisons, and between these comparisons themselves. However, as we would now expect, this ordering is spatially determined. Mary both belongs to the time of Old and New Covenants and is also a space in which these can belong together.[71] Likewise, Mary

---

71 Perhaps, then, it is also in the belonging to each other of the partners of each of these pairs and of these three pairs to each other that Mary's existence is to be seen as 'between belonging-to-ness'.

both belongs to the time of paradise and fall and is also a space in which both can belong. In both these cases, her dual function is secured by the anterior ground of her dual nature as woman. However, in the third comparison, between eternity and time, this problematic is intensified in that the logic of spatialization is at once fixed and undone as it unravels according to a deconstructive momentum that we began to trace with reference to the time before time – the so-called time of the *Mensch* 'before' sexual differentiation.

Mary: the a-temporal 'between'

For Mary, the issue is quite simply this. If Mary can in some way be between and around the times of paradise and fall, Old and New Covenants, how can this be said of time and eternity? The temporal marking that locates the passage from one space to the next in the first two comparisons can in no way hold for the third comparison. If paradise and fall and Old and New Covenants will yield to a spatialization of time, how so time and eternity? It is precisely this third comparison that will not yield to the anterior logic of spacing that provokes a dislocation in Balthasar's argument at the point of the relationship of time to eternity. For the relationship of time to eternity cannot be that of time to not-time; eternity does not, cannot only, begin where time has not yet begun, nor where time ends. One cannot tell the time of the beginning of eternity as one cannot mark the time of its borders. Such a telling would be to forget, or to misread, the analogical prefix *über*, to forget the sense in which eternity must embrace and include time and is not merely its 'beyond'. Or, to put this another way, where – or more precisely *when* – could 'between' time and eternity be? There is no such place or time, no moment outside of time and eternity – such a place, such a time, is nowhere, no time – and certainly neither a place nor a time for an existence, however much 'between'.

Now this is not to suggest that Balthasar's argument falls apart (it is unclear what this would mean), but it is to suggest that the issue of sexual difference comes to light as the question of the timing of time; and this as inflected in Balthasar's account of Christ and Mary in their *representative* roles, for in Mary's 'between-ness' lies the key to her representation. What this means is that the aporetic structure of time (of exchange and recognition) comes into view in Balthasar's account precisely at the point where telling the time as timing (spacing) fails to account for the encounter between Christ and Mary as eschatological agents – that is, as dramatic persons gathering up and representing creation in an ordering to redemption, to eternity. The elision of time in Balthasar's protological scene thus begins to unravel against an eschatological horizon whose precise concern is how the Christ can redeem the world.

Thus if, as we argued above, a phenomenology of sexual difference cannot properly achieve this, then it is of some note that Balthasar, in developing his Mariology (which must always be linked organically to Christology) reaches for an ancient logic of the Church's meditation upon the mystery of salvation: the idea of theological representation. Why is this so? Why, in order to present the mystery of God's encounter with his creation in the person of Jesus Christ born of a woman, does the idea of representation come to the fore?

Theodramatik, *representation and exchange*

In the Introduction to the fourth volume of the *Theo-Drama* entitled *Die Handlung* – *The Action* (or *Commerce*) – Balthasar remarks:

> A special concern [*or* approach] of this volume is the exact out-working of the concept of representation [*Stellvertretung*: place taking; stepping into (another's) place; *or* place exchange] which has suddenly stepped into the light after a period of forgotten-ness. (TD III, 11; ThD 4, 11)[72]

Thus, what is brought into view in the idiom of theological representation is the event of *exchange* in all its differing modalities. Moreover, representation in its very movement traces the time of exchanges as an exchanging of time, and not as some eternal view upon a preordained event. Thus, if we are to understand Balthasar's linkage of Mariology to Christology in terms of theological representation, this is because it involves the gathering of the *diastasis* of creation into the time of salvation (a gathering which is properly *without* reduction). In short, creation and salvation are not two discrete events diachronically ordered, but rather the event in which Christ as the representative gathers to himself and through himself the *diastasis* of creation riven by sin; that is, the event of Christ. Creation and salvation belong together and it is precisely this that inaugurates a radical exchange; or, indeed, is the icon of exchange – the coincidence of God and creature – which demands a new telling of time and space.

In dogmatic terms, to follow Balthasar here involves tracing the interleaving of the doctrines of the *admirabile commercium* (the wonderful exchange of places) with that of the immaculate conception (the sinless receptivity of Mary). Thus we must briefly consider the forms of representation undertaken by Christ and Mary.

Christological and mariological representation: on exchanging places

For Balthasar the form of christological representation is dependent upon his identification of Christ as the concrete *analogia entis*, which involves a profound reconfiguration of the patristic idea of *admirabile commercium* – the 'wonderful exchange of places'. In short, the determination of the event of salvation (Balthasar's singular treatment of the theme of *kenosis*)[73]

---

72 We should note, however, that the renewal of the theme of representation has already been determined by the initial decision to develop a theo-dramatic theory, for 'the outworking of the analogy between God's action and the world-play . . . is no mere metaphor but is grounded ontologically [*seinshaft*: according to being]'. Moreover, as Balthasar comments at the very beginning of the *Theo-Drama*, the dramatic encounter and exchange of God with his creature is but 'a play within the play: our play plays in his play' (TD I, 20; ThD 1, 20). And if this is so, then we are always already within the realm of representation and Balthasar can conclude, '[t]hat existence should represent itself [*sich darstelle*] dramatically, is thus a basic Christian demand' (TD I, 21; ThD 1, 22). Thus, as Balthasar turns to the idea of theological representation in order to present the drama of salvation, so analogy steps into the light as a logic of participation.

73 See Graham Ward's essay, 'Kenosis: Death, Discourse and Resurrection' (Chapter 2).

is given in terms of the *topos* or place of the Son, who is within himself the miraculous unity of divinity and humanity. Balthasar can therefore write:

> The Son . . . does not need . . . to change his own 'place' [*Stelle*] when . . . he undertakes the 'representation' [*Stell-Vertretung*: place-exchange; compare *Platztausch* earlier on the same page] of the world. He can do this on the basis of his *topos* of his inner divine absolute difference from the gifting Father. (TD III, 310; ThD 4, 334)

And this *topos*, this 'absolute distance', is 'confirmed and held open' and 'carried over to the divinity as the common, absolute gift' by the Spirit, who proceeds from Father and Son (TD III, 310; ThD 4, 333).

Following Bernard of Clairvaux, Balthasar expounds Mary's representative role as mediatorial[74] – she is situated *between* Christ and the Church – and all that this entails. Her *topos* is in the between: between paradise and fall, between the Old and New Covenants, between redemption and sanctification, and, most importantly, between time and eternity – and her place is ours. Mary's place as representative of humanity is 'in between'. This is the form of her representation; but it is also that which she has to represent.

There are, then, critical links between *diastasis*, *topos* and representation in the configuration of the economy of salvation. Moreover, the laws of representation at work in the mediator and mediatrix are different – differences which, for Balthasar, are inseparable from sexual difference. In christological representation, Christ is understood to stand on both sides of the God/world relation, for christological representation is iconic: both dual and commutative, both two ways and from two places to each other. Christ represents God to humanity and humanity to God. In mariological representation, however, Mary stands forever 'in between' as *type* – type of humanity, of the Church, of finite freedom: this logic is dual but non-commutative. Mary represents humanity to God and humanity to humanity.

These two modalities of representation, then, are not the same; they are necessarily not identical. But for all this they *belong together*. The representations of Christ and Mary are ordered to one another, they are configured so as to open the time of belonging together (in a series of different ways), which imitates no second-hand or poor approximation at instantaneous unity. If 'Adam' comes to himself instantly in the disappearance of Eve in no time at all (which is perhaps what modernity calls eternity), then Christ comes to the world by coming to Mary in the *patience (becoming) of generation*. Christ does not grasp himself as the Man would strive to do, but in and through an anterior *Urkenosis*[75] gathers all to himself by handing himself over to the Other. In this sense, then, the transcription of divine dispossession into creaturely reality can be recognized in time, or more properly in the timing of time which

---

74 See, e.g. TD II.2, 293–311; ThD 3, 318–39.
75 Balthasar's use of the idea of *Urkenosis* – an anteriority of a certain kind – is taken up in the next section.

we experience in the syntheses of gathering together, of re-ception (*Empfangen*) and re-presentation.[76]

It is precisely this belonging together that we now have to think. For here what we have to reckon with is not phenomenological asymmetry (and so the threat of violence) but thinking the possibility of the togetherness of infinite and finite freedom in the timed performance of Mary's *fiat*. Or, as Balthasar notes at the centre of the very first volume of his magisterial trilogy, in the destiny of an experience of 'the generosity of God through the patience of becoming' (H I, 327; GL 1, 339).

The immaculate circle?

In Mary, Balthasar suggests, God receives from creation the answer for which he has longed, but which he in no sense needs. But God is implicated in Mary's answer (just as the Father is implicated in the Son's obedient response to him). How? If the arrival of the angel Gabriel to Mary in the annunciation is not to mark the occasion of her rape, a violation of a woman and her body, Mary's consent to bear God's Word in her body, to become the *topos* of incarnation, must be completely free, immaculate. And yet, to be completely free and pure in this sense requires a gift, the gift of grace. If the giving of these gifts – freedom and grace – are not themselves to be a violation, then Mary must have *always already* received them; they must have been with her since her conception. The dogma of the immaculate conception is configured to the annunciation.

Here, perhaps, synchrony raises its head in another guise, that of the Althusserian 'always already' which returns us once again to a decision taken against time. However, *at the same time*, these gifts can only be given *as a result of* the fact and the event of the cross which occurs *after* their arrival; they are totally dependent upon the timed birth, life, death and resurrection of the Son whom Mary consents to bear before they happen.[77]

So, then, two characters, Christ and Mary, are held in an unbreakable, indissoluble circle of reciprocal priority each to the other, in which

> it is unarguable, that the priority of the 'immaculate' [that is, 'unmarked'] 'yes-word' is indebted to grace and the fullness of grace 'earned' on the cross, but whereupon it is just as clear that the possibility of this fullness on the cross must also be indebted to the yes-word of the mother. (TD II.2, 323–4; ThD 3, 352)

Here is a circle in which 'the effect is cause of the cause' (TD II.2, 273; ThD 3, 297) – a circle which suggests no phenomenological first, but rather the *provocation* of a crisis in the telling of the time. Balthasar claims, then, that this 'circle' of the immaculate conception is the very heart of the mystery of the encounter between finite and infinite, or divine and human, freedoms.

But is this infinitely spinning circle *salvation* – the fecundity of a 'free reception and infinite return'? Or does this circle spatialize time, albeit

---

76 Thus the ground for our thesis: something like time, something like the sexes.
77 See John Milbank's comments on Mary's reception and receptivity, 'Can a gift be given?' *Modern Theology* 11:1, p. 136.

womanly time again? In what sense does the immaculate conception deconstruct the fabrication of sexual difference through the phenomenal disappearance of woman as other? In Irigaray's terms, are we still to find here the manufacture of a 'femininity' which is precisely 'the father's indispensable intermediary in putting his law into force'[78] – a construction bound to condemnation, the condemnation of women and men to a static, essentialized account of their differences?

The inauguration of time

What would be required here to answer such a charge? Well, perhaps at least this, that the 'circle', 'in which the effect is the cause of the cause', finds space to begin *in time*. Or, in learning, as Balthasar suggests in the introduction to the first volume of the *Theo-Drama*, that '*Now* must be questioned and played [*or Now* one must question and play]: there is a Too-late' (TD I, 21; ThD 1, 22).[79]

This then is the issue of the binding of christological and mariological representation, where the question is precisely that of the inauguration of time. Of something new – of a beginning in time. A novelty that must be told, in the telling of the timing of the introduction of the stage, the opening of the play-room, which arrives only in the Word's becoming flesh, and yet which is also, as the Second Letter to Timothy would have it, 'the gift of grace given to us in Christ Jesus before times eternal [χρόνων αἰωνίων], but manifested now through the appearance of our Saviour Christ Jesus' (2 Tim. 1.9–10).

The inauguration of time is the 'temporal clue' set before us in Mary's reception of the Word, which is the bearing, and becoming of a child. For this cannot be a 'second miracle' (Karl Barth) alone, second, that is, to the first miracle of creation in which we are 'distanced' from God; rather it must be to us the 'always overtaking' of God's love for the world. For sure, Christ lived on earth in place and time, but not as it were as a second act in his divine existence, or to his pre-existence.

Creation, redemption and the reception of time

We are to tell time in God's coming to the world in the Word made flesh. We are, as it were, to tell time on the undecidable limit of the outside with the inside – of the difference of the world from God (*diastasis*) which allows, bears, a creaturely integrity and freedom interleaved with (ordered to) the difference that God (outside) enjoys with himself. We should not tell this difference as a counting or folding back, nor even as a bracketing out, but only in the performance of reception. The ordering of God's life is not analogous to the order of time (as serial succession) but rather to the timing of time as its becoming – the event of reception.

In this context Balthasar's recovery of a theological account of representation as operating as a logic of threshold inexorably supports, as

---

78 *Marine Lover*, p. 95.
79 We return to this locution in our conclusion, for we shall argue that it harbours within its silent binding of these two clauses the 'temporal clue' to the divine life we are here developing. It is but another performance of that logic which would have grace prepare nature for the reception of grace.

it undermines, any mimetic recovery of that which is represented – which is to say the transcription of divine life into finitude. But it does not do this by way of some miraculous overturning of finitude. Rather, in one of Balthasar's favourite metaphors, God in the Son *overtakes* the finitude of human being precisely as its enjoys its existence as always existence-in-relation (relations, and so encounters, marked by time and space). Balthasar's proximity to, engagement with and distancing from the thought of Hegel at this point is treated by both Ward (Chapter 2) and Quash (Chapter 4) in this volume.

Finite human being cannot alone cope with nor gather up all the words and acts that could be posited, or presented to it, in any given set of circumstances. For the human being is dependent, and more radically so by way of origin. This is again and again his or her experience of space and time – becoming so easily the prison of existence from which he or she seeks the key. But this trembling of creation (*dia-stasis*) is the ground of creaturely *ek-stasis*, for creation is the time and place where representations and proxies are inevitable (gifted) and this not merely contractually or historically but ontologically. Most profoundly, then, representation is grounded in the relational existence of human being. Representation is originary to (it bears) human being – it is not the name of an a priori horizon.

Time is the gift of exchange, which is to say it is that which allows what is not identical to belong together, through and in its patience, so to speak. And this is precisely a patience with 'where' things are: side-by-side, near and far, proximate and distanced. The fecundity of free reception and infinite return in the dramatic encounter between Mary and Christ sets before us the 'order' of this event of belonging together as precisely the order of God belonging with himself transposed (through creation and the creature's belonging to God) into the order of creaturely generation.[80]

The grace Christ gives to Mary is the grace of reception (life) – which is the inauguration of time won on the cross – as the patience of becoming. But more than this, this transposition of belonging together is no mere dwelling side by side (rubbing up against the edges) but more a dwelling within of creaturely dependence and growth – the bearing of a child. Creation as *diastasis* is, as it were, overtaken from within as it has always been but now comes to be. And so we witness the irrevocable proximity that temporal difference enjoys with sexual difference: that is to say, the 'spring' of origin (*Ursprung*) into becoming: generation.

So, then, the 'second miracle' of incarnation does not overturn this; rather Christ comes to dwell in this world through the overtaking, the exceeding, of creaturely representation. He is borne by a mother but on the condition that he bears her. How?

Christ, time and the representation of creation

As we have already noted Balthasar writes:

80 Our exposition of Balthasar's thought at this point parallels and participates in his much commented upon 'trinitarian inversion' (TD II.2, 167ff; ThD 3, 183ff). This is, as it were, to construe the difficulty of trinitarian representation as the problem of time; time is *time*'s problem, not God's.

> The Son ... does not need ... to change his own 'place' [*Stelle*] when
> ... he undertakes the 'representation' [*Stell-Vertretung*] of the world.
> He can do this on the basis of his *topos* of his inner divine absolute
> difference from the gifting Father. (TD III, 310; ThD 4, 334)

The Son, then, does not swap or substitute places with anyone according
to a place they already hold (hold, that is, in the time–space of creation).
But nor, as seemed the fate of woman, does Christ become the place in
which other exchanges occur, which amounts to the other side of the same
coin.

Rather, he is the exchanging of places (the exchanging of exchange)
and this 'on the basis of his *topos* of his inner divine absolute difference
from the gifting Father'. He is the exchanging of the here and now
'becoming' of creation for what it is that allows and bears the marking of
this present place as a place of freedom. A place in which I am already
gifted into relationship, into reception. To represent creation, then, does
not require a prior decision on time (which amounts to its spatialization)
but only that Mary should utter her 'yes' as response – that is, in freedom.
One could almost say that this 'yes' is accidental – it just happens, occurs,
becomes, in a place, in a human person – *in a voice*.

And this time of utterance, although long prepared, is also the
inauguration of time; no moment, point or sheer presence, but the
displacement of time – its ownmost *aporia* – inclined to the place of its
belonging. That is to say, something like time in God demands that this
time is not erased (and so with it every other time). And this space of
utterance is no empty container which marks the limits. Mary is no void
waiting to be filled with God, but the already excessive possibility of
human living in its prodigality.

Anteriority as the ontological difference?
However, in all that we have said thus far, we must note that a
fundamental dimension of Balthasar's account has remained almost un-
named. A dimension which, as it were, should bring us to name the
belonging together of time and space as the belonging together of the
events of salvation. The issue is this.

If time and space belong together as the possibility of free reception,
and in this they do not plot an a priori horizon or screen from which
things (the giftedness of creation) may be received, then the difference
they mark is, as it were, the difference of receiving gifts – the gift's arrival.
But still the gift, the entity, the being, is there to be received and it is this
which demands that we name in some way the difference of being and
Being – that is to say, the difference of the ontological difference.

This does not mean that we now set out to discover an 'older difference'
to that of the *aporias* of space and time – and thus a difference into which
they can be folded. This means only that the arrival of anything, if it is to
be received, is precisely the arrival of everything – or rather a participation in Being-as-a-whole, *Das Ganze im Fragment*. Being arrives in beings
(and beings in Being) precisely in the differencing of the difference which
allows beings to stand out, not merely as things or locations, but as the
continual arrival of Being itself in its sheer poverty and fullness together.

To remark at this juncture on the ontological difference (in an essay on analogy in Balthasar's theology) is not, as it were, to open up a new avenue of thought. It is, rather, to name a central thought in and through which both sexual and theological difference are always thought for Balthasar: Being gives itself in beings; to be is to be given. This is the *analogia entis*, the arrival of a difference. It is also, then, in some sense the arrival of Christ, understood as 'the concrete *analogia entis*': Christ lives as the arrival of time and difference; it is thinking upon *this* life that onto-logical and theological difference can be understood as always arriving together. This can too easily, and once again, become a valorized interval. Moreover, as such it can also become a fixed and finite interval (even if an 'infinite abyss') between the creature and God.

It is part of the intention of this essay to demonstrate the negotiations and elisions involved in Balthasar's attempt to speak of the *analogia entis* as precisely no valorized interval, as no fixed gap between the world and God, but as the granting of (and so reception of) a participation in participation. It will be our claim in the next section that to recognize this involves thinking through the interleaving differences of creation (including the difference of the world from God) which for Balthasar can never be thought apart from any claim made on the ontological difference. For thought of the ontological difference will always provoke thought of the beginning – of creation (even in its denial) – precisely in the recog-nition and reception of the givenness of Being.

We turn, therefore, to attend to the matter which is now unavoidable in this thinking both with and against Balthasar; that is, his orchestration of 'the secret law of analogy'.

The order of thought

Perhaps it is indeed on the side of analogy rather than identity, that we will have to search for the site of the 'principles of thought' in order to fathom more deeply the secret play of their oppositions.

Jean-François Mattei

Thus far we have traced the themes of sexual difference and time as they occur in, and order, Balthasar's theodramatic telling of the ordering of creation to redemption. In so doing we have also remarked upon their binding in this history of salvation. In this section, we turn to consider the *theo*-logical significance of each of these themes, not only in telling the order of creation and redemption but also in telling the events of creation and redemption as events occurring from within the divine life. In the first two subsections (A. Something like time and B. Something like the sexes), we find that the telling of this participation provokes the sugges-tion that there is *something like time* and *something like the sexes* in the trinitarian differencing. This brings us to the third subsection (C. The analogy of becoming and the coming to be of analogy) and a consideration of the thoughtful structure of this analogical participation in the divine life.

A. Something like time

Telling the time and the timing of creation

In what time can the immaculate conception occur? In what time can *Mary* open her lips in order for *Christ* to utter and perform God's loving 'yes' to creation and creation's responsive and receptive 'yes' to God? The only time in which these creative events can happen is created time, and yet they also have their part to play in the creation of time. We thus turn to a contemplation of the world's beginning, and so to the origin of time or the very timing of time. And this, we suggest, is the issue of the event and the timing of analogy – an event which, in Balthasar's thought, is in danger of being collapsed into the synchrony of a gendered priority (or the priority of gender). For the timing of analogy, which is the timing of time, is also the analogy of analogy. This should properly be the occurrence of analogy, or the participation in participation, but in the attempt to ground it in something entirely other (woman, for example) it can tend towards an expulsion from analogy.

Here, then, we would learn to tell the time in a way which does not attempt a 'timeless' account of time. This attempt to tell time should in no way represent an attempt to get 'beyond', 'before' or 'away from' time into an eternity or infinitude from which time has (always) already (a priori) been excluded. It refuses any such exclusion of time from eternity and infinitude, but remains, nevertheless, an attempt to tell the relationship of time to eternity and infinitude.

In this, the timed telling of the timing of time is aporetic. For this telling of time must itself be timed in at least two senses: (1) this *telling* of time is timed, because *we* are timed and all our speech and understanding is likewise timed; but (2), this telling of *time* is timed, for, since 'beyond' or 'before' time there is neither nothing nor not-time (which is to say that 'before' time is not the negation of time), the beginning of time happens, as it were, only in time, only as a timed event.

And in these two senses of being timed there is also at least a similar double sense in which the beginning of time must be told analogically: (1) to speak otherwise would be to posit 'super' time or 'time' outside time, therefore we must speak analogically of that which is not time (but is not not-time) as if it *were* time; but also (2) time's relationship to its own beginning is analogical – and this is the significance of the inverted commas about 'before' and 'beyond' in the attempts to tell time's beginning. To tell the timing and the origins of time is to speak of beginning, and is thus also to speak of the beginning and the temporality of analogy.

How, then, does time come to be? How can it ever occur? What is the nature of its creation?

The grounding of difference and trinitarian differencing

For Balthasar, all difference and all distance (including the difference of the creation from God, and ultimately the distance of the sinner from God) can only occur within the infinite difference of the Son from the Father. All difference and distance (including the infinite distance of the Son from the Father which is the Son's procession from the Father as far as the descent into hell and his apparently paradoxical return) occurs within God. But, as John Milbank has eloquently argued, this ('original') difference between the Father and the Son itself also only occurs within the Spirit's (a 'second') difference from them both. The Spirit, however, also only receives *this* difference of *its* identity as God in its apparently prior procession from Father and Son.[81]

This 'trinitarian differencing', by virtue of which each of the three Persons (including the Father) receives its identity as a Person and as God, and also its non-identity with the other two Persons, is the 'event' of God. It is the 'event' of the identity of the Triune God, for this differencing also *is* God. It is only within this eternal event (only within God) that any other event can occur. This is true of the event of creation and so of the creation of time.

But, more than this, Balthasar claims that

> inner-worldly Becoming [*Werden*] is an image [*Abbild*] of the eternal Happening [*Geschehens*] in God, which is, as such, ... identical with the eternal Being [*Sein*] or Nature [*Wesen*]. (TD IV, 59)

Becoming and coming to be in the world are a copy of – are analogous to – the eternal Happening of God, which is God. *There is, then, something like becoming in God (God's Happening), such that created becoming is like something in God.* But there are important differences to be maintained in these likenesses. The eternal trinitarian 'event' which is God is not a 'becoming' in the worldly sense of the coming to be of something that at some time was not. In the 'event' or 'happening' of God, God 'becomes' God (God 'happens') in God's being God. God 'is' only (in) this 'Becoming'; God is this 'Happening'. But this should not suggest that God becomes something that God was not, nor that God becomes something that God is not. This would be to posit a beginning or an end for God, and to understand analogy in the 'wrong' direction.

The direction and asymmetry of analogy and the conjecture of God

For, properly speaking, the world does not bear an analogy to God such that God is analogous to the world. Analogy has ultimately only one proper direction, which means that we can never deduce or induce what God must be like from an observation of the world (from phenomenology, for example). In such a case one would argue that since 'becoming' in the world implies a change in being, requires a not-being and then a coming-to-be, or a being and then a ceasing-to-be (requires, that is, finitude – beginnings and ends to being), then, if God 'becomes' anything in any sense (even 'God'), God either was not God, or God must cease to be God. Rather, the world bears an analogy to God such that its reflection upon its possession of a reflection of God can allow it to *conjecture* God, and so allow it to understand itself as like God, but always more like God than God is like it.

81 See note 13.

This 'analogy of becoming', then, in which we can *appropriately*, if always inadequately and with a proper reticence, speak of a certain 'becoming' in and of God which is identical with God's very Being, is not 'another' analogy alongside the analogy of being. It is rather the very same analogy: the relationship between infinitude and finitude *is the same as* the relationship between infinite Being and finite beings, such that neither being nor becoming (neither space nor time) can be seen as grounded in or privileged over the other. Both must always be seen as belonging together.

This thoroughgoing analogy, this rigorous account of the nature of the asymmetric, sacred ordering of the world as created by God and as reflecting and 'containing' its Creator, is the ancient telling of the world with which Balthasar interrupts modernity's account of the abyss and limit between the infinite and the finite. For in modernity's account, time has been excluded from eternity and eternity excluded from time, to the extent that that infinitude has in fact been limited by the finite: the infinite starts where the finite stops, but then the infinite is no longer infinite, limitless and without end, but has become another finite.

In Balthasar we are presented with a contrary logic: there must be something like becoming in God, which in being something like worldly, finite becoming, is also something not like it. Thus, in response to the question 'Is there suffering in God?' (in the sense of 'Does God suffer?'), he can reply:

> There is in God the point of departure for that which can become suffering, if the carelessness [*Vorsichtslosigkeit*] with which the Father gives himself (and everything that is his) away ... encounters a freedom which does not reply [*or* correspond] to this carelessness, but rather transforms it into the care of wanting-to-begin-by-oneself. (TD III, 305; ThD 4, 328)

His is a resolute account of the participation of the world in God, of beings in Being, and of time in eternity, such that God can be present not only *to* the world but *in* the world, such that Being can be present to and in beings, and such that time occurs within the eternal eventing of eternity. This account of analogy as participation – the world only *is* at all in its being in God, *and* God is in the world – also draws attention to the asymmetry of analogy and hierarchy. In so far as it is a ratio at all, analogy is always a proportion of disproportion. It is a linkage of likeness, but not the symmetrical mirroring of two similar things measurable one against the other. The *world* can *only* be within God's Being, whereas *God* is *also* without and outside the world. In this sense the world is more like God than God is like the world: the image is more like, more defined by its likeness to that which it images, than the 'original' is like or defined by its image or copy.

The analogy of being on this reading, therefore, is not based upon two terms (God and world, or Being and being) having become co-terminus in their sharing of a prior, common, third term which can be known apart from these two ('to be'). It is, rather, the participation of the second within the first, the asymmetric relation of two without 'a' third. And yet, there is a relationship between two and three to be told here.

The originary moment of Urkenosis

To learn analogy (to learn analogically) is always to learn identity and difference together. In what ways is worldly becoming *like* divine Becoming? In what ways is it different? And what is divine Becoming *like*? To suggest that there is between God and the world an analogy of becoming which is the analogy of being is already to suggest that there is a 'movement' in and of Being, even in God's being God. This movement in God, a movement which is *of* God and which also *is* God, is that which we have named 'trinitarian differencing'. It is the differences between and the differencing of the Persons of the Trinity; and it is thus also the *ordering* of God. Balthasar traces the ordering of this differencing and of these relationships in a controversial explication of the unfolding of the Father's *Urkenosis*.

Following Sergei Bulgakov, Balthasar describes the self-expression of the Father in begetting the Son as a 'first, inner-divine *"kenosis"* which undergirds everything' (TD III, 300). In this *Urkenosis*, the Father dispossesses himself of his Godhead, without remainder, and hands it over into the possession of the Son, such that he does not share his Godhead with the Son in the sense of apportioning certain parts of it to the Son and the rest to himself.[82] At the same time, the Father does not 'exist' in any sense 'before' or 'apart' from this handing over or *Urkenosis*. He is (only in) this handing over, just as the Son only is (in) his reception of the Godhead. This giving and receiving are two different possibilities for participating in the identical Godhead: there is no Father without Son and no Son without Father, and no God without either. But Father and Son have also never been without the Spirit, without their breathing together, without the un-over-takable Love which is both their separation and their bond.

This 'not temporally-processory *Urdrama* of God' (TD III, 303) is for Balthasar, as for Adrienne von Speyr, the *irreversible ordering* or hierarchy within God:

> These emergences in God are without doubt not free in the sense of an arbitrariness, even if there is no necessity which is foreign to God which underlies God; they correspond to a will of nature or necessity in God, which grounds an irreversible order from Father to Son and from Father and Son to Spirit, which, there where this will of necessity is 'recapitulated' 'to its very grounding' in absolute freedom, represents a 'hierarchy' which is also valid in the absolute freedom of the Persons. And precisely this 'is the *Ur*-form of freedom. In order to be able to be free, a will must be within a hierarchy.' (TD IV, 77; quotations are from Adrienne von Speyr, *Die Welt des Gebetes* (*The World of Prayer*), pp. 50–1.)

---

82 This distinction is protected in Balthasar's playful distinction between *mitteilen* (to communicate) and *teilen mit* (to share with).

The ordering of the three Persons of the Trinity, therefore, is to be understood as a certain becoming. This gives rise to the suggestion that *there is something like time in God*: a differencing which can only be conjectured or imagined in terms of 'something like time', such that there can be movement and genuine giving, receiving and exchange – the movements and differences constitutive of the Persons themselves and so constitutive of God. Bound together with this perception are the suggestions that time is grounded in eternity, that the difference of the world from God only comes to be within trinitarian differencing, within the divine, eternal, unending, originless, originary Becoming, which nevertheless has its eternal 'origin' in the primacy of the Father.

However, it is at precisely this point in his thought, and his commentary upon the thought of Speyr, that sexual difference comes into view, such that we cannot follow the conversion and transcription of the divine Becoming in(to) time and the generation of the Son into the act of creation in the unfolding of the world out of Trinity, without first returning to attend to this motif.

B. Something like (the) sexes

Divine sexuality?

These 'divine emergences', which 'happen in eternal simultaneity'[83] (TD IV, 76; *Die Welt des Gebetes*, p. 223), present us with a particular configuration of 'active' and 'passive' in the exchanges of the Becoming of these Persons: the Father actively hands over Godhead to the Son; the Son responds to this handing over with his own handing over; in his reception, in his taking, then, the Son is both 'active' and 'passive'. Both reception and handing over contain a certain thankfulness, such that even in his handing over, the Father is thankful to the Son for allowing himself to be begotten, and is similarly thankful with the Son to the Spirit for allowing itself to be breathed. This 'thankfulness' thus reveals a certain passivity in the Father's active act which is defined by the passive act of the reception and 'allowing-to-happen' [*Geschehenlassen*] of Son and Spirit. In the complex interplays between action, activity and passivity, and between an 'imprinting love' and a 'loving allowing-to-happen', Balthasar and Speyr perceive an 'interpretability' within creation of the dualisms 'between act and potential, between action and contemplation, and between the sexual differences'[84] (TD IV, 77). There is within God an irreducible duality: the duality of three.

And this language is 'already' conditioned by the analogy between these differences and sexual differences in that the relationship between Father and Son is imagined, indeed witnessed (*gezeugt*) to, as a Begetting (*Zeugung*). And yet it is not only, or even primarily, within the relationship of Father to Son that we find the exchanges which are to be reflected in creaturely regeneration. The divine Being, God (and thus that

---

83 *Gleichzeitigkeit*, '(at-the-)same-timeness': the significance of this recurrent theme of simultaneity will become one focus of our conclusion.

84 It is of note that Balthasar speaks here of sexual *differences* rather than simply of a (fixed) sexual difference as in his mariological phenomenology.

which we have named the divine Becoming), consists in the exchanges between Father, Son and Spirit. Balthasar and Speyr name this giving and receiving of identity, non-identity and even 'property', which is trinitarian differencing, as the 'liveliness of the eternal Love' (TD IV, 79). And this 'liveliness of the eternal Love' is the 'original unity of action and contemplation ... within the divine Being [*Wesens*] as in the creation' (TD IV, 79; *Die Welt des Gebetes*, pp. 35–6). Which is to say that it must also be the differentiation of action and contemplation and even unity.

From the creaturely side, this divine unity of acting and allowing-to-happen is only to be seen and learnt in its translation into the temporal, a translation which occurs only in and via the sexual:

> Finally [*Endlich*], the divine unity of Doing and Letting-happen – whose equal-worth was shown in Love – translates itself worldly-ly into two-genderedness [*Zweigeschlechtlichkeit*: double sexuality]. (TD IV, 80)

And this, such that there is not only *something like becoming* in God, but also *something like the sexes*, not only in an irreducible duality, but also in an irreducible three-ness:

> Trinitarianly, the Father appears as the [masculine] originless Begetter admittedly primarily (super-)manly; the Son [appears] to start with as the One-allowing to happen as (super-)womanly, but then again as the One actively Breathing together with the Father as (super-)manly; [and] the Spirit [appears] as (super-)womanly. And in that the Father, as has been shown, in his begetting and breathing allows himself always already to be defined with and through the Ones processing from him, there lies even in him the (Super-) Womanly, without thereby his order-primacy being touched. (TD IV, 80)

The ascription is contentious and dangerous, doubly so in its coupling with the suggestion of something like a divine Becoming. And of this Balthasar is acutely aware. For, whilst something like becoming has indeed been conjectured in God, this is only alongside the denial that there is any becoming in the eternal life of God. A denial which in turn repudiates itself in the assertion that there is nevertheless the 'ever-more, the surprise of love', which despite the eternal event and movement cannot be understood as being any change 'in God's view' (TD IV, 79). A similar ban is placed on the 'direction' in which the analogy of sexuality and fruitfulness is to be understood:

> But precisely that which is Trinitarian about God forbids a projection of the worldly-genderly into the divinity ...; one must suffice oneself with seeing the ever new opposition of doing and letting-happen, which on its [his?] side is a form of activity and fruitfulness, as the over-powering origin of that which in the created Life-world is translated into fruitfulness as the form and making-possible of love and its [love's] fruitfulness. (TD IV, 80)

Our question to Balthasar's text is whether he can satisfy his own ban – or whether he projects the worldly-genderly and the individuality of creaturely differences into the Godhead. Indeed, can he do otherwise?

C. The analogy of becoming and the coming to be of analogy

Analogy and origin: the translation and interpretation of God
Before tracing the theme of sexual difference and fruitfulness further, let us return to the beginning of time and analogy and ask: But what of the analogy of creation? What does this account of analogy suggest for an account of the origin and with it the coming to be of analogy?

Here, as the previous quotation shows, Balthasar's thought hangs on thinking *translation*: the divine unity of doing and allowing-to-happen translates itself in and into time. It interprets itself, folds itself outwards, in a 'new' setting apart within itself which requires no change in itself. It translates itself, *sie übersetzt sich*: it places itself over, across, beyond; it makes for itself a place beyond itself, a place that is more than itself, which is nevertheless a place within itself (for there is no other place). It increases itself, without changing itself – for it is its own increase.

For the world (in the world) this has always happened. This is the moment for which there is no one time, for which there is no moment – in the world or in God – because it is the moment, the movement, of time itself: the grounding or beginning of time, the kenotic creation of a space and a time for being. This movement, this moment, is an extension of the difference of *Urkenosis* between Father and Son, but it is also a movement, a moment, which only happens within (at the same time as) that 'originary' movement and moment and not in any sense only after its completion or outside it.

This, the act of creation, the translation of God by God to and into the world, to and into not-God, is the aporetic beginning of time. It is the *aporia* of creation which timed being must always know and not know, at which timed beings can only guess. This is the thought which faith can touch, can conjecture: 'the secret of all secrets, which must be posited as the ungroundable Ground for the possibility of worldly salvation history' (TD III, 302).

Time, sexual difference and belonging: the question of the analogy of analogy
Time and sexual difference, then, belong together because they can 'reveal' something of God. They are both privileged moments in words about God; quasi-transcendentals, perhaps. But they also belong together, in Balthasar's thought at least, because they both talk of *order*, because they both name a 'first' and 'second' which must remain always undecidable, and precisely not two separate, distinguishable, discrete events or sites. They are, that is, two different forms of the thought of belonging together. These two belong together because they are both ways of belonging together. They are also, therefore, both ways of thinking the together of that which has been created in its relation to God.

These two can, therefore, both be used to talk of sacred order, that is, of *hierarchy*. They are analogous to each other because of the analogy they bear to God, an analogy which they (and only they) can bear only because of God's translation, interpretation, explication or unfolding of God. Wolfgang Treitler refers to this unfolding in the term *catalogy*, which he takes, as it were, to be the linguistic form of *kenosis*: the form formed and 'filled' by God's emptying God of God; the form which is, therefore, itself also only ever a 'handing over'.[85]

There is then in God 'something' (God's 'Becoming') which can become, give rise to or translate itself into time. There is also in God 'something' (God's 'Desire-to-be-One' or God's 'Unity', the 'Unity-of-Three') which can become, give rise to or translate itself into sexual differencing. The movement is in each case the same. It is the movement of creation; that is, the movement by which God creates, and in which God becomes present to and in the creation. For each creature and for all creatures, this movement is the relationship to God. This movement can only come from within God and from God. It is a kenotic, condescending, unfolding, interpretative movement, which has its ground in the movement which is God, in the movement and moment Balthasar has called *Urkenosis*.

And yet, the coming to being of sexual difference and the coming to be of time are two different (though not separate) events. Sexual difference and time are not identical in the sense that God's Becoming and God's Desire-to-be-One are the same; just as all creatures both are and are not the same. They are the same, because they are created; they are not the same because each is created different: they are not identical.

From within *Urkenosis*, from within trinitarian differencing, a new difference comes to be: the difference of not-God from God. But this 'new' difference is always plural, always at least dual, since it always includes and gives rise to the difference of not-God from not-God. (To be a being is always to be amongst beings; Being is only present in beings.) The difference of not-God from God only occurs within the differences of God, only within that which we have named trinitarian differencing, the difference of God from God.

This emergence of not-God within God is the *aporia* of creation as a limit 'within' God, rather than only 'from' (and therefore also 'to') God. This is a limit for creation, a limit towards creation; although it is a limit in and in some sense from God, it is not and cannot be a limit to God. It is God's limiting of the world, God's giving form to the world, in an 'extension' of the *Urkenosis*. For the creation, this is a standing in and through God which Balthasar, with Gregory of Nyssa, calls *diastasis*.

The difference of creation from God is the difference of creation. This difference occurs in, participates in, the difference of God from God – of Father from Son and Spirit, of Son from Father and Spirit and of Spirit from Father and Son. This trinitarian pattern itself already suggests the plurality of 'not-God'; difference in God is never only the difference between two. The difference of the creature from God is never only its

---

85 'True foundations of authentic theology' in *Hans Urs von Balthasar: His Life and Work*, pp. 169–82.

difference, but the difference of creatures, the difference of creatureliness, the difference of creation.

The difference of creation, then, is analogous to – but not the same as – trinitarian difference. And so this 'new' difference in some sense images trinitarian differencing, such that trinitarian differencing appears to creation as 'like' time, as 'like' sexual difference, as 'like' the difference of creation itself. But how can this be asserted without equating or confusing God with creation? For God has been understood in such a way that God 'is' God's differences; God 'is' the differencing of God in God. There is therefore a danger that God will also be understood as the difference of not-God from God (or vice versa) because this difference also occurs in God. What is the difference between the differences of God from God and the differences of not-God from God and of not-God from not-God? To what extent and in what ways can these differences be told together and apart?

Here we must pay attention to the themes of necessity, order and number to which we have already frequently alluded. These themes seemed to threaten violence in the reductive logic of a phenomenological account of sexual difference. They also first began to reveal the proximity of sexual difference and time, particularly in the matter of revelation.

The coming to be of analogy cannot be told outside analogy, nor can it be told as the coming to be of something itself without analogy. For Balthasar, differences within creation (differences which are included in and also include the difference of creation from God) are analogous to (other) differences in God. That is, both the differences of not-God from God and the differences of not-God from not-God participate in trinitarian differencing.

But trinitarian differencing is itself a participation: the participation of God in God. Differences within creation are analogous to the differences between the divine persons of the Trinity. Even the difference of creation from God bears an analogy to the differences between the divine Persons of the Trinity. The difference between the creation and the Trinity, however, is the difference of analogy (the participation of participation in participation). At first glance, analogy appeared to be grounded in an interval or distance – a static difference, a particular account of *diastasis* as a spacing, or a spatialization of time, a clear first and second. Here, analogy begins to emerge as grounded in itself, perhaps even as grounded in this undecidability.

This observation might lead to the suggestion that the relationships between the three Persons of the divinity are something like analogy. Time arises from something like time; sexual difference arises from something like sexual difference; analogy itself arises from something like analogy. Nothing, not even God, not even nothing, can be excluded or expelled from analogy. Such an observation serves to mark the catastrophe of any attempt to fix analogy, and of Balthasar's apparent anchoring of analogy in woman and woman's body in particular.

Under the direction of kenotic difference
And yet, of course, the observation of the grounding of analogy in analogy continues to risk speaking, as it were, in the wrong direction. It can be

again to misunderstand or mistake the direction of analogy. For the secret of analogy is that time is *more like* 'something like time' than 'something like time' is 'like' time; that sexual difference is *more like* 'something like (the) sexes' than that something is 'like' sexual difference, or the sexes. Similarly, analogy itself is more like 'something like analogy' than that something is like analogy. It is creation which is the image, not God. The ascending movement of ana-logy in which time is recognized as 'like something in God' (translated into the suggestion that 'there is something like time in God') is always in fact a recognition of a prior movement in which time comes, descends even, from God. At the same time, for Balthasar, the halting ascription of analogy does not happen only *after* cata-logy, but rather always only ever *within* it; the human ascent to God, and so the ascent of human *logoi*, can only happen within God's kenotic condescension, within, that is, the speaking of God's Word.

Human, creaturely words about God are only ever the analogical re-marking of divine catalogy; they are only ever to be heard or spoken within the hearing and speaking of God's Word. The Father's self-expression in begetting (*zeugen*) the Son – the bestowal of a Word, his witness (*Zeugung*) of himself to the Spirit – is an always first and originary movement and moment. It is always complete, and yet never completed. This *Urkenosis*, then, is 'Ur' not only in the sense of primal or first and original, not only in the strictly temporal sense. Rather, this *Urkenosis* is Ur because it embraces and encompasses – is *über*, above, over, around and not only beyond – everything. It is the original moment and movement, an anterior differencing which cannot be fixed before, outside or at the beginning of a series of successive moments and movements as anteriority. It is a moment within which all others occur. It is a moment which does not have or recognize *first* a first and *then* a second (moment, movement, being, Person, mood or even gender). It is a moment, a movement, in which 'first' and 'second' (of sorts – Father, Son and Spirit) are, belong, together.

This *Urkenosis* is God's definition of God; but this is not a limiting definition, nor a limiting in any sense. It is the form in which God grants God form. It is the un-finishing of God, rather than the limiting of God; it is the *explicatio* – the unfolding, the explaining, the self-expression, the interpretation – the translation of God. And so it is the opening up of God; the always, ever 'more' of God, to which our limitations and their limited fruitfulness are analogous.

This opening up of God, which only occurs within God, also only 'occurs' in one 'direction': *from* Father *to* Son, whilst yet neither the Father nor the Son is ever without or apart from this giving and receiv-ing. It has, then, something to do with the 'order' of God. It is a moment. And yet, it has no end, is never finished. Moreover, it only occurs within the differences between the Father and the Spirit and between the Son and the Spirit. It overtakes and embraces these differences, but is itself held within, overtaken by them. Again, this *kenosis* is Ur in no usual sense.

This order of *Urkenosis* leaves its mark in its translation of itself in and into creation, and particularly in the nature of time. For the meantime, it will suffice to comment that this mark is remarked in Balthasar's description of the God-creature differential by the word *Gefälle* – an incline, a fall.

The excess of analogy and the Evermore of God

This unusual sense of *Ur* as applied to God, then, has important resonances with the prefix *über* – above, beyond, over, super, supra, meta – which seems so readily to emerge when analogy is being thought. For Balthasar, the Father is, for example (at least) 'Super'-masculine, the Son 'Super'-womanly, but also 'super'-masculine, etc. But this 'super' does not mean 'extra' in the sense of 'very' (or external to), but nor does it mean 'super' in the sense of only above and beyond (again, external to). It is the prefix of God's Evermore *within* which everything is embraced. It is the prefix of analogy: time participates in something above and beyond time, which is more than time, which includes, embraces, overtakes time; sexual difference, similarly.

Both God's 'Becoming' and God's 'Desire-to-be-One' are (analogical) descriptions of this 'Evermore of God'. The 'Evermore of God' – God! – can translate itself into time, as time, and into sexual difference, as sexual difference. But this translation is only ever partial and only ever across an inclination. It can only ever provide a flashing recognition of the Evermore of God. This translation cannot embrace, contain, limit or de-limit God. It is, therefore, irreversible; it cannot be folded back into itself.

Not only does God not need the world to interpret or translate God (God can do that to and with God in being God – trinitarian differencing), but the world cannot deduce or induce God from itself or from the fact of creation. Whilst creation always bears analogy to God, that analogy is incomplete. It allows only a *conjecture*. Even when the world has finished, God's *kenosis* and God's interpretation of God will not be completed, will not be finished. God's Evermore will continue. And this because the *Urkenosis* is complete, is total, includes nothing of a holding back but is rather a handing over 'without reserve'. We mistake the translation which gives rise to the creation if we understand it as partial in the sense of half-hearted or safe. The Evermore of God is not withheld from creation, and yet creation cannot contain it, and so it overspills creation. This is the sense in which creation itself can become ecstatic: the sense in which it is always being overtaken by the Evermore, by the un-overtakable Love of God.

And so, despite their common origin (God) and despite their common origination (the translation of God into not-God by God which is the act of creation), time and sexual difference belong together but are not the same, are not identical (and indeed, could not belong together if they were). Each is analogical to 'something in God'; each bears an analogy to the 'Evermore of God'; and it is because of this relationship that they are analogical to each other.

The difference of order and the order of difference in number

But it is in thinking necessity and order that we begin to glimpse the differences between the differences of God from God on the one hand and the differences of not-God from God and of not-God from not-God on the other. Human words are necessarily dependent upon divine words. Creaturely beings are logically necessarily dependent upon the divine Being. (They happen 'after' divine Being – but also 'before' any 'end' of divine Being; they are both different from God and yet always only ever within God – only ever in God's 'time', never 'outside' or 'after' its completion.)

Time and sexual difference can only occur within trinitarian differencing – can only be like something in God. And yet, neither God nor the 'Evermore of God' *has* to translate itself into not-God in order to be or to become God. God's words do not have to be translated into human, creaturely words in order to be heard and spoken. The 'necessity' by which God is three Persons is very different from the necessity of any creature or of the creation itself. God is necessary for the creation. Given creation, certain things must have happened. But those things did not themselves 'have' to happen.

But what of number? And what of the ordering of this order, the ordering of the secret of secrets?

For analogy would, at first glance, appear to be a relation between two. And yet, repeatedly, there seem to be (at least) three in play: world and God – and Christ; man and woman – and child, or God, or Christ; before and after – and now; sexual difference and time – and God, or space; Christ and Mary – and Church; giving and receiving, doing and letting happen – but three Persons; and perhaps most puzzlingly, the hypostatic union (two) as the concrete *analogia entis* and also as an image of the relationships of the three Persons of the Trinity.

Trinitarian differencing seems at once to establish and to question an ordering of 'primacy': the Father is first, Son and Spirit are in some sense second; but they can only 'be' this within the Spirit, which then appears to be secretly 'first'. Or again, the relationships of the three Persons of the Trinity are to be understood in the proper ordering of active and passive (two) and to translate themselves into the relationships between two sexes. In what senses do we need two to tell three and three to tell two? What is the duality of three which is the duality of analogy?

First, then, to consider order and number, let us think what this duality is *not*. Analogy is not to be fixed. It is not to be fixed as a difference or a distance – a valorized, valorizing interval – between two, nor as a difference which can be decided apart from those which are two. It is not a difference – first–second; man–woman; God–world; active–passive – which is to be decided or fixed in the fixing of another. Analogy is not to decide any difference as first (not the difference of time, nor of space, nor of the genders; nor even 'difference' itself), but to learn the belonging together of differences, to learn difference not as (only) same and not-same, but as the belonging together and setting apart of those which are both same and not same, and here, in particular, the chiastic interlocking of space, time and gender.

Difference, then, is always plural, is always more; it is always opening on to more. Difference is always the differencing of difference. Difference is never only two, even when it is 'a' difference between two things, because that difference will make a difference.

God is the Evermore of God; this is the differencing of God which is God. This is imaged in an evermore, the fruitfulness, of creaturely difference. With difference, given difference, there is an unstoppable multiplication of differences. There is no one analogy in which all others co-inhere. Analogy is rather the co-inherence of creation in itself and in God, a co-inherence which images the relationships of the Persons of the Trinity. This is life; this is that into which the lively eternal Love of God has been and is continually translated and yet never exhausted.

Analogy within the creaturely realm, then, is a being grounded. But it is not and should not involve the prior or anterior fixing of a first in order then to be able to ground a second in a potentially infinite regression. It is rather always a being grounded together. Always a belonging together, always a participating in each other. Always the proper undecidability of 'first' and 'second', of active and passive, of begetter and begotten; their occurrence together as the same and different.

And yet, there is here a beginning to be conjectured: the creation. But this, teaches analogy, is not the past and sealed event of creation, but rather the ceaseless continuing event of creation. Nor is this a relation which not-God has in order to be able, subsequently, to have other relationships; it is the condition of all creaturely relationships. There is a hierarchy, a sacred order, a holy beginning to be thought.

This *aporia* of creation is to be thought analogically. It is to be thought as 'a' difference, or better a differencing, of the world from God, of not-God from God. This is a difference which can only be thought of as out of God, whilst remaining always in God. It is a difference which is always being established and maintained; and which has not yet been set out and finalized. This difference only 'is' in the other differences of creation. It is not a difference which we can find or think apart from the other differences of creation. And yet it is precisely this that enables the confusion, the elision, of the God-creature 'differential' (inclination) with time, or space, or sexual difference.

This difference, then, is not 'a' 'first' moment of creation, not a moment of anteriority, but the continual moment, the time, the being of creation, the uncontainability of anterior differencing. It is already, always was, always will be, not 'a' difference, but rather the thinking together of the difference of the world from God together with the difference(s) of God from God, such that the difference of the world from God belongs to the differences of God. (And to tell this, as Balthasar has argued, we need Christ.)

The order of thought
This thought is analogical because we cannot think the differences of God before or apart from our thought of the difference of world from God; and we cannot think the difference of the world from God before or apart from our thought of the differences 'within' the world of creature from creature (of not-God from not-God). Nevertheless, we must also think the differences of God from God as being 'before', anterior to, this difference – as always before, as always during, and as always afterward.

Creation has an order, a direction: it comes from God. It is in some sense 'secondary' and 'passive', with regard to God; it is (and has been and will be) generated by God, such that it is not secretly primary or necessary for God. But as second, it can only think itself second before it thinks – or perhaps *as* it thinks – God first. Creation can, as it were, only think itself in reverse.

This order, this direction, of creation is clearly (and analogically) re-told in the direction of time. For even given the telling of the immaculate conception, time moves only in one direction, from beginning to end – from one end towards another. Indeed, time *is* this movement; it is our movement from birth to death and, as Ward has shown, through death to resurrection and beyond.

Difference, also, has traditionally been marked in the English language as occurring only in one direction: something is different *from* another, and not (properly speaking) different *to* or *than* another. Difference is always a moving away from, even a folding out of – hence the sense of the word 'differential' used to translate *Gefälle*: a differential is, in some sense, always an uneven difference, always a falling away. It is not simply a distance or a space, but a distance or a space with a sense or a direction: an inclination. And yet, it is not the linear addition of successive point-like instants, nor the repeated piercing of a membrane. It is, rather, the movement of difference in its direction.

When the attempt is made to fix this patterning of two and three (of two and more) in the security of a first, the second will always appear as a precondition for the first. Similarly, when an attempt is made to fix two, a third will always appear as their necessary precondition – an appearance which is particularly traumatic in the attempt to think a pair as first (Father and Son). Woman is well acquainted with this trauma: she appears to be nothing other than the necessary, self-effacing precondition for man; and then again as nothing other than the withdrawing pre-condition for the relationship of God and man. In this, as we have remarked, she shares a burden with the Holy Spirit, who can likewise appear as a necessarily self-effacing precondition for the relationship between Father and Son (between divinely masculine and divinely feminine), and as therefore 'super-womanly', something like woman, something like the feminine.

But what then of direction and order in sexual difference? What is the direction, the inclination of the sexual difference, of sexual differences? Here, surely, Balthasar has suggested a first and a second, an active and a passive, two discrete, eternal stations, one of which is intended to be prior to, but finds itself secondary to, the other. And surely this is 'wrong', surely this is an unobservant phenomenology, a distortion of the truth of the mutuality and exchange and undecidability of the relationships between the sexes. Does not the violence threatened in this text warn us against suggesting *any* order or *any* direction for sexual difference?

Conclusion: The silences of reception

The greatest difficulty doubtless consists more essentially in deciding what silence says.

Jean-Luc Marion

Promise and violence: the proximities of two readings

In 'Sexual difference as *diastasis*', we traced two accounts of sexual difference, following as it were the *Mensch*'s gaze as he looks upon woman. Here already, sexual difference is summoned to perform a critical function in Balthasar's theology and this in response to his reading of the times. Its significance, therefore, reaches far beyond the scope of a 'sexual politics' narrowly construed. And yet, the questions upon which such a politics would insist cannot – should not – be postponed indefinitely.

That man and woman are first and foremost equal persons is a theme that Balthasar insists upon more than once in the texts we have considered. And indeed, the question of how this equality is to be construed is an issue that in other places draws some of Balthasar's most explicit judgements concerning the end of modernity and the levelling tendencies of an insistent demand for equality-thought-as-identity.[86] However, the question of the problematic construal of this equality is raised in the *Theo-Drama* not least by an apparently contrary logic evidenced in Balthasar's texts, in which one or the other of these persons (now man, now woman) is made to appear more significant than the other. Within this equality, then – and perhaps ultimately above *and* beyond it – it is the persistent, irreducible difference(s) between man and woman which attract Balthasar's attention as far more illustrative of equality, but which also enable an absolutizing ordering of one over the other from which any equality appears very distant.

In the first account of sexual difference, Balthasar traces these differences as relative to each other, fluid and in some sense undecidable. This is an account which appears to promise much to women who have been

---

86 Thus for example, in an essay on women priests, Balthasar asks and suggests: 'At such a late hour of history, can we still hope for a return of this sense-giving balance – which is only symbolically intimated in the sexual, but in reality extends much farther as concerns the human being in his place within being as a whole? If we can do so, then certainly only through the woman who perceives and understands her role as counterpoise to and spearhead against man's increasingly history-less world' (NE 191).

And so we return to a proximity in the thought between Balthasar and Irigaray, who suggests that the demand for equality amounts to genocide, if not suicide: 'Demanding equality, as women, seems to me to be an erroneous expression of a real issue. Demanding to be equal presupposes a term of comparison. Equal to what? ... Men? A wage? A public position? Equal to what? Why not to themselves? (*The Irigaray Reader*, ed. Margaret Whitford (Oxford: Blackwell, 1991), p. 32). If sexual difference is the issue of our age which could, if only we knew it, be 'our salvation' (*An Ethics of Sexual Difference*, p. 5), then for Balthasar this salvation resides within the Catholic Church, for '[b]ecause of her unique structure, the Catholic Church is perhaps humanity's last bulwark of genuine appreciation of the difference between the sexes' (NE 195).

repeatedly assigned to lesser places on account of a lesser nature and a lower status, for here first and second are resolutely *not* translated into place. In thinking after Christ and the events of salvation history, however, Balthasar's Christian theology will rest content with a preliminary, hesitant, fluid description of *neither* the relationship between man and woman, *nor* that between God and world to which it bears an analogy: too much hangs on the determination of each, and in particular their binding one to the other.

Thus, a second view of sexual difference becomes a fixing of sexual difference in woman – all the more *man's* second view of woman as *his*, rather than any thought of their *belonging together*. The *Mensch* is called to recognize the significance of its sexual differentiation, but for this man the significance of sexual difference has become the significance of woman. Indeed, sexual difference has become the significance of woman, her very *esse*, making her the occasion of the binding of creaturely difference to theological difference. This binding amounts to and depends upon the spatialization of woman, for it requires woman to be that place in which the ontological difference is not only contained, but reduced and collapsed: in her there is no difference between Being and being, she becomes – or at least tends towards – their union in oblivion, in the nothing of not-being. And so, as the most-significant, as pure sign, woman loses her own meaning and is denigrated in her exaltation: it is precisely Balthasar's recognition of the significance of sexual difference that threatens to distort his representation of this significance.

And this all on account of Christ's appearance in the world. A mysterious appearance which is at least doubly surprising, for since Christ is God, and since Christ is a man – a male *Mensch* – he might be thought of as 'absolutely' and 'essentially', 'in himself' *first*, and yet, as man, he is 'second' to the 'first Adam' and, as the Logos, he proceeds from the Father and so appears to be at least quasi-feminine (and apparently not masculine) – and all the more so in his duality (divine–human). In this observation, with which Balthasar's Mariology begins, woman's significance is told as it were in advance of woman.

Balthasar's provisional attempt to answer and quieten (perhaps even *silence*) this riddle provokes further surprise and unease: in order to represent Origin in the world (and this is his procession from the Father), the one who appears to be quasi-feminine must nevertheless be a man. In addition, in order to establish him *as man*, the feminine will be made to proceed from him. And, to 'reassure' still further, we are guaranteed that there can be no question of parthenogenesis – of feminine from feminine – here.

In this moment, in the (surprising and disturbing) appearance of Christ as quasi-feminine and yet both evidently and necessarily (and so all the more disturbingly) a man – sexual difference is fixed as that which will tell the relationship between God and *Mensch* in Christ.

At the same time, the dissymmetry of man and woman is also decided as a symmetry of inversion. The different differencing of man and woman is forgotten in securing a measured difference in which theological difference and analogy can in turn be secured. And so, in a lifeless mirror logic, woman is made to be all that man is not (including not-*Mensch* and not-being); a move which will always threaten violence to women (and men).

Thus, in Balthasar's delineation of sexual difference there is a tendency to fix, to sever or to still the hovering oscillation of first and second as chronological and logical, as spatial or temporal absolutes (as only relatively undecidable), rather than to preserve them as relative un-decidables. And this not only in order to allow a view on to theological difference, in order, that is, to allow the God–creature differential – creaturely *diastasis* – to appear in the world, but also in order to make preparation for God to be born and salvation to be received.

Releasing the promise: the order of temporality and a third account of sexual difference

In 'The ecstasies of time', we turned to consider further the *temporal* aspects of this ever-tightening logic, in which sexual difference is, as it were, *forced* and granted no time in which to emerge. For it is precisely in order to *fix* sexual difference that first and second must be construed as occurring in a certain sense *at the same time* – as, indeed, the very same time. Or contrariwise, in an (a-)temporal logic in which cause and effect can increasingly no longer be told apart, first and second are construed as only *at the same time* as an immediate result of this fixing.

At first sight, the concentration on *time* after the reading of an over-spatializing account of sexual difference might have appeared an attempt to provide a stabilizing counter-balance: if sexual difference has been read too much as space, then consideration of its timing might prove able to redeem these accounts. Our pursuit of this theme, under Irigaray's directive, however, could provide only an intensification of our diffi-culties. For in the over-spatialization of sexual difference, and in par-ticular of woman, a similar over-spatialization of time itself was harboured: it is precisely in their temporal ordering – as first and second – that man and woman have been spatialized in an elisory logic of 'at the same time'.

However, rather than only returning to its beginning, this problematic intensification (as might be expected of the theologian who seeks not to 'dissolve' problems, but rather to plumb their mystery) opens on to 'another' telling of both time and sexual difference in contemplation of the interleaving of the different forms of representation evidenced (represented) in marian dogma and christological doctrine. Thus, in telling the interleaving of the time of creation and the time of redemption, this third account attempts to release the promise of the first through the determinations of the second. In this account, therefore, the ways in which the first two accounts made preparation for this third in which salvation is to be received begin to emerge; at the same time, and by the same token, the ways in which those first two accounts belong together, for all their apparent incompatibilities, also become apparent.

In this third account, then, woman's temporal placing is explicitly problematized, for Mary, who above any other is *the* woman (and not least the Woman of the Apocalypse), appears to come, to be, 'before' and 'after' the man Christ, from whom – or more properly with whom – her sexual difference is to be reckoned. Moreover, this general problematic of woman is rendered more acute in Mary, for she is not only *dual* – bride (to one *Mensch*) and mother (to others) – but also *first* bride, bride in her *fiat*, in her assent to union with the Word and so *then* mother *to the same man*, in order, at the last (that is, eschatologically) to become again his bride. And so we might suggest that she is at once his bride and his mother, whilst also being (becoming) his bride in order to become his mother, and then his mother *in order* to become his bride. Indeed, she is – becomes – first his bride in order to become his bride at (the) last.

Here, in the telling of the apparently 'simultaneous' preparation for, and reception of, salvation (the reception, that is, of the reception of grace), there emerges a persistent and irreducible interleaving of two and three. There are two persons (Mary and Christ) joined in two relations (mother–son, spouse–spouse). But these two relations are in fact three, for there are differences to be told between the first and the second marriages. And this is not least because we are told the relationship of these two at three different times (Mary's *fiat*, Christ's birth – the two 'sides' of incarnation – and the last days: corresponding to creation, redemption and sanctification), all of which are prepared in and unfold from the time and the timing of the immaculate conception.

This apparently circular ordering of two and three is also to be seen in the description of Mary and Christ as being held in an unbreakable circle in which effect is cause of cause. Here, again, there are two persons (Christ and Mary) and two terms (effect and cause) of one relationship (causality), which appears twice (Mary 'causes' Christ and is caused by Christ), thus combining two 'causes' and one 'effect' (a total of three) in an unconventional manner. And so there appear again to be three terms (cause : effect/cause : effect; or, effect/cause : cause : effect) bound by two moments (: and :), or three moments bound by two movements. It is this convoluted interleaving of two and three that is reflected in our formulaic representation of salvation history as told in the immaculate conception in the locution 'grace prepares nature to receive grace'.[87]

In this, the question of undecidability returns – but this is always an undecidability within, perhaps of, a certain order or direction: for this undecidability does not mean that cause is effect, nor that effect is cause, that first is second and second first, nor that grace and nature are the same thing. But it means that these are only distinguishable in relation to each other; there is an important sense in which they will always only ever *fall together*. There is no first without second; there is no nature without grace; which does not necessarily mean that either second term (second, grace) is secretly anterior or prior.

This falling together is temporality: it is the timing of time, the time of 'at the same time'; it is the time of creation and redemption (and therefore also the time of sanctification). This is a *structural* undecidability, resting

87 Here, too, we must note that this binding of two and three, which is perhaps at least the undecidability of first and second, has never been far from the trauma of trinitarian doctrine, which has – as has frequently been commented upon – again and again seemed only able to represent three in terms of two (even in Milbank's essay on the *Second Difference*, which in some sense seeks to reassert the Spirit's place – the place of the third person – the relations between *three* persons appear to be reduced to *two* differences).

upon the structure of the 'translation' of God into not-God – a translation which, whilst it is complete, is never completed and so is only ever partial. These undecidables, then, are 'at the same time', but it is precisely this simultaneity which can be misread or absolutized into a relation of absolutes – an absolute relation or difference of anteriority – within and for creation, such that they are intepreted as the completion of the translation of God as an absolute and anterior ground. Such an interpretation amounts to the exclusion of God from the world and the closing of God's ever opening and awakening love – moves which still and silence the trembling into life of the Word and creation.

Nevertheless, it is precisely in the failure of 'at the same time' (and *not* in its winning out), through, that is, time's own-most *aporia*, that there emerges an order or direction of relation (first and second must tell at least a temporal ordering, a *particular* – relative – direction) in which the divine life may be glimpsed. In one sense, this is the direction of time, the order of creation. But it is also the only order for the telling of a relationship to God. In both senses it is irreversible. In being 'retraced' (which is not the same as reversed) this order can lead thought on and back to thoughtful conjecture (not deduction, nor induction) of God, something like time and something like sexual difference.

Life and thought after God

In 'The order of thought', therefore, we pursued the links between sexual difference, temporality and theological difference as they appear in Balthasar's construal of human thought after God (and in particular Christian theology's trinitarian thought of Trinity). All human thought – words, *logoi* – of God can only ever be thought after God; thought, that is, after and within (not beyond) God's thought – God's Word, the Logos.

In thinking this thought, thought finds that the world – including thought – bears an analogy to God: it comes 'after' and yet occurs 'within' God; it bears a likeness to God who is ever more dissimilar. At the same time, although this is, as it were, the persistent structure of thought in general, this thought – the analogical thought of thought – can never be thought 'in general', but only in and at particular moments, through time. In this sense, then, thought knows 'privileged' moments for its thought of thought and for its thought of God. The two which this essay has sought to outline as they occur in Balthasar's thought are that of sexual difference and that of time.

And so we have found that, for Balthasar, not only are the differences between the sexes – and in particular sexual regeneration – *something like* 'something in the life of God', but that these differences have been reduced to one difference which would also tell the difference of not-God from God, the translation of God into something like God. But in this, the direction, the order of sexual differencing appears to have been fixed and over-determined as a difference in a way which either depends upon or grounds (how would we be able to tell the difference?) a misunderstanding of the sacred order of creation and the divine *kenosis*. These decisions upon sexual difference are coupled with (are simultaneous with) an exclusion of the world from God and of God from the world, which amounts to a restriction of God and a limiting of the divine life.

Sexual difference is pressed into this over-determined service as a result of Balthasar's insightful and persistent recognition of the analogy borne by creaturely sexual regeneration and fruitfulness to the Evermore of God and the divine creation of the world. This is the thought, at once elegant and disturbing, which captivates Balthasar's theology. It is quite simply the thought that the *Mensch* has always begun, and knows its own coming to be as sexual and as always from within a woman. Sexual regeneration participates in the act of creation, and so sexual regeneration must be *something like* creation. There is then a proper sense in which the *Mensch* can know the difference of creation from God (and hence the differences of God from God) only in and with sexual difference.

But this privilege and those dependent upon it reveal the pressure for a decision to be taken upon sexual difference. If so much can be recognized in sexual difference, then it can seem vital that sexual difference be determined. But this train of thought always ignores that we can also only recognize sexual difference in, and at the same time as, all that to and with which it is analogous. It cannot be fixed in advance of – as anterior to – all these other differences, as the difference of anteriority. In the over-determination of the direction of sexual difference (first–second, man–woman) which threatens violence to woman, this direction remains in fact unthought and serves to order and similarly over-determine the whole of Balthasar's thought.

To remark upon this tendency is not to reject Balthasar's central insight. It is, rather, in the *reception* of his thought upon reception and receptivity, to note the provisionality of reception; to remark upon the aporetic structure of reception itself as temporal event and the manner in which it provides. For, as Balthasar's logic insists, reception should properly be without reservation. And yet, precisely because one cannot choose only to receive part of this thought, we have to be prepared thoroughly to think that which has been received in its reception.

At the same time, and from within these accounts of sexual difference, we have also attempted to trace the privilege of *time* in human thought after God, and in particular the thought of that thought. And here, again, we would suggest not only that time is like something in God (such that we might say that there is something like time in God), but that talk of time also provides a modality in which we can talk about the creaturely, and particularly the human, relationship to God, as 'after' God and yet also 'in' God.

In tracing Balthasar's attempt to tell the timing of sexual difference, we have found an almost unremarked-upon temporal clue to the divine life: the necessity and the impossibility – the *aporia* – of the thought of 'at the same time'. This thought can only ever occur 'after'; it is an urgent thought which is always both 'now' and 'too late'.[88] 'At the same time' cannot be

---

88 In recalling the lines from the beginning of the *Theo-Drama* to which we have already referred and in which Balthasar expresses the urgency of his (of the human) task, '*Now* must be questioned and played: there is a Too-late,' (TD I, 21; ThD 1, 22), this thought not only returns us to the beginning, but questions the *sense* of the silence by and in which these two clauses are bound together – that is, the silent binding of 'now' and 'too late'. Perhaps it is not only necessary to play (to act) and to question *now*, because there will (otherwise) be a 'too-late' ('too-late', then,

thought *at* 'the same time' – it can only ever be thought *after* that 'same time'. In its failure, this thought provides an aporetic opening on to (thought of) the divine life which is above and beyond, before and after, within and without all that is.[89] Although urgent, then, this thought need not always be (as it often is) frustrated, or short-circuited – always already too late, always after something which it would have but which has already finished. It can be patient thought of the world as (timed) from and in God; a patience, that is, with the patient delay in which God arrives to and in the world precisely in divine withdrawal. This thought of 'at the same time', then, is the *density* of thought – its 'reflective substance'.

Theo-politics and the strangeness of silence

By way of conclusion, let us speak of three strange silences – and thus of the almost silent theme of silence which has run throughout this essay. We would not wish to remain silent on this motif, but to speak (or to write) into this silence is always to run many risks.

First, at the heart of Balthasar's account of woman as 'answer', we have noted *woman's* silence. Her voice is recorded in neither Balthasar's account nor the Genesis texts which he would recount. The 'strangeness' of this silence – its significance – is redoubled in the context of a theology which also attributes so much to Mary's 'yes-word', when, once again, we have no record of her saying 'Yes'.

These crucial answers have always already happened, in the time and memory of the text. They can be, they are to be, taken as read. And yet there are questions which become – should become – unavoidable: Were these women always silent? And if so, were these answers in fact – in the time of creation – never given, never spoken: is the memory of these answers a fabrication? Or were they perhaps always and for ever silent

---

always awaiting its timely appearance). For 'too late' has always already arrived in and with (thought of) the 'now': 'now' is (always already) too late. For, if there *is* a 'now', then not only is there a 'too late', but 'now' is a 'too late'.

Now, this time, our time, is the time in which we must play, the time in which we must act; 'now' is always the (only) time we have in which to act; 'now' is the only time that can be enacted and it must be enacted. At the same time, 'now' is always to be questioned, precisely as to *what* and *when* this 'now' is; precisely as to the sense in which 'now' is always (already) too late. And this is not necessarily in the tragic passing by of salvation as unreceived and unreceivable, but in the necessary delay of the reception of salvation (grace – and indeed creation) as always giving itself and always (already) being (and having been) received. Perhaps it is precisely this disjoint that is to be received at the end of modernity?

89 This essay was completed shortly before Donald Sheehan and Olga Andrejev's translation of Fr Pavel Florensky's remarkable monograph, *Ikonostasis* (Crestwood: St Vladimir's Seminary Press, 1996), came to our attention. In an extraordinary contemplation of the inside-out, upside-down nature of the timing and substance of dreams and the imaginary, Florensky prepares his exposition of a theology of the icon, which is always theology of revelation, by engaging with the *aporia* of time in the relationships between the visible and the invisible, between time and the eternal. (See 'Introduction', pp. 33–42.) In this his thought recognizes the 'temporal clue' to the divine life in the eschatological grounding of all creaturely differencing. No doubt subterranean lines of filiation remain to be traced between Balthasar's thought and Orthodox theology here, and this not least via Balthasar's appropriation of Bulgakov's theme of *Urkenosis*.

answers (silent answers which have been rendered all the more silent in their over-determination and over-interpretation)? And what if these women did speak? Have they then *been silenced*? And which of these last two would be the lesser violence?

And so, second, there is the at-once strange and unsurprising silence of the *tradition* precisely upon these silences, precisely in the many words spilled into these silences, speaking about these silences as if they had never been (silence). What would be the differences between the silence which masks silence in speaking so many words (refusing to recognize that it is silence that is being so interpreted) and the silence which would mark, and even remark upon, silence *as silence*?

Third, then, and at the heart of these silences as their silent binding, we remark upon a *structural* silence (and not merely the silence of structure), precisely in the difficulty of the recurrent pressure to recognize and to say *what silence says*. To be sure, theo-politics demands (and this not always silently) an attention to the violences of silences imposed (howsoever silently imposed); an attention which would not always remain silent. However, this runs deeper into a structure which is a risk taken not only on interpreting silence (on translating into the ambiguity of language the ever greater ambiguity of silence) but on a (sometimes almost silent) promise. This promise is the possible-impossibility (the *aporia*) of the stumbling procession of speech (and the Word) from silence in a manner which does not (will not) erase silence as its other, its limit or its beyond, but which serves precisely only ever to preserve it (silence) within itself (the Word) as that with and in which it always belongs. A procession which is analogous to the trembling into life of creation from and within the divine life.

4

❧

Drama and the Ends of Modernity

BEN QUASH

In his celebrated meditation on a public execution and the crowd which gathers around to see it,[1] Michel Foucault articulates what is the presupposition of every interpretative endeavour: the interpreter finds herself always already 'in the middle'.[2] 'The eternal game', Foucault writes, 'has already begun'. We are players in its movement. The drama of life and death displayed on and around the scaffold invites us to consider this fact in a particularly concentrated way. It prompts us to ask with a certain urgency how we are to read this 'eternal game', for it is not at all a text whose meaning lies flat on the surface.[3] It is with Hans Urs von Balthasar's remarkable attempt to attend to this problem – a problem raised acutely for us 'moderns' by the various inadequacies and gaps in our post-Enlightenment schooling in *how to read* – that this essay will deal.

The relationship between the crowd and the spectacle in Foucault's account is complex. It is they, in a sense, who have constructed the very stage on which their experience now comes to them, so that in some way their 'poetic' (constructive) imagination has a certain priority over what their senses now communicate.[4] And this experience, already framed in

---

1 For his stimulating reading of the Foucault passage, I am grateful to Adrian Poole. His inspirational lectures on 'Tragedy' (which I heard in 1990 in the University of Cambridge) have played a very significant role in shaping my approach to Balthasar's theology, and this chapter is in very large measure indebted to him. I am also grateful to Nick Adams for his insight and advice both before and during the writing of this essay.
2 The phrase is given the dignity of opening Dante's great masterpiece: 'In the middle of the journey of our life . . .' (Dante, *Inferno*, 1.1).
3 This obscurity remains despite all the strategies Foucault examines, which seek to table exact correlations between the pain inflicted and the guilt admitted to, or between the offence given *to* and the punishment exacted *by* the monarch's power.
4 The role of the poetic imagination as 'the transcendental possibility of revelation' is powerfully articulated by John Milbank in his chapter entitled 'A Christological Poetics' in *The Word Made Strange: Theology, Language, Culture* (Oxford: Blackwell, 1997), pp. 123–44; see especially p. 130. He describes the 'poetic' existence of humankind as related (as 'a mode of knowledge') to the 'integral activity' by which we develop as human beings. Our products (which are the scaffolding for our own experiences) carry 'the presence of our human community' (p. 125), even as they 'dispossess' us and act in new ways upon us.

part, will now be turned and interpreted in a thousand minds' eyes, giving some a glimpse of justice and some of martyrdom, some an intimation of paradise and some of the place of the damned. There is, as Foucault says,

> an ambiguity in this suffering that may signify equally well the truth of the crime or the error of the judges, the goodness or the evil of the criminal, the coincidence or the divergence between the judgement of men and that of God. Hence the insatiable curiosity that drove the spectators to the scaffold to witness the spectacle of sufferings truly endured; there one could decipher crime and innocence, the past and the future, the here below and the eternal. It was a moment of truth that all the spectators questioned: each word, each cry, the duration of the agony, the resisting body, the life that clung desperately to it, all this constituted a sign.[5]

What this tableau illustrates is the *dramatically social* character of all our searching for truth. What is taken for true is true *in*, and not *apart from*, its negotiated, discursive, reception: a reception in which 'all the spectators *question*'. The work of reading the wounded world (and the activity of poetic imagination which such reading both feeds and presupposes) demonstrates the inextricability of the dramatic and the social in truth's appearing.

Truth, then (like the social life in which it comes to be for us), is not just 'brutely given', to use John Milbank's phrase.[6] Truth (like the social life from which it is inextricable) is in motion in the interpretative reception and activity of all those who participate in it. Just as the social emerges from (indeed *is*) a kind of perpetual rehearsal – a tempering into solidarity which is never complete, because the list of characters is greater than we can conceive, and because new circumstances are always arriving – so too truth is under construction. It is never (as Hegel knew) plausible in abstraction from its informing particulars, which are ever new. The scaffold which a society sets up for the staging of its shared experiences does not stand in neutral isolation from the play of passion and interpretation which presses around it. It is *scaffolding*, with all the provisionality which that implies. And true to this, the shared experiences themselves are never absolutely framed. In other words, there is an irreducibly dramatic character to socially-borne truth.

There is, correlatively, an irreducibly social dimension to drama. There cannot be proper drama without social life (or, to put it another way, without responsibility). The alternative to the 'brutely given' is not the 'banally free' – a romp of private fancy and indulgence. We may be tempted to deny the common placing (or implication) of ourselves with others in time and space; in history and society; in the 'eternal game'. But we cannot, in the end, escape our obligation to read what the god-riddled

---

5 Michel Foucault, *Discipline and Punish: The Birth of the Prison*, tr. Alan Sheridan (Harmondsworth: Penguin, 1979).
6 John Milbank, 'Magisterial ... and Shoddy?', *Studies in Christian Ethics*, 7:2 (1994), pp. 29–34.

world has inscribed on those around us – in bodies both physical and social. Together – like the crowd at Foucault's scaffold – we have to account for it. When we encounter the otherness written into one another and the world, we have no choice but to read these (often disturbing) marks as part of a story (however mysterious or incomplete) about the gods and about human beings and the world in which we live. We find ourselves responsible for trying to give an account of ourselves and what we have received. The task of a certain kind of framing, however inadequate it turns out to be, calls us back from the spurious belief that we can be left alone with ourselves (in an *unframed* 'inner space', as it were). To deny this responsibility is a flight from the stage – from what we have in common; from temporality, embodiment and language; and so from truth.

Hans Urs von Balthasar sets out to honour all the complexity of this task. He enacts, in his theology, a reading of the wounded world and of the 'eternal game' which will expose those traditions and practices of 'modernity'[7] which have evaded their dramatically social, embodied, temporally unsettled, mysteriously inscribed character. He does so not in order to be able definitively to bring the curtain down on an epoch, or to write 'FINIS' beneath it and then set it aside. He does not announce the end of modernity in that way – that would, after all, be a rather modern thing to do: too tidy an objectification, too hubristic a claim to overview. Rather, he seeks to redramatize the traditions and practices of modernity. We will be concerned in this essay to assess what this means: whether Balthasar is successful in his aim of shaking modernity from pursuit of its tidier and more hubristic 'ends', or whether the 'ends' of modernity are too determinedly held (too influential even in Balthasar's own thought) wholly to be escaped.

Epic, lyric and dramatic

Questions of genre are at the centre of our considerations here. Balthasar's attempt, we have said, is to redramatize the traditions and practices of modernity. But this presupposes a certain notion of what the dramatic is.

7 I necessarily rely to a large extent on the analyses of others for my notion of 'modernity': most of all (with Nicholas Lash and others) on the history of ideas and practice told in Amos Funkenstein's book *Theology and the Scientific Imagination: from the Middle Ages to the Seventeenth Century* (Princeton University Press, 1986); as well as Michael J. Buckley's *At the Origins of Modern Atheism* (New Haven: Yale University Press, 1987) and Stephen Toulmin's *Cosmopolis: The Hidden Agenda of Modernity* (New York: Macmillan, 1990). While acknowledging the difficulty of dating its origins ('Some people date the origin of modernity to the year 1436, with Gutenberg's adoption of moveable type; some to AD 1520, and Luther's rebellion against Church authority; others to 1648, and the end of the Thirty Years' War; others to the American or French Revolution of 1776 or 1789 ... [and] if we see Newton's creation of modern science as the start of Modernity, the starting date is in the 1680s' (Toulmin, pp. 7–8)), nevertheless, a consensus emerges that 'thanks to Galileo in astronomy and mechanics, and to Descartes in logic and epistemology' the seventeenth century was a period in which an agenda was set which focused on the 'pursuit of mathematical exactitude and logical rigor, intellectual certainty and moral purity' (Toulmin, p. x). As Funkenstein puts it, the 'ultimate prospect of science' became in that period 'a *mathesis universalis* – an unequivocal, coherent,

So in order to understand what for Balthasar makes drama *drama*, we begin in the middle of an actual play: Aeschylus' *Agamemnon*.

If we attend to the *Agamemnon*, we begin to see how various genres, or poetic perspectives, represent moments which contribute to the dense and complex effect of drama; these are moments rescued from their one-sidedness by being interrupted, taken up, patterned, mutually disciplined by drama's combining of them. And from this there can come that devastating attack upon the audience which is so effective in achieving capitulation to an engrossing dramatic moment.[8]

So, for example, we witness the extraordinary power of the prophet Cassandra's lyric utterances at the point when Agamemnon has vanished off-stage into his palace to meet an unsuspected death at the hands of his wife. It is a moment of high tension, in which the intensity of anticipation provides a ground for the poetry to take effect. Cassandra enters a frenzy which alarms the chorus intensely. Why? Because the chorus clings to a hope that it will be able to read its experience straightforwardly and without itself being implicated in the dark prelude and ghastly entail of what it is witnessing. But at the heart of this vain attempt Cassandra opens up an unbalancing reminder that no-one stands apart. The disturbing truth that in the mind's eye (the lyric imagination) of every interpreter there is a different reaction to this experience (a disordering challenge to neat consensus), and that every reaction is always also an investment *in* this experience (a sharing in what is to become of it), this disturbing truth plays itself out violently in the medium of her impassioned plunge into wild song. Like the execution on Foucault's scaffold, the clash of perspectives initiated by Cassandra's song precipitates a crisis in *how to read*.

---

and artificial language to capture our "clear and distinct" ideas' (Funkenstein, pp. 28–9); and this mechanical, mathematicized natural philosophy, as Buckley argues, was allowed to 'ground' religion, along with all the complexity of the human experience of reality.

8 What is at issue in this discussion of poetic genres or styles (and, similarly, poetic 'moments' or 'voices') is not a narrow characterization of the poetry's metre (though the metre of course makes an important contribution to the overall effect of the poetry). I am making a broader point about the poetry's various ways of 'styling' (and that means presenting *and* interpreting) its material. In other words, 'epic', 'lyric' and 'dramatic' stand for entire ways of looking at things: they are three different kinds of poetic perspective. Thus it is quite legitimate to talk in terms of 'lyric memory and forecast' as of things proper to lyric's own distinctive perspective, and as different from (for example) 'epic' memory or recall. It is possible to describe lyricism as that which works 'by association of ideas [through the power of imagery and the restless configuration of symbols] rather than in obedience to order in time, [taking us] deep away into the past, the future, and the elsewhere' (Richmond Lattimore, 'Introduction' in David Grene and Richmond Lattimore (eds.), *Aeschylus I: Oresteia* (University of Chicago Press, 1953), p. 20). In the highly developed tradition of nondramatic poetry (both epic and lyric) on which the early tragedians drew, these differences of perspective and approach were already in place, and in tragedy we can witness the chorus (for example) moving distinctly from speech 'in character' into long choral lyrics, into epic recountings, and back into character again. We shall see shortly that this identification of poetic style as more than merely metrical or formal style is in line with Hegel's own typological approach to poetic genre.

The chorus tries to frame the experience, and Cassandra blurs the frame. The chorus seeks to maintain an objective distrust of the substance of Cassandra's prophecy:

> Indeed we had heard of your prophetic fame;
> but we seek no interpreters of the gods.[9]
>
> (ll.1098–9)

but recognizes the unsustainability of its pretension to objectivity even as Cassandra speaks. It is unable, however hard it tries, to avoid a certain turbulent imaginative response to what she says.

Thus the power of lyric utterance to affect and involve the imagination and emotions is demonstrated in this scene, as the resistance of the chorus is broken down and suddenly its members are *within* an unframed dramatic moment. Their position as observers and commentators is compromised and complicated by their failure to remain detached, and the experience is characterized by questioning. The chorus asks Cassandra:

> From where have you the *boundaries* of your prophetic way?
>
> (l.1154)

and, later, remarks

> ... the *end* I do not know.
>
> (l.1177: my emphases)

It is the added ingredient of the unrationalized, inexplicable and open-ended prompting (the prophecy, the hunch, the *image*) that is overwhelming:

> Thyestes' feast upon his children's flesh
> I understand and shudder at, and fear possesses me
> as I hear it truly told and not in images.
> But when I hear the rest I lose the track and run off the path.
>
> (ll.1242–5)

Their alarm is related to the alarm of a tragic audience, which feels with some intensity the contagion of overwhelming emotive utterance which threatens to swamp a sought-for objective stance (something we might describe as an 'epic' distance). Like the *Agamemnon*'s chorus, the audience to tragedy is coaxed by images into a relationship with the facts of a situation where it no longer retains its bearings. The lyric voice in a play is to us – the audience – what Cassandra is to the chorus. It reminds us of a dimension in which songs and memories and intimations enthrall our reason. We inevitaby 'lose the track' of narrative, even when we know the play's plot beforehand. The playwright commits himself in this way to persuading the audience into a position where it can be knocked severely off balance.

9 Aeschylus, *Agamemnon*, tr. Hugh Lloyd-Jones (London: Duckworth, 1979).

This is not, of course, to say that dramatic experience is constituted by the lyric moment alone and undifferentiated. Rather, it is lyricism as it issues into the dramatically social dilemma of how critically to respond to the sequence of events being played out before us; how to monitor and judge what we receive together. I have just sought to show that drama awakens impulses in us which are beyond any notion we may have of individual rational control (and the 'control' of 'reason', we may note, is a particularly dominant conception in certain strands of modern thought). But there is more to take account of. Our agency is also conditioned by the related fact of being ineluctably *social* (it involves entanglement with the things experienced by other people). In this way, drama raises with a particular, authoritative urgency the question of what it is not only to be free, but (more than that) to be free in the company of others.

Another brief example shows how the tragic playwright wields the force of both lyric and non-lyric forms: this double battery is far more disturbing and heady than either on its own could possibly be. In *The Medea*, the audience first hears the agonized, primal (yet recognizably 'lyrical') groanings of the protagonist, coming from off-stage:

> Ah, wretch! Ah, lost in my sufferings,
> I wish, I wish I might die.[10]

> (ll.96–7)

Again, it is in the tension of anticipation that the lyric voice first begins to take its effect, feeding on the circumstances in which the audience's imagination can run away with itself. What monstrous and desperate figure *is* it that can groan as Medea does?

> Oh, I wish
> That lightning from heaven would split apart my head.

> (ll.143–4; translation altered)

Yet, shortly afterwards, Medea appears on stage and is unexpectedly analytical and lucid in her explanation of her plight. Fully aware of the way that society forms its judgements on issues and people (ll.218–19), she makes a case for herself. This quality of articulate advocacy she retains in arguments with Creon, Jason and Aegeus, often winning the assent of the chorus. Medea shows herself adept at the language of political life when she wants to be: her skill at it (especially following on the heels of the dark and primitive rage of which she gave a token before appearing on stage) sets up a deeply unsettling tension in the audience – especially, we can imagine, in a normally xenophobic fifth-century Athenian audience. An instinctive fear of the foreign and uncontrollable (fuelled by the sound of Medea's initial groaning) is followed by the shock of hearing one's own language (the language of formal supplication, and all the proper procedures that go with it – touching the beard, clasping the knees and so on)[11] used by a stranger. The easy distinctions between monsters

---

10 Euripides, *The Medea* in *Euripides I: Four Tragedies*, David Grene and Richmond Lattimore (eds.) (University of Chicago Press, 1955).
11 Ibid., ll.324, 709–10.

and barbarians on the outside, and civilized interlocutors to whom one owes respect and fair treatment on the inside, are utterly blurred. The monster is *inside* the city walls, while the 'civilized' figures are themselves implicated in the monstrousness (witness the cruelty of Creon's refusal to recognize Medea's case, plausible though it is in every aspect). The mixture of poetic forms – wild song and clear argument – stand in their interweaving combinations as evidence that clear distinctions between outside and inside are not to be made in this dramatic situation. The audience responds, then, both intellectually and emotionally to the powerful figure of Medea on stage, but is rocked between both kinds of response.

Epic, lyric and dramatic in Hegel and Balthasar

It is time to introduce Hegel. He steps on to the stage alongside Balthasar both as the epitome of modernity's quest for absolute knowledge and also, ironically, as a most nuanced student of embodied particulars, and the dramatic interchange of human beings in their shared existence. As Graham Ward has recognized in his essay, 'Hegel's position remains profoundly ambivalent'.[12] Ward talks of the 'egoism of modernity',[13] and yet (as we shall see) Hegel is not a pedlar of illusions about an asocial autonomy of the self. The subjectivity which Hegel articulates is not an egoistic but rather a dramatic one, and in this respect, Balthasar can acclaim him in volume I of *Theodramatik* as 'touching the nerve of our endeavour'. Hegel is both the icon of modernity's titanic aspirations, and the prophet of their subversion. And, I will argue, Balthasar lets both these facets of Hegel's thought interact with his own thinking. Hegel is both mentor and foe, but in each case he is given a role in the play. This essay will take seriously the task of measuring the thought of Hegel and Balthasar against each other, in the belief that to understand Balthasar's relationship to this one thinker is to appreciate crucial features of his more general attitude to modernity.

What we witnessed in our encounter with Aeschylus' *Agamemnon* was the dramatic combination of a presumed 'epic' distance belonging to one kind of poetic stance, and a passionate, self-involved 'lyricism' belonging to another kind. Their consummation was dramatic. It was just this distinction between the three styles – epic, lyric and dramatic – that Hegel set up as the culmination of his *Aesthetics*.[14] And, as Francesca Murphy mentions in passing in a 1993 article, and again in her recent book, Balthasar directly derives this typology of genre from Hegel and proceeds to use it theologically.[15] With whatever suspicion we come to regard the

---

12 Above, p. 35.
13 p. 50.
14 G. W. F. Hegel, *Aesthetics: Lectures on Fine Art* (2 vols), tr. T. M. Knox (Oxford University Press, 1975) (from now on referred to as *A*).
15 Francesca Aran Murphy, '"Whence comes this love as strong as death?": The presence of Franz Rosenzweig's "Philosophy as narrative" in Hans Urs von Balthasar's *Theo-Drama*', *Journal of Literature and Theology*, 7:3 (1993), p. 236; *Christ the Form of Beauty: A Study in Theology and Literature* (Edinburgh: T. & T. Clark, 1995), p. 163.

content of Hegel's analysis of the genres, there is no doubt that the broad lines of the typology offer a brilliant instrument for appreciating the nature of drama. Balthasar, whose academic training was as a 'Germanist', takes up the challenge of recasting dramatic theory in a theological way by taking the baton which Hegel proffered at the close of his grand aesthetic project and running with it.

It is a passage in volume II.1 of *Theodramatik* (TD II.1, 48–55; ThD 2, 54–62) which stands out as being of key importance for understanding Balthasar's choice of the dramatic genre as *Theodramatik*'s dominant motif, and for that reason it sheds important light on the whole of the central section of his theological trilogy. It is all the more relevant for our purposes because it manifests the deep debt to Hegel's typology of poetry which we have just noted, without feeling the need to draw attention to the fact in a laboured discussion. This point of contact with Hegel is of much greater interest than the explicit (and often polemical) treatments of his thought which occur elsewhere in Balthasar's work. It shows Balthasar taking Hegel's dramatic theory, without being bound to the letter of its original formulation, and creatively reapplying it for highly suggestive theological ends. He is not talking *about* Hegel – that particular debate is entirely secondary here to the work of creative theology. What it *does* show is that an awareness of the Hegelian sources enables one to be fully sensitive to the 'nerve' of Balthasar's endeavour.

Balthasar takes up Hegel's distinction between epic, lyric and dramatic, and shows how each can be used to characterize the relation of God's action to the world and to his creatures. He concludes that the dramatic (in this case the *theodramatic*) must have priority. Each of the first two perspectives (epic and lyric) is important but incomplete without its joint presence in the third, dramatic perspective. As we trace this argument, we shall see that it is an argument about far wider issues than are immediately apparent; implicit within it, in fact, is a characterization of (and attack on) modernity's construal of the stuff of human knowing and doing.

Epic, says Balthasar, 'smooths out the folds' of past history by reporting it under closure, so to speak. It assumes a standpoint from which one can observe and report impartially on a given sequence of events. Hegel had provided a precedent for this statement when he described epic as presenting us with 'an action complete in itself and the characters who produced it', and the form of the presentation as 'the broad flow of events'.[16] Balthasar begins to weave this theme theologically. Confronted by Jesus' suffering, he says, the epic view regards it as 'past history'. In a way that recalls the *Agamemnon*'s chorus as it tries to deny its investment in the events before it, epic's attitude to eucharistic celebration is to keep its distance. It prefers to make the eucharistic action narrowly an anamnesis of Jesus' suffering, and 'a mere calling to mind of a past event' (TD II.1, 48; ThD 2, 54–5). Systematic (systematizing) theology, for similar reasons, is prone to using this voice. Its concerns are often with the careful appropriation of the historical and textual traditions about God's action, and their redescription in terms of some kind of abiding 'universal

16 *A*, p. 1037.

significance'. By extension, the epic voice is also the voice used for 'external' relations, 'at councils and in the theological and polemical treatises dealing with heretics or the threat of error'. In the epic mode, God is referred to in the third person, as 'he', and the subject matter of the discourse is 'his' nature and action. In such cases – 'with a kind of bad conscience', as Balthasar puts it – one must speak 'about' (*über*) God, as though one were able to stand somehow 'over' (*über*) such subject matter. What Balthasar calls an 'epic-narrative theology' along these lines will 'assume the role of judge over the events and their actualization' (TD II.1, 50; ThD 2, 56).

That there are lines of continuity with Hegel's conception of epic is clear: epic summons up an entire narrative world in a way that proceeds tranquilly and steadily, comprehending all kinds of detail. An understanding of individual action as the direct expression of a broader teleology is the established criterion on which a reading of epic is grounded. The particular action and the individual agents are always, to use Hegel's phrase, 'conciliated' with 'the general world-situation'.[17] There is an element of *necessity* at the heart of the events and happenings that take place (Hegel also calls this element of necessity 'fate'). And this is one way of choosing to read the interaction between God and his creatures. But from Balthasar's point of view, it will almost certainly be an inadequate way of reading the world. At its worst, according to Balthasar, epic is the genre of a false objectification. It reifies what is given to it to know. It substitutes monological narration for dialogue, without supposing that this is a loss for truth.

Balthasar continues his appropriation and reapplication of Hegel as he turns to the lyric genre. The lyric voice stands at the opposite pole from the epic. Hegel had described lyric as the genre of the self-contemplating mind 'that instead of proceeding to action remains alone with itself as inwardness'. Its *telos*, Hegel had said, is 'the self-expression of the subjective life'.

> Here therefore there is no substantive whole unfolded as external happenings; on the contrary, it is the intuition, feeling, and meditation of the introverted individual, apprehending everything singly and in isolation, which communicate even what is most substantive and material as their own, as *their* passion, mood, or reflection, and as the present product of these.[18]

We will sense the spirit of Cassandra evoked here: the whole substance of an action is transposed into a volatile, highly individual, immediate, and emotionally coloured mode of response and expression. The *present* moment utterly dominates the foreground of lyrical subjectivity. 'What matters', Hegel had said, 'is only the soul of feeling and not what the object of the feeling is';[19] and 'what is satisfied . . . [is the need] for self-expression and for the apprehension of the mind in its own self-expression'.[20]

17 *A*, p. 1080.
18 *A*, p. 1038.
19 *A*, p. 1114.
20 *A*, p. 1113.

Drawing on this characterization, Balthasar is able to show how, in the lyric moment, an individual finds him or herself able to enter into a vivid representation of some past event, and to be enriched there imaginatively. The objective circumstances of the past event are filtered and appropriated by the subjective consciousness. They act as the 'external stimulus', to quote Hegel, which the individual uses 'as an opportunity for giving expression to himself'. Balthasar puts it this way: '"Lyrical" . . . means the internal motion of the devout subject, his emotion and submission, the creative outpouring of himself' (TD II.1, 49; ThD 2, 55). Eucharistic celebration in such a voice is an entirely different thing from its epic counterpart. Not only is the past event awakened by memory, its content is made present through reflection and imaginative participation, and brought alive 'just as if the event itself were here and now'. The lyrical is not the voice of councils and controversies, and of external relations; it is the voice which speaks in edification, from faith to faith, 'in the bosom of the Church'. In the lyric mode, God is addressed as 'Thou'.

Balthasar concludes that at a point very near its source, 'the river of Christian utterance splits into two streams' (TD II.1, 49; ThD 2, 55–6), and this is a split which has parallels with the traceable divergences in the modern West between a quest for reification and control (on the one hand) and (on the other) an involutedly lyrical obsession with an asocial and atemporal subjectivity – the subject's presence to herself in a consciousness around which the world revolves. Both are denials of an open, dramatically social future. As Catherine Pickstock argues, both undertake a kind of war on time, in reaction to the perceived impermanence of things. Both attempt to deny the difference time makes, trying instead to *organize* the flux'[21] (this is, in Pickstock's terms, 'a process of spatialization'), and this often issues in an architectonic and therefore forcibly ordered structuring of the things that occur in the world in their various proportions and relationships.

Epic's pretensions to objective distance, on this account, become the pretensions of modernity in its belief that there can be a single vantage point on history and creation (which is no longer, of course, creation – for that would concede its character as gift – but rather 'nature', and therefore an object of our manipulation). Situations, arguments and problems, modernity claims, are always and in principle treatable under the terms of a universal method. Rationality is singular, determinate, unambiguous. Where it is ostensibly resistant to consensus, it is necessarily aberrant. Paradox, indeterminacy and spontaneity are not reasonable. Modernity at its most epic, then, presides over a shift 'from the oral to the written'; 'from the particular to the universal'; 'from the local to the general' and from the time-specific to the time-independent.[22]

And yet modernity must 'turn to the subject' in order to anchor this universal, epic reason, and here is one of its greatest paradoxes. It must depend (with an unjustifiable faith) on a speculative wager which can never adequately be underwritten: that human reason is not assembled

---

21 Catherine Pickstock, 'Necrophilia: The middle of modernity', *Modern Theology*, 12:4 (1996), pp. 407–8.
22 Toulmin, *Cosmopolis*, pp. 30–5.

out of the midst of contingency, but has an authoritative, structured, interpretative centre which time and chance cannot alter. This abstraction from the movement of time asserts something like a steady, eternal 'present', which is always nearer to the subject than anything generated by passing events and experiences. Convinced of this 'present', one can presume to deny the fragility and indebtedness of human subjectivity. On this view, one need never adopt an attitude of thanksgiving for what comes to one (unasked for and groundless) as the gift of one's self; nor need one adopt the (equally eucharistic) attitude of *anticipation* – anticipation of that 'knowing even as I am known' which keeps Christian life in motion and free of solipsism.

That Balthasar concurs with this diagnosis of modernity as both too epic and too lyric (and as too often at a loss to know how to heal this rift) becomes apparent in the introduction to *Herrlichkeit*. Modernity's taste for epic generates 'exact sciences' whose exactness pertains to only 'one particular sector of reality' because of its 'abstraction'. It cannot express the rich particularity and love of 'the living bond between God and the world'. At the same time, the breathing world is disowned by the subjectivity to which it gave birth – the subject asserts its autonomy and self-subsistence, so that the world is concomitantly devalued as 'but an appearance and a dream – the Romantic vision'. But these evasions can only be a prelude to a very modern despair: the world resists both moves (is 'unmastered'), and the human creature is left 'to live with the object of his impotence', which he cannot bear (H I, 15–16, 17; GL 1, 18, 19).

What therapy is there for this rift between the brutely given and the banally free which the illegitimate aspirations (these 'ends') of modernity have opened up? In the specific context of divided Christian utterance, this is the question that Balthasar tries to answer by a turn to drama. He turns to consider whether there is an alternative to mere alternation between the voices of epic and lyric respectively, and finds that their unity rests only in the dramatic dimension of revelation. Hegel still proves useful here, as we see by the fact that Balthasar's is a classic dialectical formulation in Hegelian vein:

> We shall not get beyond the alternatives of 'lyrical' and 'epic', spirituality (prayer and personal involvement) and theology (the objective discussion of facts), so long as we fail to include the dramatic dimension of revelation, in which alone they discover their unity. (TD II.1, 50; ThD 2, 57)

Hegel had said that drama brings us nearer than any other form of poetry to 'the spirit in its wholeness', because it does justice to the 'objectivity which proceeds from the subject' as well as to 'subjectivity which gains portrayal in its objective realization and validity'.[23] Drama, in other words, joins the dimensions of both epic and lyric into a new whole, which shows the relationship between certain kinds of events (or 'objective developments') and their 'origin in the hearts of individuals'. The result is that the object is displayed as belonging to the subject, while

23 *A*, p. 1039.

conversely the individual subject is brought before our eyes ... in his transition to an appearance in the real world.'[24] The significance of the *acting subject*, therefore, is the key difference between epic and dramatic poetry. Happenings that arise from external circumstances and not from an agent's 'inner will and character' are not *dramatic*, in Hegel's terminology.

Balthasar's theological transformation of Hegel's concept of the acting subject focuses on the figure of the *apostolic witness*, as the dramatic 'person' whose voice is most nearly a unifying and heightening of both epic and lyric ways of speaking. The faith of the apostle speaks to those within faith *and* to those outside faith – his witness is not one of impartial report, but is witness vouched for by the participation of his whole life. Paul's letters put God's action at the centre, but include himself (taken over by this action on the Damascus road) as *part* of the testimony to the truth of revelation. Paul 'pulls out all the stops of his existence in order to convince those to whom he is writing that they too are drawn into this action just as much as he is'. Only in this dimension can it be seen how Jesus' death and resurrection are alive and present. The evangelists, too, 'do not recount stories in which they are not involved; in fact, they know that their only chance of being objective is by being profoundly involved in the event they are describing'. Imaginative participation is actually the proper form of their objectivity, to the extent that God is never *simply* spoken of as 'He', without the 'Thou' (which acknowledges that the One spoken of is always present) being implicit at every point. The essentially dramatic activity of bearing witness before both Church and world – of personally handing on the drama of Jesus' life even as it lives in oneself – overrides the epic/lyric distinction. (Thus the drama is equally alive in all good catechesis.) Meanwhile, Scripture does not 'stand at some observation post outside'. It, too, is inside the drama. Its content points beyond itself to the Spirit which makes the drama present and alive in each new scene. Scripture mirrors the drama which is manifested by the Spirit, and Scripture 'can only be understood in reference to' this drama (TD II.1, 52; ThD 2, 58).

Balthasar is here living and breathing Hegel's analysis of drama. When Hegel says that in drama 'the *entire* person of the actor is laid claim to' and that 'the living man himself is the material medium of expression',[25] he unwittingly sets a pattern for Balthasar's apostolic witnesses who 'with their lives ... vouch for the testimony they must give' (TD II.1, 51; ThD 2, 57). Individual characters (like the apostolic witnesses and catechists of Balthasar's scheme) and their aims are important inasmuch as they generate action. They are dramatically significant *for the sake of* the action. And the action is significant, in turn, inasmuch as it is penetrated by and fitted to the characters and their aims. The intentions and aims of acting characters are not to be separated from external happenings and deeds. There is a striking interdependence of the subject's mind and character (on the one hand) and the *telos* of the action (on the other), and this last point in particular (about the *telos*) is something that Balthasar's

24 *A*, p. 1038.
25 *A*, p. 1039.

understanding of drama has inherited very substantially from Hegel. In fact, Balthasar's theology of mission positions character in line with the broader aim or *telos* of action in more or less the same way that Hegel's *Phenomenology* shows Spirit aligning individuals with the movement of rational necessity (each individual event properly finding its goal in teleological relation to the embracing system). The mediating function of the Church in Balthasar's theology of mission is closely comparable to the notion of mediation (between collections of acting people) which Hegel sees not only in drama, but also (on another level) in the State, right down to the language of sacrifice or extermination (*Vertilgung*[26] and *Aufopferung*[27]) as the means to freedom from the 'extreme of individuality'.

But Balthasar's theology of mission has another influence, beyond even Hegel's – and that influence is St Ignatius of Loyola. Even when he ceased to be a Jesuit, Balthasar remained an Ignatian to his core. Drama's power to draw one into the truth was always recognized by Ignatius. *The Spiritual Exercises* are an extraordinary kind of rehearsal for taking part in the action, in a way that reconstitutes the self in a life of praise and dramatic sociality. They know the necessity of creating a 'culture' by which truth can be borne. They are an education in *how to read* from a position 'in the middle' of existence, by a loving act of interpretation and participation. They therefore hold, for modernity, a remarkable potential for healing.

And yet there is an ambivalence in Balthasar's Ignatian, as in his Hegelian, heritage. For Ignatian dramatics stand famously at the threshold of modernity, even as Balthasarian dramatics look back on it – and there is in Ignatius a strongly lyrical strain. Balthasar recognizes this. The *Exercises'* invitation to 'Imagine Christ our Lord present before you upon the cross, and begin to speak with him'[28] is a moment which exemplifies a particularly lyrical kind of spirituality. Ignatius is sometimes accused of a concentration on the individual (to the detriment of the 'discursive character of life')[29] which is already modern. Balthasar must deal with this legacy.

He must also deal with the legacy of Hegel, whose role as both potentate and ironist of the modern quest for certainty we have already noted. Hegel too identifies (from the middle of modernity) drama's therapeutic powers. As Rowan Williams (echoing Gillian Rose) has affirmed, there is in Hegel a profound insistence on 'the "speculative" projection of a continually self-adjusting, self-criticizing corporate practice' in his thinking about thinking.[30] This is not blithe theorizing about a total, reconciled historical unity. If Hegel presents us with truth as system in

---

26 G. W. F. Hegel, *Phenomenology of Spirit*, tr. A.V. Miller (Oxford University Press, 1977), p. 137.

27 Ibid., p. 213.

28 *The Spiritual Exercises of St Ignatius*, tr. Louis J. Puhl SJ (Chicago: Loyola University Press, 1951), p. 28 (§53).

29 George P. Schner (ed.), *Ignatian Spirituality in a Secular Age* (Ontario: Wilfrid Laurier University Press, 1984), p. 5.

30 Rowan D. Williams, 'Between Politics and Metaphysics: Reflections in the Wake of Gillian Rose', *Modern Theology*, 11:1 (1995), 14.

the *Phenomenology*, it is nevertheless not a system that can be grasped from any one partial position. Thinking, on this account of Hegel, has the character of 'engagement', and of 'converse, conflict, negotiation, judgement and self-judgement'.

But this account cannot bypass the fact that a 'steady formal presence'[31] remains in the process, as Milbank – calling it the 'myth of negation' – has remarked. This myth of negation is the underpinning of the Hegelian dialectic, whereby, by a kind of logic, the initial positing of an object or state of knowing leads to its negation (and consequent preservation or sublation). This logic of negation intrudes its determining operation upon a realm which might otherwise be occupied by *poiēsis*: the positive, constructive *imagining* of alternatives to any given state of affairs. In this way, as Milbank points out, Hegel 'subordinates the contingencies of human making/speaking to the supposedly "logical" articulation of a subjectivity which is secretly in command throughout'.[32] Contingency is consigned to the level of the merely indifferent: the indefinite base of Hegel's pyramidic construction. And this is Hegel's epic side.

The work of excavation should have given us by now a sufficient sense of Balthasar's substantial debt to Hegel, and his approval and appropriation of Hegelian insights where the value and character of drama are concerned. But Hegel's very modern *betrayal* of drama in certain other (key) respects is something against which Balthasar has to guard. This will help us to understand Balthasar's more general position of antagonism towards Hegel, and his endeavour to recover a sense of divine glory and sovereign freedom over against Hegel's depiction of unfolding process. But we cannot rule out the possibility that Balthasar will succumb to the same pitfalls as those to which he alerts us in Hegel.

The case against Hegel

Hegel correctly saw, according to Balthasar, that a 'spiritual horizon ... was ... the precondition for a meaningful play, whether it was tragic, comic or simply dramatic' (TD I, 66; ThD 1, 71). His depiction of the actualization of Spirit as embodied consciousness against which individuals could be observed and judged dramatically or, later, historically, was an attempt to adumbrate just such a 'given, absolute meaning' in a rational way. Balthasar does not dismiss this attempt out of hand, but implies that *the 'spiritual horizon' opened up by his own vision of God's 'bestowing freedom' maintains a sense of the dramatic better than Hegel himself ever managed*. Despite providing so rich and subtle a typology of genre, Hegel's characterizations of drama, so Balthasar seems to imply, never make the grade, and this is because they can never break free of certain epic undertones. Hegel's dramatic persons – even in the full extent of their freedom – are shown to be subordinated to a wider realm of operative circumstances (*poiēsis* subordinated to the myth of negation). 'A genuine end', writes Hegel, 'is ... only attained when the aim and interest

---

31 Ibid., p. 15.
32 John Milbank, *Theology and Social Theory: Beyond Secular Reason* (Oxford: Blackwell, 1990), p. 157.

of the action, on which the whole drama turns, is identical with the individuals and absolutely bound up with them ... and at the denouement, every part of the whole thing must be closed and finished off.'[33] Thus, for Balthasar, Hegel's understanding of tragedy fades off into a vision which becomes merely epic in its immanence. He asserts that Being in Hegel and the other philosophers of Spirit 'loses its freedom' in the '"Odyssey" of its cosmic evolution towards itself' (H III.1/2, 965; GL 5, 636).

In the Christian perspective, by contrast, Balthasar wants to say that the epic undertones of the Hegelian dialectic are overcome at the same time as lyric individualism is kept at bay. The things that happen to an individual do not matter only to him or her and only in a series of discrete moments (a 'lyric' view which at its worst degenerates into the 'banally free'). Nor, at the other extreme, do the things that happen to an individual have meaning only in relation to vast and impersonal forces which underlie the world as we know it (the 'epic' or 'brutely given'). No 'superordinate sphere' is set over against the significance of individual lives in the Christian vision. As Balthasar puts it, 'the divine dramatic *answer*' has taken place 'in the form of the human dramatic *question*'. The cry from the cross 'is the very antithesis of that kind of religious resignation which surrenders to an undramatic, absolute horizon'. And the answer that is given in response to it is

> relevant in all ages, being both the answer to *this* particular cry and ultimately, eschatologically, the answer to every cry. It cannot lose its relevance because it is itself entirely *act*, although it only shows itself to be such where people are themselves acting and questioning dramatically. The precise meaning of *eph-hapax*, then, is that there is a unique answer to all instances of the question. Not an answer definitively known and kept safe, obviating the question. (TD I, 20–1; ThD 1, 21)

On Balthasar's account, the trinitarian God of Love as Christians understand him (and only that God) makes absolutely secure the conditions upon which drama relies for its effect. This God shows that the touchstone of what is true lies not simply in the subject's presence to self, and certainly not in the subject's abject irrelevance to some abiding and overriding completeness, but in the giving and rendering back of freedom between a 'Thou' and an 'I'. He shows that such loving freedom stands in analogical relation to the ultimate trinitarian freedom, and is dependent on its creative gratuity. The dramatic differentiations of creatures are situated within the relational 'super-differentiations' of the Trinity. Thus the integrity of the creature as creature is preserved and intensified; it is situated in a mysterious relation (a relation in which there is no room for a secret, underlying identity) to what is ultimate in and beyond the life of the world.

The resources yielded by analogy are Balthasar's key safeguards against that presumption of an identity between human consciousness

33 *A*, p. 1167.

and the self-consciousness of Spirit which he suspects has been per-
petrated by Hegel – a move in which 'Thou' and 'I' are made to mean less
than they should. The mutual self-gift of the persons within God's own
trinitarian being, seen with the eyes of Christian faith, affirms human
relationships of love in all their ungraspability and their irreducible
differentiation (as well as their freedom from any assumption of self-
sufficiency). It affirms them because it sees in each case as an
analogue (indeed, inasmuch as they are loving, a uniquely privileged
analogue) of God's trinitarian being. Relationships of love, for Balthasar,
show that personal self-possession and identity are not things to be
counted on, except by grace. The creature becomes dramatically
significant only as related to, only in relationship. Yes, the person's
subjectivity is his or her own, but it is entirely a gift, which is first received
from another:

> [The Christian's] faith teaches him to see within the most seemingly
> unimportant interpersonal relation the making present and the
> 'sacrament' of the eternal I–Thou relation which is the ground of the
> free Creation and again the reason why God the Father yields His
> Son to the death of darkness for the salvation of every Thou. (H
> III.1/2, 977; GL 5, 649)

Jacob's ladder: the exercise of analogy

We have just witnessed Balthasar's case for a more really dramatic drama
than Hegel ever comprehended, argued (with the help of analogy) on the
basis of an understanding of the unbridgeable difference between creator
and creature over against any understanding that conceals an assumption
of ultimate identity. His theological construction on this basis seems
admirably to meet the requirements for a safe passage between the
'brutely given' and the 'banally free'. But perhaps a little more pressure
can be applied before we rest satisfied – and this will be an exercise which
(importantly) enables us to tease out with greater subtlety what is at stake
in Balthasar's handling of analogy.

Lucy Gardner and David Moss identify what it is that Balthasar must
achieve in order to make good his case against modernity. He must
develop his doctrine of the analogical relationship between divine and
human being 'as precisely no valorized interval, as no fixed gap between
the world and God'.[34] The suspicion that a theological aesthetics (like that
presented in *Herrlichkeit*) relies too heavily on mapping the harmonious
proportionality between creatures and their creator must be allayed by a
presentation of the moving image which is Theo-Drama. This will restore
to theology the forgotten knowledge that we can only think towards the
truth 'from the middle' of creaturely existence, and that this necessarily
involves a continuous activity of imaginatively constructive participation,
in which we develop our own interpretative readings of God's ways in
the world alongside the readings of other people. There is no clear sight of

34 Above, p. 115.

the whole pattern here – this is the danger of the *Gestalt* language developed in Balthasar's theological aesthetics. Rather – in dramatically social fashion – one must think with the help (and the discipline) of analogy.

Now the language of analogy needs extremely sensitive handling, as Balthasar knew from his long association with both Erich Przywara and Karl Barth. The kind of analogy resisted by Barth is precisely that crude assertion of proportionality between God and creature to which we have just adverted. Balthasar answers this concern by his rehabilitation (following Przywara) of the Fourth Lateran Council's vital emphasis on the God who is 'ever-greater': 'However great the similarity between God and the creature may be, the dissimilarity is always greater [*maior dissimilitudo*]'.[35]

This is an acknowledgement first of the analogical ordering of being, in that God's being-God and the creature's being-created are not identical kinds of being. They do not draw on some independent repository of being *per se*. No neutral notion of being is presupposed, of which God and humans are equally exemplifications. The *analogy* in being is that these non-identical ways of being are in some way ordered to one another, which is to say that createdness is posited by God's creatorhood, preservation and sustenance, not as continuous with it, but as corresponding with it in its own proper and distinct way. In this sense, despite Barth's suspicions, it has the same character as the relationship between faith and grace in the *analogia fidei*.

An analogical mode of *knowing* corresponds to this analogical ordering of *being*. Given that God's being is 'ever-greater', and that every similarity is enveloped in dissimilarity (so that we cannot adequately frame it – we 'lose the track and run off the path'), our ways of *reading* the divine must display not only a passionate commitment to acknowledging God's intimacy, but also the reverent reserve that is called forth by a God 'ever-greater'. Balthasar is convinced that the best way to express this is in terms of comparatives – they foster a more properly Christian 'reading' of God than superlatives ever can. Superlatives are static abstractions; they become, in the hands of modernity (and in Pickstock's words), objects 'to end all objects', and they represent 'the once-and-for-all termination of desire' rather than its limitless enrichment and play.[36] In refusing to delimit the operation of this comparative principle, one acknowledges the uncloseable character of what we might call the 'vertical' analogical relation to the 'ever-greater'.

But then there comes another (analogous) kind of analogical expression. As Moss and Gardner suggest, there is an analogical relation between the 'vertical' analogies that keep open the space between divine disclosure and creaturely appropriation, and the 'horizontal' analogies which emerge from all our myriad readings of the world and the interchange within it – our interpretations of the superabundance of the world's particulars and their 'wonderful commerce'. This horizontal movement, too, can say with the *Agamemnon*'s chorus, 'the end we do not

---

35 See Balthasar's use of this text (drawing on Denzinger) in H III.1/2, 881; GL 5, 548.
36 Pickstock, 'Necrophilia', p. 405.

know'. Here, too, we can participate (constructively) in an ecstatic movement which promises truth without closure. Joining, with mind and heart, in the rich 'horizontal' conception of analogies is our most legitimate way of involving ourselves in the creation's movement through time, and it protects us from falsely trying to make the world and our reading of the world stand still.

The horizontal *ekstasis* (set in motion when we recognize analogies in created being) is not without relation to the vertical, though we do well to respect analogy's charge not to finalize the similarities. There is much to be gained from showing (in the face of modernity) that all acts of knowing – as much our knowing of the world as our knowing of God – are more 'traversals' than 'appropriations'.[37] It may be that the 'ever-more' that is evoked by our pluriform 'horizontal' itineraries of analogical recognition becomes a nearer way than any other of honouring God's 'ever-greater' relation to us – which is, after all, given *in creation* as a 'luminous invitation'.[38] The analogies we conceive, if we dare to believe this, can become like Jacob's ladder: 'Unaccountably scaffolding skyward', in the words of a contemporary poem.[39] Of the building of this ladder the poem remarks 'How long it must have taken', and 'What endless patience' it must have demanded. And indeed the angels 'tread upon it cautiously' – as they and we must. But our activities of knowing, provisional though they must be, orientate themselves in faith to an inconceivable richness of possibility promised to us by God in the passage of time – most especially the gift of himself.

The truth of revelation, Balthasar says, acknowledging all this, is found in movement; in 'a continuous forward striving (*diastasis*)':

> [This *diastasis*] is the truth of the *cor inquietum*, of hope and love for what is absent. It is into *this* human experience that the divine truth comes to embed itself. This delicate network of temporal relationships is strong enough to hold the absolute truth, which is itself a truth of eternal relations in an eternal life. (ST I, 85; ExT 1, 80)

Thus Balthasar himself asserts what we have already supposed his theology to imply: the fittingness of temporality's motive incompleteness (and our never-finalized explorations of truth in time) to the analogical expression of God's otherness. There is a 'fit' between *diastasis* in time and the *diastasis* of God's otherness. The restless heart's hoping and loving through time are not wholly distinguishable from its restlessness in ('vertical') relation to God's ungraspable plenitude. This acknowledgement of temporality is an important one in Balthasar's thought – particularly in conjunction with the suggestion that 'unaccountably' the 'scaffolding' of the temporal constructions of our human experience may form a ladder by which heaven draws near to us. We are reminded here again, as we were before, that Balthasar's task in *Theodramatik* must be to reconceive form as more than just pulchritudinous structure. He must

---

37 Ibid., p. 421.
38 Ibid.
39 Sally Bushell, *Night Thoughts* (Cambridge, 1997).

demonstrate something other than the 'spatialization' of time. He must communicate a notion of form not architectonic but diachronous.

Gardner and Moss are optimistic that Balthasar's theology does not entail 'any riveting of "parts" on to an empty frame, nor ... any correlation of God to his creature'.[40] And indeed, at first blush, it seems as though Balthasar's turn to drama gives his notion of *Gestalt* added mobility. But even Gardner and Moss must admit that he manifests a tendency to 'encode temporality', and they know that 'this move is not unconnected with a general feature of the logic of modernity'. Gender is an area in which Balthasar is particularly tempted to attempt this 'structuration' – but the larger question raised is whether all his gestures towards diachronicity do not in the end fall back into an organization of the flux which is 'strategic and studied'.[41]

For the terms of a rather static idea of form can be used to interpret even the relations which drama displays. Dramatic interchange can succumb to a composite patterning, and because this patterning aspires to the wholeness of *Gestalt*, it becomes precisely a pseudo-spatialization. Such form – such composite patterning – can be almost as architectonic as anything implied by the aesthetics. It can become a *matrix* (and therefore an intermediate middle ground) which regulates the properly unframeable relation of creator and creature (as well as the relations between creatures and creatures). To allow this to happen is to deny dramatic insights with regard to human existence. It shares the deficiencies of modernity's epic perspective in its ambition to read the ways of God in the world.

The alternative has the potential to be dangerous, too. The 'flux' which is the passage of time can invite the 'lyrical' interpretation that it is *just* flux – in other words, 'banally free'. Christian theology which seeks not to be epic faces the problem of how to interpret the 'flux' as not totally random and undefined (which is to say unjudgeable and unredeemable).

It must find a way of doing this which does reintroduce an element of dramatic articulation, but does not bring us back in subjection to epic's attempts at marshalling command. It must work on the basis that epic need not be the only alternative to lyric. Yes, the successiveness of time (and our conceiving of analogies in time) calls out to be treated theologically in a way that allows it a certain integrity and coherence, because God creates and sustains it through his redemptive faithfulness. Augustine, and theologians after him, have used an analogy with music to show how flux can be thus articulated without ceasing to be open-ended. But (theology has the resources to say) this is not necessarily an *epic* perspective. The key aspect to the belief that 'all ... limited perspectives ... are themselves beautifully integrated into the cosmic poem' is that it is *belief* – it is participatory faith, not epic sight. The flux may be articulated, but it seems we cannot (ever) view the totality of those articulations, because they are intimated only *in* the flux. We learn to read 'from the middle', and this is necessarily an activity of faith. It demands what I will call an existential register.

40 Above, p. 72.
41 Pickstock, 'Necrophilia', p. 408.

Nicholas Lash takes the idea of 'metachronics' from Bishop Christopher Butler to illustrate this. Music for him, too, provides a reminder that 'temporality has structures'. He reflects, then, that

> If we take metaphysics to mean our general sense and under-standing of the structure of the world, beyond particular categories and things and instances, then we might describe as 'metachronics' our attempts to understand the whence and whither of the world, its 'metatemporal' structure beyond particular episodes, epochs, stories and occasions.[42]

Now Christians, because of the fact that they have an 'unsurpassable particularity of memory' which furnishes their faith with its 'defining centre', are bound to seek a certain 'metachronic understanding' around which their activities of 'remembrance and expectation' structure them-selves.[43] But this is *faith* seeking metachronic understanding. Meta-chronics is every bit as vulnerable as metaphysics to the 'quite unwarranted imperialistic claims to theoretical finality' which this essay has associated with modernity. The restraint a Christian theology must exercise is governed by the fact that 'metachronics will remain, as long as there is time, unfinished!'[44]

Making the relations that emerge in time 'accountable' by forcing them through a supposed matrix which is pre-emptively exhaustive of all their possible combinations is an overweeningly epic gesture – it is bad metachronics, and therefore a false reading of the world. The mere notion of 'harmony' or 'resolution' can act as a matrix of this prefiguring kind, and so occlude the significance of time. And where time suffers, so does analogy. Analogy, wrongly understood in terms of 'valorizing intervals', represents precisely that kind of grid which interferes with a full, free differentiation between God and humanity in history.

In this section, we have raised the question of whether much of Balthasar's honouring of diachronicity (and, with that, of the poetic exploration of the world's truth) does not in the end fall back into an architectonic act of spatialization, which predetermines all the human possibilities of participation in this drama. It seems as though Balthasar is too ready to take the Hegelian path of allowing history to empty itself into system, rather than overturning the tables of modernity, and tipping system back into history again. This Hegelian instinct is confirmed by his association of drama with the notion of harmonious resolution: dramas, on such an understanding, give formed, generalized expression to human patterns of encounter (and therefore, by extension into theodramatic terms, to *divine*/human patterns of encounter). We perceive this debt to Hegelian thinking when Balthasar talks of drama's 'unificatory endeavour that sheds light on existence' (TD I, 241; ThD 1, 262) as mirroring 'the eternal, divine plan' (TD I, 109; ThD 1, 119), or of

---

42 Nicholas Lash, *The Beginning and the End of 'Religion'* (Cambridge University Press, 1996), p. 30.
43 Ibid., p. 31.
44 Ibid., p. 70.

'the indivisible unity of the play's ideal content', or of 'the pleasure of being presented with a "solution"' (TD I, 242, 243–4; ThD 1, 262, 264). He fuels the suspicion that he is often in danger of looking for an innate stability in the constitution of human life and its interactions which it is not theirs to possess. This can only compromise Balthasar's attempt to restore to life once again a *'cor inquietum'* in modernity's breast.

And this in turn risks playing into an ecclesiology which attributes a dimension of 'objective' holiness to the Church. Any such notion of the Church, like any over-resolved notion of the integrating power of dramatic form, seems to represent a theologically questionable stage or arena for the working out of the truth of the relationship between God and human beings. In order to see whether this is indeed what happens in Balthasar's thought, it is to his theology of the Church that we now turn.

Crystallized love: the birth of Balthasar's theology of the Church

We have found ourselves compelled to say that Balthasar's dramatic theory has many of modernity's failings – failings showing up most noticeably, in this case, as Hegelian debts. These failings play directly into the weaknesses of his otherwise promising attempt to construct a 'theodramatics' that will do justice to the experience and existence of believers in relation to God.

Balthasar is difficult wholly to impugn here, because the ends he sets out to achieve are sufficiently distinct in his own mind from the ends of modernity (as we have characterized them for the purposes of this essay) to resist assimilation in any obvious way. In particular, he is vocal in his rejection of Hegel's immanent teleology, and can call on extraordinarily powerful rhetoric to evoke a horizon of eschatological possibility which is dramatically open. Some of the best examples of his passion on this point arise from his self-definition against Karl Barth, whom he accuses of having 'gone a bit too far into the light' (KB, 368; B, 358). Barth's tone, he says, 'veritably thrums with a hymnic certainty of eventual victory' (KB, 364; B, 354). It seems that Balthasar, by contrast, is the advocate of a far more radical existential irresolution.[45]

Balthasar's failure properly to confound modernity's persistent pursuit of its ends is not, therefore, at its most visible in his explicit treatments of eschatology. Rather, it only comes into view when one begins (as we have begun) to be sensitive to the way in which a dynamic conception of analogy can turn into an act of reification; time's movement can end up being construed as bad metachronic architecture; the pluriform nature of creaturely interactions can end up obscured by a matrix which believes that it contains in itself (in logically prior fashion) all the relevant possibilities for human relationship. Of course, the material resists it, and that means that in practical terms the only way of sustaining an impulse to 'frame' things in abstraction from the

---

45 For a more extended discussion of this contrast, and some suggestions why it is not quite as easy to draw as it first seems, see my article 'Von Balthasar and the Dialogue with Karl Barth', *New Blackfriars* 79:923 (1998).

contingencies and bountiful vagaries of time is through a forgetfulness of history – what P. J. FitzPatrick in his book on the eucharist calls 'selective amnesia'.[46] In this section, I want to suggest that this is what enables Balthasar in his ecclesiology to structure atemporally what is a phenomenon that ought to have an irreducibly temporal aspect, namely, the Church itself.

The saints – and centrally the saints of the New Testament – constellate, according to Balthasar, around the form of Christ, and become *types* of the various forms of life which can take shape in the Church in response to the generative Word. In this way, they participate in the overall event of revelation. They function as typical (emblematic) figures of ecclesial life, and are ordered to one another accordingly. So, for instance, John (with Mary) represents 'love', Peter 'office', and Paul and James alongside them make up a fourfold structure which determines the form of the Church's existence (in imitation of its Lord) and the form of its theology.[47] Balthasar is scrupulous in inserting at every point the caveat that the 'unity' which reigns between these 'pillars' is not primarily a unity 'on the level of "brotherliness", but in their common looking upwards to the one personal centre of all theologies' (i.e. Jesus Christ). But the unity he intuits in these New Testament types seems nonetheless like a relatively strong and unreserved claim to perceive the dimensions of the form of revelation as it takes shape in its specifically *ecclesial* medium. It is a vision in which the (analogically) unfolding transposition of Christ's form into the lives of countless saints in Christian history is 'contained' by the placing of something like a grid (or net) of exemplary relations at its source. It is also an intuited unity that, in order to give itself any legitimacy, must sit fairly light to traditional exegetical concerns, and must depend on some decidedly idiosyncratic interpretations of New Testament passages. The fact, for example, that Peter and John run together to the tomb of Jesus is taken as evidence of the birth of 'a Church with two poles: the Church of office and the Church of love, with a harmonious [!] tension between them'.[48] But how securely can one make the assertion that what John's Gospel seeks to present in this resurrection narrative is a comparison between two 'ecclesiologies'; that there is ecclesiological significance in the fact that one runs faster than the other; that Peter arrives second because encumbered by the preoccupations of office; that John holds back and allows Peter to enter the tomb first because he recognizes Peter's distinctive authority? Balthasar owes much to Karl Barth in his self-consciously literary reading of the presentation and interaction of character in the Gospels,[49] but the elaborateness of his readings exceeds the critical reservation exercised by Barth, and is difficult to dissociate from his speculations in *First Glance at Adrienne von*

---

46 P. J. FitzPatrick, *In Breaking of Bread: The Eucharist and Ritual* (Cambridge University Press, 1993), p. 237.
47 H III.2/2, 101; GL 7, 111; cf. also ST I, 129–30; ExT 1, 122.
48 German text in *Mysterium Salutis: Grundriss Heilsgeschichtlicher Dogmatik* III/2, J. Feiner and M. Löhrer (eds.) (Einsiedeln: Benziger, 1969), p. 315.
49 Cf., for example, Barth's drawing of formal correspondences between Paul and Judas, discussed in David F. Ford, *Barth and God's Story* (Frankfurt am Main: Peter Lang, 1981), p. 87.

Speyr about the quasi-mathematical structure of the communion of saints and its capacity to configure the fullness of the Church's sanctity.[50] Balthasar's treatment of the Church mutates at times into a masterpiece of spatialization. The missions of the saints have their analogical relations (interpreted as a 'variety in unity') displayed as 'a whole spiritual geometry of heaven' (ST I, 242; ExT 1, 225).

Behind all the other saints in their various configurations, there stands Mary, who manifests for Balthasar the consummate ecclesial disposition. Because she makes herself more available in God's service than any other person in the drama, her mission is the most comprehensive of all the missions of the saints – it has the furthest 'reach'. *Everyone* is affected by Mary's *fiat*. Mary is so fully receptive to the will of God for his redeemed people that she becomes the 'real symbol' of what the Church perfectly is, so that Balthasar is happy to talk at times of 'Mary–Church' as of a single entity.

The marian form of the Church, however – like the ecclesial constellation of saints – is yet another encroachment into the area of the *maior dissimilitudo* by means of a privileged mediation of the super-form. Indeed, Balthasar sees it as the perfect *Gestalt* of that divine form which has been transposed into the creaturely realm. It is thereby the inclusion and completion of the exemplary interrelations of all the other saints. So whereas the notion of transposition (like the notion of analogy, in whose ambit it is) *could* be used to describe an open-ended series of new improvisations on the christological form, it ends up here (like Balthasar's use of analogy in wider respects) slipping back into an assertion of timelessly harmonious proportion. In this case, the proportion is between the divine kenosis, and marian self-surrender (cast by Balthasar as a kind of Ignatian *indiferencia*).

This, in turn, demonstrates the historical forgetfulness which FitzPatrick called 'selective amnesia'. Can any consenting act of availability to God be abstracted in the way that Balthasar abstracts Mary's? Is it right to forget the *particular* circumstances and the *particular* occasion on which Mary said this *particular* 'yes' to a *particular* call?

We should take a moment to trace just what effects this move to *generalize* Mary's self-surrender (and thereby make it something like a 'still centre' for the divine–human relation, impervious to time) can have. A way to test it is to see what it does to the theology of the eucharist, which prima facie ought to be theology particularly sensitive to the role that temporal extension and non-identical repetition play in the 'scaffolding' of the Christian life and its 'reading' of God.

The eucharist does indeed play an important part in Balthasar's theology. It appears at a significant moment in his Christology (TD II.2, cf. especially 223; ThD 3, 243), and is positively central to his treatment of soteriology (TD III, 295–395; ThD 4, 317–423).[51]

---

50 *First Glance at Adrienne von Speyr* (San Francisco: Ignatius Press, 1981), pp. 82–5; *Erster Blick auf Adrienne von Speyr* (Einsiedeln: Johannes Verlag, 1989), pp. 72–6.

51 As we have already noted, there are also important considerations of the eucharist in the final essays of ST II (502–24; ExT 2, 491–513).

The once-for-all event of Christ's *eucharistia* – or self-offering – meets the sins of the world at every point; confronting them wherever they arise. This is so not only in the past but also in this present time (the time of God's patience) which precedes Christ's second coming. Christ's *eucharistia*, in other words, has an eternal aspect, and this means the continual and present operation even of the human suffering (the 'wounds') of Christ in relation to human sin. It is almost as though (from one perspective) the persistence of human sin keeps the wounds alive and concrete 'from below'.

And such 'distribution' of Christ's suffering and death by means of its eternal aspect seems not to compete with, but rather to enhance, a certain existential seriousness in terms of the human response. As Balthasar puts it, '[i]n the transition from the Old to the New Covenant, "night" has become intensified; at the crucifixion, it covers the whole universe (Mt 27:45); the sword has become sharper, death more radical' (TD III, 335; ThD 4, 359). This cannot but affect the Church's existence, and the lives of individual believers. The Church can expect, with Mary, to be taken into 'utter forsakenness and darkness' (TD III, 334; ThD 4, 358).

Yet Balthasar, as so often, does not sustain this note. Even at the heart of his most explicit attempt to show how the Church is inwardly involved in Christ's eucharistic sacrifice (TD III, 368–73; ThD 4, 394–400), there is placed the perfection of the attitude of Mary, and the strength of the consequent language of nuptial consummation weakens the existential register. Consummation is the dominant note:

> Insofar as the Woman plays the part allotted to her in [the eucharistic] drama, she can be drawn in the most intimate way into the Man's fruitful activity; she can be fructified by him. Thus (and only thus) can we say that, in the Eucharist, the community is drawn into Christ's sacrifice, offering to God that perfect sacrifice of Head and members of which Augustine spoke in celebrated terms.

An always-already 'perfect' response acts here as the condition for all true human involvement in the eucharist. Though Balthasar acknowledges the dimension of Mary's 'utter forsakenness and darkness' at the cross, he goes on to interpret it as only the beginning of her 'nuptial relationship' with Christ: 'she is the only one able to receive the seed of God, eucharistically-multiplied – thousands-fold – into her womb' (TD III, 334; ThD 4, 358). This 'fruitful motherhood' of the Virgin is 'a fruitfulness that extends to the whole world' (TD III, 336; ThD 4, 361). Thus Mary's ability to receive and distribute 'the seed of God' is, for Balthasar, to be understood in a priori terms, as the condition for all eucharistic encounter and participation. Her perfection sets a term to the existential register and to the importance we are permitted to accord it.

It will have become clear that Balthasar's treatment of the eucharist as a theological *topos* is complex, and that we would be foolish to see in it a complete evacuation of the area in which human participation comes to expression. That would be to go too consciously against the grain of his theological project, which – inasmuch as it is theological dramatics – seeks to recognize all the scope and wealth that is proper to human freedom.

But his treatment of the eucharist nevertheless manifests many of the tendencies which we have identified as problematic in his theology. The eucharist may not be a theologoumenon which can or should be dealt with *exclusively* in terms of its impact on human existence (on our aspirations, emotions, compulsions, practices and so on). But though not *exclusively* existential in significance, it is *at least* existential. By giving it a marian still centre which operates, apparently, as the resolved a priori condition for its human dimension, Balthasar makes the eucharist less dramatic than the terms of his theology encourage us to expect, undercutting its existential significance. This ought to make us concerned.

As well as being the marian *Ecclesia Immaculata*, animated inwardly by a subjective holiness like Mary's, the Church also, of course, has an objective and institutional 'casing'. It is, to use Balthasar's words, necessarily 'a positive institution'. In relation to the Church's structures and ministry, as in relation to the eucharist, Balthasar has an opportunity to admit – even celebrate – the derivedness and situatedness of the forms they have taken, forms poetically (which is to say constructively) participated in by believers in the power of the Spirit and down the ages. But here, too, he elides time. The Church's structure, he says, like her basis, 'cannot grow' (ST II, 348; ExT 2, 331). Her forms of ministry are not to be relativized, whether 'in a liberal manner or by means of a theology of history (Tertullian, Joachim of Fiore, the Protestant Reformers)' (ST II, 336; ExT 2, 319): 'the particular *form* of the ministeriality [of the Church] … is no foreign element that has been added on *ab extra*. It is crystalized [*sic*] love, like water that has taken on the form of ice for a period.'

We may ask how long this period is, in which the Church's structure has this crystalline *stasis*. The answer Balthasar gives is a stern delimitation of the difference time makes. He denies here what elsewhere he tantalizes us with as a remedy for the ills of modernity (that is to say the dramatic reinstatement of time as the medium of our involvement in the true, the good and the beautiful). He states that the time of the crystallization of love is the *whole* of time, until the end of time. The time of this crystallization is 'the time of the winter that lasts until the Last Day, the time when "we are on pilgrimage far from the Lord" and need discipline and impersonal severity because we are not yet separated from the sinful world' (ST II, 335; ExT 2, 318).

By making this move, he 'frames' and reifies time, as if it were a surveyable unit. This is a *betrayal* of time, and serves an abstracted depiction of the Church which removes it from its situatedness in a 'poetic' history of Christian practice. Von Balthasar conceals the 'derivedness' of the Church in all its contingent, institutional details, and instead instantiates an 'imposed mysteriousness' on its behalf.[52]

Resistance to this move can only be shaped by the following theological affirmation: that the kind of 'totality' imparted to the Church by the Crucified One is a 'form' mysteriously traced by his corpse-like obedience in Hell, which *still waits for its full revelation*. The analogies drawn with any kind of dramatic resolution or harmony of form ought to be disciplined and limited by this intuition of the christological super-form,

---

52 Pickstock, 'Necrophilia', p. 407.

which, like Lash's metachronics, is as yet unfinalizable. Yet *Balthasar's* theodramatic super-form, in which the saints struggle and spiritual powers clash, and in which the life of faith is enacted in the tension between the aeons, is all too capable of mirroring the clear resolution and definition which, as we have seen, characterized the *Hegelian* dramatic form.

In sum, and to reiterate, the consequences of this tendency to impose resolution are a serious undercutting of the effectiveness of Balthasar's use of analogy as a safeguard against Hegel's assumption of identity, by making the field of analogical relation into too finalized and too incautious a middle ground for depicting the interaction of God and the creature; by making it a field in which too much is assumed to be perceptible. And where the doctrine of analogy is thus debilitated, the doctrine of the Church is bound to suffer too.

'[People] whose concerns are essentially ecclesiastical', writes FitzPatrick, '... are likely to be prone to habits of accommodation, so that past and present may be rendered straightforwardly harmonious in the service of religion.'[53] By 'habits of accommodation' he means that 'blurring and obscuring of history'[54] which facilitates our fabrication of unassailable-looking edifices which we convince ourselves are meant to be as they are in every respect, now and always. Balthasar's theology of the Church (and of the lives of individual Christians as subordinated to it) is just such a fabrication: an intermediate realm in which drama, rather than being intensified in its implications, is relativized. And here we should perhaps be ready to acknowledge an element in 'modernity' which actually still *serves* the dramatic quest for truth – an element in modernity which (were Balthasar really to put an 'end' to it) would leave his theology the victim of an amnesia either sinister or pathetic. There are in modernity, as FitzPatrick sees, certain disciplined habits of mind which should be highly prized:

> willingness to question and to doubt, perseverance in absorbing and often expensive enquiries, openness in free and irreverent debate, and refusal to grant privileged exceptions to what has custom on its side.[55]

Balthasar's tendency to betray time in the construction of a doctrine of the Church that sells his theodramatics short needs to develop these important disciplines. They are disciplines which modernity still harbours for its own healing. And this is an important reminder that a theological task like Balthasar's will not be the complete obliteration of the traditions and habits of mind of immediately preceding centuries, but their restoration to a full role in the on-going 'live' drama which is Theo-Drama. This drama cannot ever be evaded, which is why all our disciplines and techniques will in the end be better exercised when we *embrace* the drama – when we recognize that our life is not 'a given', but that (in every

---

53 FitzPatrick, *In Breaking of Bread*, p. 237.
54 Ibid., p. 262.
55 Ibid., p. 236.

particular and at every moment) life is the medium of God's active self-bestowal, as well as the medium of our call to respond. The task of theology at the 'end' of modernity is to pull modernity on to the stage, so that it will learn to do the things it does best (to question, to doubt, to debate) aware that it is in the middle of being related to, and not under the illusion that it can have a privileged vantage point from any fixed place of upholstered security.

Theological dramatic theory at the end of modernity

I dreamt our world lost careful hold of time
Instead of March the daffodils became
A Yellow-while when smell is in the air,
When green explodes and warmth upon the back
Is neither too much nor a dream denied.
The age of the infant is measured by
A sudden budding of the cherry tree
On the day of birth so warm, so softly pink.
Each year the petals thickly pile until
He sways aloft with eager reddened mouth
In eager reddened boughs fifteen springs high.

. . .

Only the old believe in metal tongues
Communal hours secure and understood,
The rest of us must do the best we can
Each pocketing his own continuum.
Though Jacob on the sand had little need
Of face of watch (to him the angel spoke)
Yet we have luminosity controlled,
Each wink asserts possession of the scythe.
Fear not, for when the church bells cease to ring
In darkest night we'll be sure of the hour.[56]

This has been, to some extent, an essay about time. The fact that it is not the only essay about time in this book shows what importance the theme has for a proper appreciation of what Balthasar promises even when he disappoints.

Drama needs time. More than that, it relishes time, instead of trying to mitigate its effects. While lyric tries to find a medium for the operation of subjective self-consciousness which is not timeable, and epic narrates time under closure and in that way seeks to manage it, drama blurs the frame. It is the art form truest to life and the manifestation of complex, pluriform, multiply-interpreted truth in changing circumstances.

The way it achieves its ends, as we saw right at the beginning in attending to the dramatic wealth and intensity of Aeschylus' *Agamemnon*, is to explode the fantasy that we can have 'careful hold of time'. Drama shows that the self-assertion involved in our quest to measure time has a dark irony: the only possession it achieves is possession of deadness. The

---

56 Sally Bushell, *Night Thoughts* (Cambridge, 1997). Reproduced by permission.

'sureness of the hour' which modernity has is a hollow gesture against its lost ability to know what (and whose) 'hour' it is. Modernity has taught us to 'pocket our own continuum' – epically to commodify time, lyrically to privatize it. To modernity, we can be sure, the 'angel does not speak', and there is no 'unaccountable scaffolding' to convey the divine light's appearance.

However we quantify and specify time (calling this moment, for example, 'March'), we cannot, without recovering our more real investment in it, articulate its *quality*, in which all the senses participate and 'green explodes' and there is 'warmth upon the back'. Only then, dramatically, does 'March' become 'a yellow-while'.

And 'while' is a concept that cannot be pocketed: it is a blurring of the boundaries of our experience; more an invitation than a concept, in fact. It is something we are 'in the middle of'. It is not a word that modernity celebrates. Yet, as Jesus Christ told his closest disciples (his first constructive interpreters), it is just this sort of time that is the time in which Christian life must be lived: 'A little while and you will see me no more; again a little while, and you will see me' (John 16.16). With these words he initiates the time of the Church, which is a time dynamic in every way; a time where the disciples must learn new ways of asking and new ways of receiving (vv. 23–24), in a transformative process (v. 20) which leads towards fullness of joy.

Theology has long had the resources to school Christ's disciples in citizenship of this 'while' – in all the existential, unfinalizable, dialogical seriousness of human self-determination. Theology has known the importance of time's passing in manifesting Christ's presence. Christ is given to the Church never as an object of manipulation or something 'under the command of our gaze'; never 'in the mode of a punctual moment', but as a continual gift (eucharistically), through the movement of rituals made new time after time, and displaying many of the quirks and accidents of our poetic reception of that gift.

That is why John Milbank is right to hint at ways in which truth must find expression in a 'genuinely public', 'traditioned', 'collective' but 'embodied' and above all 'eucharistic' voice.[57] That is why Balthasar makes his potentially vitalizing move to drama – because his theology acknowledges fully the ever-greater dimensions of that drama which includes every other: the drama between God and human beings in and beyond history. His theology speaks acknowledging that in every approach to truth we speak from *within* the drama, *before* the end of the play. Because the drama (made present most compellingly in the eucharist) is indeed a drama wider than any other conceivable drama – the drama of God's action – therefore it cannot completely be 'framed'.

That is why it is so disappointing that Balthasar at key points keeps alive modernity's destructive polarization of epic and lyric. We set ourselves the task at an earlier stage in this essay of assessing how Balthasar dealt with strains both of epic and lyric in his inheritance. The conclusion we seem bound to draw is that whilst his instincts about the importance of drama for healing the fissures that have opened up in

---

57 Milbank, 'Magisterial . . . and Shoddy?', p. 34.

modernity are good – and are in great measure realized (for example in his essays on the eucharist, which stress how the commanding activity of 'seeing' must be complicated by the more receptive and uncertain function of 'hearing' and the highly *participatory* activity of 'eating'[58] – nevertheless he seeks at other times to 'have luminosity controlled'. He will not accept the full implications of his own choice of drama – particularly in the area of ecclesial life – and so he will not allow that hope to open up which theological dramatics might yet offer to the modern era: the reconstitution (in the face of Enlightenment rationality) of cultures which teach people to read and speak with authenticity because their memories, understandings, passions and wills are permitted to interact in ways that are not predetermined.

We must be disappointed that even in that most innovative area of his theology – the meditation (with Adrienne) on the descent into Hell – Balthasar tries to control the dazzling darkness with strategies that mitigate the drama. The Hell of Balthasar's theology is *outside* and *beyond* our own time. It is narrated in 'epic' time, which is to say (as Gary Morson and Caryl Emerson put it in their discussion of Mikhail Bakhtin), it is 'fundamentally different and totally remote'.[59] The irony of Balthasar's theology is that at the moment when it aims most concretely to concern itself with struggle, suffering and death, it also becomes most mythological. The Hell of Balthasar's theology of Holy Saturday is *outside* and *beyond* our own time: it is, in effect, 'totally remote'. And it is this Hell which is emphasized as the realm in which the trinitarian relations are acted out for us and for our salvation. Here again, I think, we see that recurrent epic tendency in Balthasar's thought, which is prepared to sacrifice some of the existential, unfinalizable, dialogical seriousness of human self-determination. Attention is diverted from the struggles and suffering that characterize the social and material aspects of human history, and the structural and political aspects of sin are not considered. This has led Gerard O'Hanlon to remark that '[f]rom one who is so conscious of the reality of evil there is a curious lack of engagement with the great modern structural evils'.[60] Balthasar misses his opportunity to conceive the search for justice as a project, 'something with respect to which each of us has obligations in the immediate future of our lives'.[61] Instead, we find the same urge to concentrate on intuiting the wholeness and integrity (the *resolved* dramatic shape) of the Christ-form – a form which is now confidently seen to stretch to include even that which is utterly contrary to God.[62]

58 'Seeing, Hearing and Reading within the Church' and 'Seeing, Believing, Eating', in ST II, 484–513; ExT 2, 473–502.

59 Gary Morson and Caryl Emerson, *Mikhail Bakhtin: Creation of a Prosaics* (Stanford University Press, 1990), p. 420.

60 Gerard O'Hanlon, 'Theological Dramatics', in Bede McGregor and Thomas Norris (eds.), *The Beauty of Christ: An Introduction to the Theology of Hans Urs von Balthasar* (Edinburgh: T. & T. Clark, 1994), p. 109.

61 Morson and Emerson, *Mikhail Bakhtin*, p. 398.

62 I am indebted here to the insights of Craig Arnold Phillips in his dissertation 'From aesthetics to redemptive politics: A political reading of the theological aesthetics of Hans Urs von Balthasar and the materialist aesthetics of Walter Benjamin' (Duke University, 1993).

Meanwhile, alongside this somewhat too 'readable' epic narration of the descent into Hell, there is a curiously lyric fascination with the consciousness of the Christ who goes there. This has its roots in Nicholas of Cusa's thoughts about the so-called *visio mortis*. He writes:

> The vision, *visio*, of death by the mode of immediate experience, *via cognoscentiae*, is the most complete punishment possible. And since the death of Christ was complete, since through his own experience he saw the death which he had freely chosen to undergo, the soul of Christ went down to the underworld, *ad inferna*, where the vision of death is.[63]

Like Ignatius of Loyola, Nicholas of Cusa shows himself in certain respects to be a forerunner of modernity's concerns – in this case, the peculiarly intense fascination of modernity with human consciousness. Nothing is accepted as real except as it is *cognized* by a human subject whose consciousness is therefore projected as having a certain uninterrupted continuity and command of its material. Balthasar's German Idealist habits of thought filter this tradition of the *visio mortis*, leading him to rehearse the myth of an unbroken, self-possessing consciousness as the index of the world's truth, now raised to a unique importance by its centrality to the person and work of the Son. Thus Balthasar asserts:

> The Son must 'take in with his own eyes what in the realm of creation is imperfect, unformed, chaotic' so as to make it pass over into his own domain as the Redeemer. (MP, 175)

That which is contrary to God – 'the entire object of the divine eschatological judgment' – is existentially 'measured' by Christ in the mode of consciousness (MP, 174).[64]

Balthasar's work on Christ's death is an extraordinary feat of imaginatively attentive theology. But what it propounds is a model of human being which asserts the ultimacy of an individual's controlling gaze when it ought rather to allow the full force of death to unbalance it. In other words, if it wants Christ to be dead, it ought to allow him really to be *dead*, and thereby hold out a new ('theodramatic') possibility for understanding the true integrity of human persons less in terms of their presence to themselves (alive or dead) and more in terms of their presence to an ever-greater Other. In the space opened up by this especially extreme unbalancing of lyric self-centredness (which only death prompts, and of which only Theo-Drama can offer – in faith – an account) there is then room for lesser but surely important recoveries in the face of modernity – for example, the recognition that in life as well as in death our *visio* is interfered with by flaws and fantasies, and that who we are and what we are doing cannot authentically be construed except through our being built together with other human beings into something whose boundary

63 Nicholas of Cusa, *Excitationes* 10 (Basle, 1565), p. 659; quoted in MP, 170 (German text in Feiner and Löhrer, *Mysterium Salutis*, p. 245).
64 German text in Feiner and Löhrer, *Mysterium Salutis*, p. 248.

or frame is continually being reshaped. Ironically, then, the challenge presented by death (a challenge which Balthasar ducks in ways both epic and lyric) is a confirmation of the importance of the dramatically social (of how we are held even when we cannot hold, or possess, ourselves), that is to say, a confirmation of the importance of 'the middle' with which this essay began and must now end.

John Milbank suggests that theology needs 'a looser and more mystical (more eucharistic) account of the Spirit's guarantee of continuing truth in the body of the Church',[65] and it is to a contemplation of the eucharist (its disruption of our attempt at a 'careful hold' on things; its articulated but unbounded scaffolding through time) that we turn again here. The eucharist is the medium of dramatic sociality in which we may find a kind of therapy for our damaged attempts at reading the world and God's ways in it. It expresses a powerful interplay between concrete account and passionate song which knocks us off balance in order to engross us in a new form of relationship, which is communion. What begins as an invitation to do certain things (for example, to go and make peace with one's neighbours before approaching the table) proceeds to take dramatic shape as a call to have certain things done to one. The boundaries of our relationship to one another and to the eucharistic events are blurred, and there is the re-initiation of a drama of encounter and response, and a sequence of giving, receiving and giving back. In this movement *through* submission (or 'immersion', to bring alive the baptismal imagery which accompanies the eucharist) we are reconstituted in freedom and sent out to 'do' once again. Thus eucharistic celebration takes on those qualities of dramatic openness, spontaneity and commitment to the world which reflect the real nature of witness to Christ's incarnate presence. The eucharist is acknowledged as something to be celebrated by the world in the active presence of God, while the history that makes a 'present' of the eucharist is not left behind (or selectively forgotten), but is caught up in anamnesis. History is cast in its true light as the place of specific encounter between God and human beings, and it is not foreclosed, inasmuch as new histories are being generated by it all the time.

Alongside the *epic* component of 'account' (the definiteness of subject matter which we are not to forget) there is a *lyric* summoning of the whole person, 'with all his heart, with all his soul, with all his mind, and with all his strength' (Mk. 12.30). The bringing of the works of God into the present should provoke that internal imaginative wrestling which seeks to find the appropriate response, the right interpretation and form of obedience. This issues in prayer: a prayer which will reflect, perhaps, the lonely prayer of Jesus in Gethsemane, though the works of God that are recalled are also wonderful, and with equal validity evoke an attitude which Audet calls 'admiration and joy'.[66] This, too, issues in prayer.

The account, effectively, spills over into a present continuity of its own subject matter, a new, various and improvised enactment. In forgiveness, proclamation, witness and communion 'the concrete image of the actual

---

65 Milbank, 'Magisterial . . . and Shoddy?', p. 34.
66 J. P. Audet, 'Literary Forms and Contents of a Normal εὐχαριστία in the First Century', in *The Gospels Reconsidered* (Oxford: Blackwell, 1960), p. 19.

assembly itself' becomes 'three-dimensional'.[67] It takes on dramatic shape, in a communal interaction between people which is itself the dominant eucharistic sign of the reconciling sacrifice of Christ. The people become invested in one another, and together are 'incorporated' into the Body of Christ. Even the element of questioning can be the beginning of an important enactment between the individuals involved. In the words of MacKinnon, 'The men and women who allow themselves to be questioned are, by the scrutiny to which they submit themselves, permitted and enabled to become part of the question set for others.'[68] This is a movement of concrete testimony articulated (necessarily) in the witness of those passionately engaged – a movement which does not pretend to be able to step back and do justice to its subject matter from a position of cool neutrality, and so a movement which is the essence of apostolic witness. This quality of apostolic witness partakes of the eucharist's own ability to overcome the epic/lyric dichotomy, in the way that both are deeply self-involving at the same time as being historically alert and having things to say with respect to the world. The element of apostolic witness – which finds perpetual expression in Christian people's encounters with the world in obedience to their 'missions' – is so integral to the eucharistic assembly that it cannot be separated from it. As Kavanagh writes:

> the statement of motive for [eucharistic] blessing ... is a veritable kerygmatic annunciation to the assembly that this same *mirabile* is present here, active now, accomplishing its purpose still within the life of each and every member of the worshipping people.[69]

The eucharist holds together the account which the Church seeks to give to the world with the self-involving passion which makes that very act of witness simultaneously an act of divine praise. In a similarly dramatic way, the eucharist holds together the Church's past with the particularity of its present, and its corporateness with the particularity of the persons who constitute it.

In the Peto Institute in Hungary, severely handicapped children are 'conducted' repeatedly through certain motions. They submit to the control of another whilst their limbs are guided to certain positions and through certain sequences of action. In this way, they begin to acquire a greater control over their own bodies and a capacity to initiate action themselves. The sequences of drama which we have looked at in this essay – and the eucharist itself – are conductive in some comparable way. And the movement through which they conduct their participants is the decentring movement of *ekstasis* and *kenosis* – the loving 'movement' of the Trinity itself.

This particular way of being conducted does not make clear distinctions between our own agency and the movements through which we are

67 Nicholas Lash, *His Presence in the World* (London: Sheed & Ward, 1968), p. 96.
68 D. M. MacKinnon, *Explorations in Theology* 5 (London: SCM Press, 1979), p. 115.
69 A. Kavanagh, 'Thoughts on the Roman anaphora', *Worship*, 39:9 (1965), 520; quoted in Lash, *Presence*, p. 81.

guided. There is here a complex tangle of involvement. The eucharist teaches this lesson. We submit to motions beyond our control (like the children in the Peto Institute) and yet we continue to occupy different physical and mental space, and the motions remain ours, at least in part. It is therefore properly drama which is taking place in our relation to one another and to God: submission placed in sometimes even physical tension with our nature as separate existents; our position as observers, commentators and actors compromised and complicated, but never eradicated, by the impossibility of remaining detached.

This movement awakes us to a sense of freedom, a sense of our personhood, and a sense of our giftedness by God, at the same time as it leaves us with a more intense desire for the ever-greater.

> [S]ince the movement of freedom opens out to the infinite, every achievement of freedom, every experience of autonomy, will itself lead to a new movement toward the God who is ever greater and can never be mastered. As Balthasar puts it, the experience of the fulfilment of freedom and the corresponding experience of the ever-increasing longing for freedom grow in direct proportion.[70]

We are never, then, to forget or ignore the properly dramatic condition of our existence: the fact that 'the end we do not know'. The gift we receive from the divine Giver is not an ending of any kind. Those claimed by Christ are not the proprietors of an ending. The gift we receive is the gift of a freedom that calls us together to discover a new and transformative love, and to give thanks for it – a very eucharistic kind of freedom.

---

70 John J. O'Donnell, *Hans Urs von Balthasar* (London: Geoffrey Chapman, 1992), p. 68.

5

❧❀❧

Afterword: Making Differences

ROWAN WILLIAMS

Difference preoccupies the postmodern consciousness. That portion of the intellectual world that can be called 'postmodernist' is in systematic revolt against the dominance of identity and the erosion of the reality of what is not said in any act of saying. Put more prosaically, the postmodern consciousness rejects the possibility of a representation of the world that harmonizes and includes any and every act, phenomenon or dictum, a representation that does not have to acknowledge its own locatedness and thus its own 'failure'. And so far from being a malign assault upon 'ordinary' human discourse, this contemporary insistence – certainly in the hands of Derrida, at least – claims to be the only adequate way (yes, of course that is a paradoxical claim in this context) of articulating what language actually is; for a searching after presence, identity and totality is a searching for the end of language. As if language were the imperfect means of knowing with which we have to struggle for the time being until something greater than language is here: which is no way to go about constructing theories of speech.

Hegel has often been the target of such revolt. He is understood (not necessarily rightly understood) as canonizing the search for the end of language under the guise of what looks like a dialogical structure. Hegel's spiritual subject posits itself and *then* negates itself; the negation is *conditioned* by the first affirmation, it is always and necessarily and exclusively the other *of* the thesis. In such an otherness, there is no real difference expressed; the semantic lack acknowledged in the thesis is the gap that the antithesis articulates, and there is no excess of what is unspoken that will, so to speak, free the second moment from the conditions fixed by the first. Even if we say that the negation of the negation means that there is some kind of excess in the second moment (its denial does not simply reinstate the first term), it remains, like the original negation, a moment of denial *of* the specificity of the foregoing moment. The Hegelian dialectic, in other words, is always bound to the model of otherness as conditioned by a *prior* sameness: at every juncture, sameness is what is primordially present and active, otherness is what reacts.

Yet what might it be to speak of a simultaneous or equipollent otherness? The characteristic seduction of literary and philosophical postmodernity is to look towards a rhetoric of unconditional difference, an unspeakable otherness that is the inevitable shadow of speech or thought; what is known, said, represented is present in its mode only because of the unrepresented and unrepresentable, which is not some substantive mystery 'behind' the speaking world but the sheer fluidity and contingency of speech itself, knotting itself around the emptiness of duration. Derrida's *différance* is still paradoxically infused with something like (almost) the numinous: the thereness of language itself, so necessarily mobile that it cannot embody 'real presence' and cannot be understood as a system of static representation, evokes something of the awe of the last propositions of the *Tractatus*. If there is speech, there is the unsayable, simply because speech cannot be everything, cannot escape its mobile, anarchic temporality, cannot do other than reflect itself and rework itself. But what is unsayable is strictly unsayable, not to be gestured towards in a timidly religious way. There is no relation between the same and the other, the said and the unsayable. The one is not even the 'opposite' of the other, as it cannot belong in one frame with it at any point.

But what makes this a seduction is precisely this refusal of a relation between same and other. If this is strictly maintained, the result, ironically, is another kind of reduction to the same. What is is speech, which finds its own otherness in its own life, responding to and reflecting on itself. Its temporality is curiously discarnate, as the passage of time is markable only by the play of linguistic events with one another. It is as if what is crudely understood as time, the time of the body's transactions, retreats, to be replaced by the variegated times of textual transaction and interaction, diverse, often reversible. If otherness is the always unsayable, what can be said about the prosaic and diurnal otherness of the processes of dialogue, the relations of concrete social power, the specific rather than general moments where speech is arrested (terror, passion, doubt; the awful fragmentations of sense we hear in Shakespeare's virtuosos of sexual jealousy, Othello and Leontes; the violent abruptness of the techniques with which Herbert ends so many of his poems; the nightmare fluency of the diabolical voices in Dostoevsky, showing by their uninterrupted movement the gulf between diabolical and human speech, with its hesitation, backtracking and marks of struggle)? If the inter-ruptions of discourse are always the sacred unsayable other of some postmodernist theory, what becomes of the temporal conflicts and resist-ances of 'ordinary' interpersonal exchange? The absolutizing of the other, whether in the hermeneutic vein of Derrida or the ethical vein of Levinas, can work to reinforce a sameness more enclosed than Hegel's (or Hegel's, at least, as understood by so much of modernity and postmodernity).

Two poles, then: a model that suggests first identity or presence, next difference (resolving again into identity); and a model that suggests always an identity shadowed by a wholly unrepresentable otherness. Neither model, it could be said, allows easily for a difference that is both simultaneous and interactive, a difference that allows temporal change, reciprocity of action, and thus avoids the two different but depressingly similar varieties of totalization that might be implied by the polar models we began with. And this is where theology stakes a claim to be heard within the cultural debate. The themes of Christian theology, above all its reflections on otherness within the divine life and the peculiar otherness between the divine and the human in the identity of the Saviour, demand, in our present context, to be read afresh, as attempts to think through otherness so as to avoid totalization. The essays in this volume examine the thought of a twentieth-century theologian who has devoted more energy than most theologians to pursuing the logic of the trinitarian and christological traditions of the Church, and has outlined a metaphysical idiom that could shed much light on the threatened stand-off between a philosophy of unproblematic identity and an anti-metaphysics of speech and the void. All the contributors to this book share a central conviction that it is in his treatment of difference that Balthasar has most to say to the present intellectual scene; and this is worked out in several different ways (which permeate all the essays in varying degrees).

To start with there is the fundamental importance of understanding analogy itself as a tool and a principle in Balthasar's corpus. The theme has been the subject matter of quite a bit of study in recent years, and these remarks will be woefully superficial to those more familiar with the material. But briefly, the important points made about Balthasar's approach to analogy have much to do with two features of his discussions. There is, in the first place, his repeated reference to the dictum of the Fourth Lateran Council: whatever the likeness between God and creatures, it is outweighed by a greater unlikeness (*maior dissimilitudo*). Balthasar connects this with the principle classically formulated by Nicholas of Cusa that God is *non aliud* in respect of creation – not *an* other, an item enumerable in a list along with the contents of the universe. Analogy is thus emphatically *not* a correspondence between two or more things exhibiting in varying degrees the same features, as if God had a very great deal of good and creatures steadily diminishing quantities of the same. There is no system of which God and creatures are both part (so much can be granted to a rhetoric of unqualified *différance*). But what then *is* analogy? It is the active presence of the divine liberty, love and beauty precisely within the various and finite reality of material/temporal reality. 'The divine' is not present in creation in the form of 'hints of transcendence', points in the created order where finitude and creatureliness appear to thin out or open up to a mysterious infinity, but in creation being itself – which includes, paradigmatically, creation being itself in unfinishedness, time-taking, pain and death. The crucified Jesus is, in this context, the ground and manifestation of what analogy means.

The implications of this are many and complex. God and the created order do not and cannot stand together as prototype and image in any straightforward sense – which means that the relation between them is not that of primordial identity and derivative response, even though it is a relation of unqualified dependence. They cannot be moments in one story. But the dependence of creation upon God is the free bestowal of God's life *in* the forms of finitude, with all their historical and conditioned diversity. The otherness of God and creation is to be conceived at once in two ways that are deeply in tension, yet equally grounded in the *non aliud* principle. On the one hand, the otherness between God and the world is inexhaustible and irreducible; nothing can bring these realities into co-ordination or – in the ordinary sense – subordination and

superordination. There is always an 'unlikeness' that defies (by definition) measure and category. On the other hand, the life of creation is not
an independent subject alongside the divine life, but that life itself freely
'alienated' from itself in a gift so absolute that it establishes the possibility
of a free response, of an authentic love. God truly loves God; yet God
truly loves God in and through what is, without qualification, *not* God –
the realm of time and vulnerability, in which loving subjects are formed.
Thus God is neither an identity into which otherness must be assumed,
nor a nameless and abstract sacredness around the corners of speech. The
representation of God is always starkly paradoxical within the contingent
Godlessness of a vulnerable and corrupted world. And because the
variousness of that contingent world is so grounded and affirmed or
allowed in this strange relatedness, the hierarchies of the world are
unsettled: we cannot simply assent to the vulgarized Platonism that
would order the creation according to whether this or that reality was
'closer' to the divine and the spiritual. The otherness of the contingent
world to itself, the dualities of body and spirit, male and female, and so
on, can no longer be thought of as higher and lower, first and second,
pure and compromised. The analogical presence of divine love in the form
of the worldly other makes differences in the world in some sense
simultaneous and reciprocal, not to be read in terms of a fall from pure
presence or transparency, or a descending *scala naturae.*

But this reading of the analogical relationship makes sense only in the
context of what Christians say of God-as-such. The Catholic faith is that
God is not *a* subject, nor even a plurality of subjects in intimate
connection. God is intrinsically that life which exists only and necessarily
in the act of 'bestowal', in a self-alienation that makes possible the
freedom and love of an other that is at the same time itself *in* otherness.
The extremity of the relation between God and the God-forsaken Jesus
is our way in to this claim for the life of God-as-such: the divine life is
what sustains itself as unqualified unity across the greatest completeness
of alienation that can be imagined; and so appears as unqualified gift or
(as I have been calling it) bestowal. The gulf between Father and crucified
Son, between Father in heaven and Son in hell, now appears as the
immeasurable measure of the way divine love 'leaves' itself, travels
infinitely from itself (from self-possession, self-presence). Here there can
be no identity prior to differentiation: the only identity in question is
precisely the total and eternal self-bestowal that constitutes the other. The
generative or originary moment in the divine life, the Father, has no
reality except in the act of generating the otherness of the Son and sustaining the unity of divine life across this gulf of immeasurable otherness
by the issuing of 'spirit': the life bestowed in its wholeness upon the Son is
both returned to the Father and opened up beyond the duality of Father
and Son as the Holy Spirit. Or, in other words, the self-alienating of divine
life in the Father's self-gift to the Son itself 'alienates' itself, posits itself as
more than a symmetry of self-sacrifice, becomes that which the Son gives,
realizes, liberates, from the depth of his distance from the Father.

These dense theological insights, by no means easy to trace clearly or
formulate economically in the terms of Balthasar's work, yet fundamental
to practically all of his immense output, return us to the starting point of

these remarks. Here is a theological language which can make some claim to have gone beyond the sterile opposition of undifferentiated presence/ identity on the one hand and unthinkable *différance* on the other. How far Balthasar realizes the promise of his own insight is a question that invites a reflection at least as extensive as his own writing, and is therefore not a question that a single book such as this is going to answer. But a highly significant area noted here, in which Balthasar tantalizingly both opens up revolutionary perspectives and intimates some very firm and traditional closures, is that of sexual differentiation. It is theologically important that humanity itself is not thinkable as a monistic identity; to be human is to be gendered. And if the unity of the divine life and love is analogically active in the differentiation of the material and contingent world, theology is bound to take the genderedness of human existence with complete seriousness. Balthasar undoubtedly does so. But what makes his analysis tantalizing is a central unclarity about how far sexual differentiation really can be said to partake of the differentiation of the trinitarian persons, a differentiation in which there is no unilateral and fixed pattern of priority or derivation but a simultaneous, reciprocal conditioning, a pattern of identity *in* the other without remainder. To engage with this *aporia* in Balthasar, we need more than an enlightened outrage at a rhetoric of sexual differentiation apparently in thrall to unexamined patriarchy. Balthasar is not so easily written off. What is needed, rather, is a response within his own rhetoric, within the terms of the extraordinary affirmation of simultaneous and reciprocal difference that his account of the trinitarian relations and the relation of God to creation insists upon (and I say 'insists upon' rather than simply 'allows', because it is so clear that his entire theological enterprise falls if these relational distinctions can in any way be reduced to a system of co-ordination and subordination).

But this inevitably brings into sharp focus the extreme difficulty of realizing in our theological speech the 'simultaneity and reciprocity' required by the formative patterns at work here. Inevitably – because our speech is temporal, like the rest of our human being – we say one thing, then another; in speaking of the trinitarian relations, theologians have always found it difficult to avoid various kinds of virtual subordina-tionism (how do you speak of dependence without at once speaking of some kind of 'coming after'?). It is not too surprising if the same issue arises in connection with speaking theologically about gender. Hence the provocative idea, central to the longest essay in this collection, that 'something like the sexes' is part of what is involved in speaking of God. And if all accounts of difference in the world other than static oppositions of competing atomic subjects are constructed narratively and drama-tically, if the way we speak of self-dispossession and gift is unavoidably the telling of a sequential process, do we not also have to say, boldly, that 'something like time' is involved in speaking of God? That is: however hard we insist upon the simultaneity of the divine subsistents, we can say nothing of this simultaneity that is not abstract and formal unless we take the necessary (not to say canonical) risk of *evoking* simultaneity by telling a cluster of 'stories' that configure in different and reciprocal ways the relations of the trinitarian persons. In short, it is not by denying undialectically the realities of time and gender that we arrive at an apt rhetoric for the divine, but by so working with the modalities of talk about time and gender that the timeless (that is, in concretely theological terms, the faithful, always active) reality of the reciprocal differentiations of trinitarian life is brought to view.

And this returns us yet again to our starting point: all this discussion has about it something of the character of a Moebius strip. God is not to be spoken of by denying contingency. The mysterious difference of God is never an abstract otherness defined simply by the negation of the predicates of contingent being. Balthasar is always ambivalent about much of the apophatic tradition in Christian theology (and sometimes, as perhaps in his pages on John of the Cross, does some of its representatives less than complete justice), precisely because it insufficiently observes the true and radical sense of divine difference that his cruciform understanding of analogy intimates. God is not different *like that*: if divine difference were the negation of all finite predicates, God would be the other belonging to a discourse about the finite world. God's life would be subsumed under that of the world, the antithesis of the world's thesis; and out of such a discourse, no possible language for divine freedom or love could be generated. Balthasar's form of negative theology is close to the fierce Lutheran conviction that it is only in that concrete otherness to God embodied in the abandonment of the crucified Messiah to death and hell that the divine difference, both within God and between God and the finite order, can be seen. Here and here alone can we begin to think the freedom of God that is entailed in the power to bestow the divine life without reserve and without limit, unconstrained by any imaginable distance, threat or absence.

Here and there in these pages, some unease or at least interrogation is expressed as to Balthasar's capacity to allow in specifics what his theological vision enjoins in general. It is not only a question about his handling of gender issues; there is the teasing and challenging abstraction from the actual history of this century, the abstraction from the specific calls to 'stake' an identity in dialogue and action (to borrow a familiar idiom of Gillian Rose); there is the sense that at times the spiralling inwards towards the 'marian' moment in the Church's reality, the unqualified contemplative self-abnegation that allows God's act to *be* in the world, slips towards a reinstatement of certain kinds of hierarchies within creation, hierarchies of transparency to the divine, and a concomitant impatience with the realities of conflict within the Church. This is expressed neatly in the charge that Balthasar's espousal of the 'dramatic' in his theology is persistently overtaken by reversion to the 'epic', understood as a narrative of unfolding and final containment. What I earlier called the temporal conflicts and resistances of 'ordinary' interpersonal exchange, what might equally be called the sense of the tragic – always a significantly difficult area for the theologian to handle – are often felt as absences in Balthasar's *œuvre*, despite the often stunningly powerful focus on the unconsoled dereliction of the crucified.

But if the overall perspective here outlined is correct, if Balthasar does indeed open up a path beyond the twin threats of an eternal return to the same and an eternal alienation between thought or speech and the void, he is proposing a programme so searching and radical that even a theologian of his stature is unlikely to realize it with uniform fidelity. Part of the hinterland of this book is a strong dissatisfaction with a good deal of the reception of Balthasar in the theological community, a reception that has become increasingly politicized. He has not been adequately located within a continuing European cultural and intellectual debate (granted that his *awareness* of the debate is at best uneven); he has been adopted as a canonical authority for certain disciplinary and doctrinal options among Catholics (Roman and Anglican), most notably in just that area where his thought is (as the foregoing pages have illustrated) most contestable and complex, his reflections on matters of gender; he has been stigmatized as a simplistic purveyor of unreformed certainties, appealing to corrupt or oppressive models of authority and obedience in the Church; or merely ignored as one of those eccentrics who assume that the whole breadth of human reality can be illuminated by the Nicene and Chalcedonian faith.

The essayists in this collection are happy to be counted themselves among such eccentrics; but they are for that very reason concerned to pursue Balthasar's own method of tracing a path towards the 'formless' form of the beauty of God's Word through the cultural agon of the end of the twentieth century. Theology is fragmented now as never before, at precisely the moment when certain of its traditional patterns and resources have extraordinary pertinence to the cultural culs-de-sac and standoffs amongst which we live or try to live or fail to live. Balthasar is one of a very small number of contemporary theologians to articulate this pertinence in a way other than simple reiteration of a sealed and finished tradition. (As one or two scholars have observed, Michel de Certeau is another, whose convergences with Balthasar – as well as some dramatic divergences – badly need more discussion.) Balthasar is too important for a renewal of Christian ontology to be left to the politics of the Catholic institutions; he undoubtedly needs to be 'politicized', but in the widest possible theatre of politics, the muddled, struggling debate, so often stifled or abandoned, as to the character of human difference – the debate in which the Christian theologian obstinately battles to understand why it might be that the concrete plurality of human life, from conception to death, demands an unqualified, attentive and hopeful contemplation and a response of nurture and of love.

Name Index

Subject Index

185